JEWISH EXEGESIS AND HOMERIC SCHOLARSHIP IN ALEXANDRIA

Systematically reading Jewish exegesis in light of Homeric scholarship, this book argues that more than two thousand years ago Alexandrian Jews developed critical and literary methods of Bible interpretation which are still extremely relevant today. Maren Niehoff provides a detailed analysis of Alexandrian Bible interpretation, from the second century BCE through newly discovered fragments to the exegetical work done by Philo. Niehoff shows that Alexandrian Jews responded in a great variety of ways to the Homeric scholarship developed at the Museum. Some Jewish scholars used the methods of their Greek colleagues to investigate whether their Scripture contained myths shared by other nations, while others insisted that significant differences existed between Judaism and other cultures. This book is vital for any student of ancient Judaism, early Christianity and Hellenistic culture.

MAREN R. NIEHOFF is Senior Lecturer in the Department of Jewish Thought at The Hebrew University of Jerusalem. She is the author of *The Figure of Joseph in Post-Biblical Literature* (1992) and *Philo on Jewish Identity and Culture* (2001).

JEWISH EXEGESIS AND HOMERIC SCHOLARSHIP IN ALEXANDRIA

MAREN R. NIEHOFF

CAMBRIDGE
UNIVERSITY PRESS

CAMBRIDGE UNIVERSITY PRESS
Cambridge, New York, Melbourne, Madrid, Cape Town,
Singapore, São Paulo, Delhi, Tokyo, Mexico City

Cambridge University Press
The Edinburgh Building, Cambridge CB2 8RU, UK

Published in the United States of America by Cambridge University Press, New York

www.cambridge.org
Information on this title: www.cambridge.org/9781107000728

First published 2011

Printed in the United Kingdom at the University Press, Cambridge

A catalogue record for this publication is available from the British Library

ISBN 978-1-107-00072-8 Hardback

For Udi, Maya, Ayana and Stav

In memory of
Leora Elias-Bar Levav and Rena Moses-Hrushovski

Moi, un peu mort parmi les vivants, toi, un peu vivante parmi
les morts.
(Albert Cohen, Le livre de ma mère*)*

Contents

vii

Acknowledgements

This book had its beginning in a reading group on the *Iliad* at the house of my friend and colleague Yehuda Liebes. When coming across a reference in the Oxford edition to Aristarchus' text criticism, I immediately asked whether Philo, known for his quotations from Homer, was aware of his fellow Alexandrian's work. It was this initial question which prompted my broader investigation into the connections between Jewish Bible exegesis and Homeric scholarship. The reading group contributed in another crucial way: I profited immensely from Yehuda's vast knowledge of Homer's epic and could not have endeavoured to study the scholia without his help in the initial stages. Later on Yehuda also read a draft of the book, offering constructive comments and encouraging me even more than usual.

Special thanks are also due to Margalit Finkelberg, who accompanied my work on this book from its beginning. I recall our first meeting at *Mishkenot Sha'ananim*, when I told her about my preliminary impression that there may have been significant links between the Homeric scholia and Jewish Bible exegesis in Alexandria. Margalit responded with enthusiasm and has encouraged me ever since, providing materials from her private library and reading drafts of chapters. Her comments were detailed and wise, saving me from mistakes and alerting me to new avenues. Moreover, my Homeric colleagues abroad have been very kind and forthcoming. Filippo Pontani immediately responded to each draft of a chapter with a few pages of bibliography as well as detailed and extremely helpful comments, which saved me from mistakes and prompted me to tighten my arguments. He has also read the final version of several chapters, taking a keen interest in the book. René Nünlist generously shared his work before it was published and read drafts of chapters with unusual attention and curiosity. His comments as well as his provision of unavailable literature significantly contributed to the book. Francesca Schironi kindly shared unpublished work and answered specific questions.

I also wish to thank my colleagues in the field of Philonic studies and
Hellenistic culture. David Runia read a draft of the whole book, offering extremely useful comments, which shaped the final version. Ellen
Birnbaum read two chapters with exceptional care. She left no word unex-
amined and offered good advice, helping me to formulate my arguments
more clearly in view of an audience unfamiliar with Homeric scholarship.
George R. Boys-Stones and Eric S. Gruen each read a draft of a chapter,
providing lucid comments from their vast scholarly expertise.

Studying Philo's *Questions and Answers*, I acquired new teachers and colleagues in the field of Armenian studies. I wish to thank Sergio de la Porta,
who offered an extra-curricular course at the Hebrew University, teaching a handful of students Classical Armenian. Subsequently, Sergio kindly
studied with me Philo's *Questions and Answers* and guided me through
the intricacies of the Armenian translation. Without him Chapter 9
could not have been written. I also wish to thank Abraham Terian, who
visited the Hebrew University during the spring semester of 2006 and
patiently helped me with my first readings of Philo's *Questions and Answers*
in the Armenian translation.

A significant source of inspiration was the interdisciplinary reading group
in the field of Hellenistic Judaism at the Hebrew University. We started
in the autumn of 2006, reading the fragments of Ezekiel's tragedy, and
developed into a lively discussion group during 2007–9, when we read
the *Letter of Aristeas* and related sympotic literature. The group provided a
unique forum for exchanging views with colleagues from different fields and
considerably broadened my perspectives. I also profited from the group's
discussion of my chapter on the *Letter of Aristeas*.

The research for this book was generously supported by the ISRAEL
SCIENCE FOUNDATION (grant nos. 810/03 and 435/08). I benefited
from the encouragement and thoughtful advice of the anonymous review-
ers. The two research grants moreover enabled me to hire outstanding
assistants: Sergey Minov, who helped from the beginning to the end with
unfailing energy, as well as Yakir Paz and Sharon Weisser. The compe-
tence, commitment and academic independence of each of them have
significantly contributed to the book. Sergey also compiled the bibliography, while Yakir prepared the index. The grants furthermore enabled me
to systematically order books from other Israeli libraries as well as from
abroad. I wish to thank especially Zemira Reubeni of the National Library
for her never fading energy in tracking down books, thus emulating the

ideal of the ancient library in Alexandria, without, however, resorting to its more notorious methods. Over the years the ISRAEL SCIENCE FOUNDATION has shown exemplary flexibility in meeting the ever changing needs of scholars, thus contributing to research in a comprehensive manner.

It has been a special pleasure to work with the editorial team of Cambridge University Press. Michael Sharp promptly responded to my initial query by encouraging me to submit drafts of ready chapters. Laura Morris subsequently took an active role throughout the editorial process, accompanying my work with foresight and gentle humour. The two anonymous readers of the Press offered useful comments for the final version of the book, inviting me to think of the wider implications of my argument. Christina Sarigiannidou was a very efficient production editor; Jan Chapman was exceptionally conscientious and constructive in her work as copy-editor. The mosaic shown on the cover of the book was unknown to me before Roni Amir of the Bezalel School of Arts in Jerusalem kindly drew my attention to it.

Chapter 5 is based on a lecture originally delivered in French at the Université Libre de Bruxelles and to appear as 'Recherche homérique et exégèse biblique à Alexandrie. Le cas de la Tour de Babel', in S. Inowlocki-Meister and B. Decharneux (eds.), *Philon d'Alexandrie: un penseur à l'intersection des cultures gréco-romaine, orientale, juive, et chrétienne, Actes du colloque de Bruxelles, 26–28 juin 2007*, which was to be published in 2010. I wish to thank Sabrina Inowlocki-Meister for her permission to use the material in this book.

I am delighted to dedicate this book to my immediate family, my husband Udi and our three daughters. Udi was always the first to hear about new questions and answers, taking a keen interest in the development of the book and offering useful comments on the introduction. My family has provided me with a firm anchor in the pleasures of life without which I would have led a rather limited ivory-tower existence.

This book is also dedicated to the memory of two special women. During the preparation of the book, within less than a year, both of them died of cancer, Leora just after Passover 2006, Rena just before Purim 2007. Accompanying them and mourning their loss has sometimes made research impossible, while at other times it was precisely my work which set me back on the track of life.

Last, but not least: during my work on this book I have become increasingly appreciative of the ancient scholars, both Jewish and Greek. Since the peak of Alexandrian scholarship there seems to be 'nothing new under the sun', both academic methods and human mistakes having been repeated ever since. I can thus only hope that this book would have been pleasing to its heroes.

MAREN R. NIEHOFF, JERUSALEM

Abbreviations

PHILO'S WORKS

Allegorical Commentary

Agr.	*De agricultura*
All. 1, 2, 3	*Legum allegoriae* I, II, III
Cher.	*De cherubim*
Conf.	*De confusione linguarum*
Congr.	*De congressueru ditionis gratia*
Cont.	*De vita contemplativa*
Det.	*Quod deterius potiori insidari soleat*
Deus	*Quod Deus sit immutabilis*
Ebr.	*De ebrietate*
Fuga	*De fuga et inventione*
Gig.	*De gigantibus*
Her.	*Quis rerum divinarum heres sit*
Migr.	*De migratione Abrahami*
Mut.	*De mutatione nominum*
Plant.	*De plantatione*
Post.	*De posteritate Caini*
Sacr.	*De sacrificiis Abelis et Caini*
Sobr.	*De sobrietate*
Somn. 1, 2	*De somniis* I, II

Questions and Answers on Genesis and Exodus (Q&A)

Q.E. 1, 2	*Quaestiones et solutiones in Exodum* I, II
Q.G. 1, 2, 3, 4	*Quaestiones et solutiones in Genesin* I, II, III, IV

Exposition of the Law (Exposition)

Abr.	*De Abrahamo*
Dec.	*De decalogo*
Jos.	*De Iosepho*

Mos. 1, 2	*De vita Mosis* I, II
Opif.	*De opificio mundi*
Praem.	*De praemiis et poenis*
Spec. 1, 2, 3, 4	*De specialibus legibus* I, II, III, IV
Virt.	*De virtutibus*

Historical writings
| *Flacc.* | *In Flaccum* |
| *Legat.* | *Legatio ad Gaium* |

Philosophical writings
Aet.	*De aeternitate mundi*
Alex.	*Alexander* (= *De animalibus*)
Prob.	*Quod omnis probus liber sit*

OTHER WORKS

Titles of other ancient works are abbreviated according to the *Oxford Classical Dictionary*, 3rd revised edition, 2003, with the following exceptions:

| *FGH* | *Die Fragmente der griechischen Historiker*, ed. F. Jacoby. 7 vols. Berlin, 1923–30 |
| *SCI* | *Scripta Classica Israelica* |

CHAPTER I

Setting the stage

From the inception of modern research Jewish Bible exegesis in Alexandria has often been regarded as a marginal phenomenon or a puzzling hybrid. It tended to be studied either from the perspective of biblical interpretation in the Land of Israel or as a forerunner of Christian exegesis. Scholars familiar with the Jewish tradition usually focused on the emergence of rabbinic literature, which subsequently became normative. If Alexandrian exegesis was at all taken into account, it was characteristically either construed as a derivative phenomenon depending on its counterpart in Jerusalem or dismissed as an alien body of literature, which reflects Greek ideas and anticipates Christianity while failing to resonate in traditional Jewish circles.[1] On the other hand, scholars familiar with the Christian tradition tended to approach Jewish Bible exegesis in Alexandria in the context of either the New Testament or patristic literature, giving special emphasis to allegory. In this scenario Philo figured rather prominently, often being praised as *the* representative of Hellenistic Judaism who prepared the way for Clement, Origen and others.[2]

Luckily, a number of scholars have appreciated Alexandrian Judaism in its own right. During the transition period from the Enlightenment to *Wissenschaft* it was praised by Isaac Marcus Jost as a strikingly modern form of Judaism. He stressed that it was based on a division of state and church as well as on a cultural synthesis of Jewish and Greek traditions.[3] Alexandrian Judaism emerged as an important paradigm for combining tradition with critical awareness. It was identified as a forerunner of the Golden Age of Jewish philosophy in the Middle Ages and liberal Judaism in contemporary Germany. Following this early impulse, additional scholars have begun to study Alexandrian Bible exegesis in its proper cultural and

---

[1] See esp. Frankel 1854; Ritter 1879; Wolfson 1947; Cohen 1995. On the history of scholarship, see Freudenthal 1869; Cohn 1892; Niehoff 1999; in press, a; J. J. Collins 2010.
[2] See esp. Gfrörer 1831, vol. i; Dähne 1834; Deines and Niebuhr 2004.
[3] Jost 1821, esp. pp. 265–99; 1857–9, vol. i, pp. 1–2, 344–93; see also Meyer 1991; Schorsch 1977.

historical context. Such pioneering studies tended to focus on the Ptolemaic period, while Philo's exegetical writings, as opposed to his historical works, have generally been examined with little awareness of their immediate context in the Roman period.[4]

It is thus time for a comprehensive study of Jewish Bible exegesis in its immediate Alexandrian context. The most relevant aspect of Alexandria, which has thus far been surprisingly overlooked, is the fact that the city was the leading centre of Homeric scholarship in the Hellenistic world. Developing Aristotelian models, it boasted of the largest library at the time as well as the famous Museum, which has rightly been identified as a type of university.[5] In contrast to that of Pergamum, Alexandrian scholarship focused on the literal text, identifying the authentic version of the Homeric epics and analysing their literary features. This detailed attention to the Homeric text led to a standardization of the corpus and a division into recognized books.[6] Glenn Most has pointed to the importance of this Alexandrian contribution to the canonization of Homer's epics.[7]

A learned Jewish scholar such as Philo would naturally be familiar with the Alexandrian division of the Homeric epics; he refers once to a passage 'in the *Iliad* at the beginning of the thirteenth song' (*Cont.* 17). He assumed that Greeks and barbarians were raised on the poets, initially acquiring basic reading skills and then launching into a 'detailed investigation'.[8]

---

[4] Freudenthal 1874 had a seminal influence on modern research, calling for a change of paradigm. Freudenthal offered a detailed analysis of some early Jewish works written in Greek and showed that they anticipate rabbinic literature, sometimes even influencing it. Equally important, yet less accessible to a wider audience is Gutman's work in Hebrew (1958–63), which offers an in-depth study of the early Alexandrian exegetes. Gutman regularly interpreted Alexandrian Jews in terms of their Hellenistic environment, arguing that they engaged with the surrounding Greek literature to treat biblical motifs. Fraser 1972, in his magisterial study of Ptolemaic Alexandria, analysed Jewish sources in terms of the city's contemporary discourse, thus giving a significant boost to the field of Alexandrian Judaism. Gruen 2002 made an important contribution by analysing the historical situation of Alexandrian Jews and their proud self-image especially during the Ptolemaic period.

[5] For details on the Library and the Museum, see Fraser 1972, vol. I, pp. 312–35, 447–79, who emphasized the importance of the patronage system as well as Aristotelian influence; contra Pfeiffer 1968, pp. 87–104, who stressed the role of Alexandrian scholar-poets, such as Philitas, who initiated in his view a rupture from the Classical Age. Fraser's conclusions have been confirmed by Pöhlmann 1994, pp. 26–40; Canfora 2002; N. L. Collins 2000; Rajak 2009, pp. 74–8; and, less emphatically, by Clauss 2003, pp. 92–8.

[6] Regarding the division of the Homeric epics into twenty-four songs, which is standardized by the Alexandrian scholars but not reflected in the early papyri, see Nünlist 2006; S. West 1967, pp. 18–25; contra Jensen 1999.

[7] Most 1990, pp. 54–8; on the *numerus verbum* see also Marrou 1950, pp. 228–9; M. L. West 2001, pp. 50–2, 61–7; 1998, p. 99; M. Finkelberg 2004, 2006, who showed that Alexandrian readings, as distinct from the number of verses, were not influential in the transmission of the Homeric texts.

[8] *Agr.* 18, *Mut.* 179; Philo also refers to his own 'reading and study of the writings of the poets' as part of his training in grammar (*Congr.* 74).

'The Poet' provided him not only with many winged expressions, but also with an authoritative proof-text for Jewish monotheism.[9] Other anonymous exegetes in Alexandria explicitly compared the biblical story of the Tower of Babel to a similar enterprise of the sons of Aloeidae recorded in the *Odyssey* (*Conf.* 4–5). Such references are not at all surprising given the known acculturation of Alexandrian Jews. They not only spoke and wrote in Greek but quickly read even their Scriptures only in the Greek translation.[10] Homer's epics, which constituted the most important pillar of Greek education in Hellenistic Egypt, were obviously familiar to them.[11]

The present book is based on the recognition that Homer's epics as well as Moses' Torah were foundational texts, irrespective of whether their canonicity was precisely the same, and as such prompted a large corpus of minute interpretations in their respective communities of readers. The hermeneutics involved in both contexts emerged in a similar historical environment and followed surprisingly similar rules. Moreover, readers of the Homeric epics and the Bible faced texts with distinct literary features, while at the same time relating to them as the basis of their religion. Given these premises, it is time for a systematic investigation into the historical connections between the ancient students of Homer's epics and Moses' Bible.

It is the purpose of this book to examine the connections between Homeric scholarship and Jewish Bible exegesis in Alexandria. Literal interpretation, both in its own right and as a basis of different forms of allegorical exegesis, will be the focus of our attention. I shall argue that Jewish exegetes were generally familiar with the academic methods developed at the Museum. Many of these methods directly applied them to the Jewish Scriptures. Alexandrian Bible scholars thus created a new synthesis and

---

[9] *Abr.* 10, *Conf.* 170; for examples of Homeric expressions in Philo see, e.g., *Fuga* 31, *Somn.* 2:53, 2:275; Berthelot 2010; Niehoff in press, b; in press, d.

[10] Even Philo, who refers to Hebrew etymologies, had no access to the Hebrew Bible but instead relied on etymological lists, as has been shown by Amir 1988, pp. 440–4; Grabbe 1988 (including an English translation of Y. Amir's 1984 Hebrew article); Kahn 1965, pp. 337–45; Kamesar 2009, pp. 65–73; contra Rajak 2009, pp. 149–50, who proposes to revive the position of Wolfson 1947, vol. 1, pp. 87–90. Note other signs too of Philo's acculturation: he not only attended the theatre and was familiar with the different sports practised in the gymnasium (Harris 1976, pp. 51–101) but is also the first extant writer to call Plato 'most holy' (Niehoff 2007). He explained many of his views by reference to Plato, Aristotle, his student Theophrastus and the Stoics, obviously taking a keen interest in the contemporary philosophical discourse (Bréhier 1908; Runia 1986, 1981; Lévy 1998, 2009; Alesse 2008; Niehoff 2010b. On Philo's views on Greeks and Greek culture, see Birnbaum 2001; Niehoff 2001, pp. 137–58. For further details on the exclusively Greek context of Alexandrian Bible exegesis, see especially Chapter 7.

[11] On the centrality of Homer in the educational programme of Hellenistic Egypt see Cribiore 2001.

offered ground-breaking analyses of their canonical text. Their achieve-
ments were outstanding and anticipated both modern text criticism as well
as subsequent developments in later antiquity. Whereas the overall picture is
one of significant creativity in dialogue with the intellectual discourse of the
environment, it is conspicuous that there were lively controversies among
Alexandrian Jews about the nature and legitimacy of academic scholarship.

THE DIVERSITY OF ALEXANDRIAN JUDAISM

Special attention will be paid in this book to the diversity of views among
Alexandrian Jews. In Alexandria, where Josephus' famous distinction of
three Jewish 'sects' does not apply and no papyri of the significance of
the Qumran Scrolls have yet been discovered, we have to rely on the
extant literary evidence for a reconstruction of the different approaches.[12]
Already the earliest Jewish sources from Ptolemaic Egypt suggest significant
diversity. While Ezekiel the Tragedian, for example, used Euripides' model
to stage his own drama of the Exodus, Aristeas denounced the use of
biblical materials on the stage.[13] Artapanus employed motifs of the Graeco-
Egyptian Alexander legends to depict Moses as a military leader, whereas
Aristobulus was convinced that Moses had established a distinct Jewish
philosophy, which was comparable to the views of the Peripatetics, Homer
and Hesiod as well as Orpheus.[14]

The *Letter of Aristeas*, Demetrius and Aristobulus provide our main evidence of Jewish Bible exegesis in Ptolemaic Alexandria. I shall argue that
they were written in the mid second century BCE and belonged to the
period when Alexandrian scholarship was at its height under the leadership
of Aristarchus.[15] The *Letter of Aristeas* will first be investigated, because
it offers a meaningful and unique account of the Alexandrian Library in
relation to the Jewish Scriptures. In contrast to current views, I shall argue
that Aristeas was conservative. Rejecting the application of critical Homeric

---

[12] The Therapeutae, depicted by Philo as a 'party' (προαίρεσις, *Cont.* 67) with separate living quarters
near Alexandria and a special style of life, will be discussed below in Chapter 9. The diversity of
Alexandrian Judaism is also stressed by J. J. Collins 2000, pp. 14–16. On the sects in the Land of
Israel, see esp. Baumgarten 1997, pp. 42–80; Goodman 2000; Newman 2006, esp. pp. 51–124.

[13] On Ezekiel's and Aristeas' attitudes towards the theatre, see Gutman 1958–63, vol. II, pp. 9–69;
Jacobson 1983; Lanfranchi 2006; Barclay 1996, pp. 132–8.

[14] On Artapanus see Gutman 1958–63, vol. II, pp. 109–36; Holladay 1983–96, vol. I, p. 235; Barclay
1996, pp. 127–32; on Aristobulus, see Gutman 1958–63, vol. II, pp. 186–220; Walter 1964, pp. 10–13,
103–15; Holladay 1983–96, vol. III, pp. 114–15, 204–6, 226–7; J. J. Collins 2000, pp. 186–90.

[15] For discussions of the dates of these works, see below in the respective chapters, especially Chapter
3, where I explain why the generally assumed third-century date of Demetrius can no longer be
maintained.

methods to the Jewish Scriptures, he provides an important mirror image of some of his colleagues' scholarship. Demetrius and Aristobulus, on the other hand, positively engage the hermeneutic methods developed at the Museum and throw crucial new light on the state of biblical scholarship in the Ptolemaic period. Both authors furthermore belong to the Aristotelian tradition and help us reconstruct the history of that school in Alexandria.

Lacking independent exegetical sources between the mid second century BCE and the first century CE, vital evidence of the diversity of Alexandrian Judaism comes from Philo. While implying that there is but one legitimate approach to Scripture, namely that of 'us students of Moses', Philo does not altogether suppress divergent Jewish voices.[16] Initially, it must be noted that he mentions 'thousands of schools' opening on the Sabbath to teach Jewish values.[17] This number cannot be taken literally but deserves serious attention, because the undoubtedly existing variety of synagogues in Alexandria implies diverse kinds of activities and attitudes.[18]

Moreover, scholars have noted the complexity of Philo's work, which reflects not only his own views, but also those of his colleagues and predecessors. Wilhelm Bousset, Richard Goulet and Thomas Tobin offered comprehensive reconstructions of such early exegetical layers. Relying on an internal literary analysis, the first two identified Stoic predecessors of Philo, while the last argued for previous Platonic interpreters of the Book of Genesis.[19] Whereas the first two studies are no longer taken seriously today, they, too, pursued the important aim of understanding Philo in the context of his discussion partners in Alexandria. The methodological problem underlying these studies, which has also aroused the impression of a too speculative approach, is the fact that in the majority of examples Philo himself does not refer to others. The analysis thus relies on exegetical tensions or contradictions, which may be explained by recourse to earlier interpreters whose views Philo integrated into his work without harmonizing them with his own position.

Significant progress has been made in this field by David Hay, who began to examine Philo's explicit references to other exegetes. Initially, he studied Philo's references to other allegorists and then devoted a seminal article to other exegetes in Philo's *Questions and Answers*. Hay concluded that Philo did not write in an intellectual vacuum but conceived of 'exegesis as a kind of

---

[16] The expression 'we students of Moses' can be found in *Her.* 81, *Q.G.* 3.8. Philo's emphasis on Jewish unity has recently also been noted by Carlier 2008, pp. 234–6.
[17] Μυρία διδασκαλεία (*Spec.* 2.62).   [18] See also Clauss 2003, pp. 150–1.
[19] Bousset 1915; Goulet 1987; Tobin 1983.

dialogical enterprise that involves debate partners and opponents'.[20] Such discussion partners included both allegorists and literalists. Hay stressed that the latter were sophisticated and critical readers of Scripture, thus correcting Shroyer's earlier view of them as naïve, orthodox Jews.[21]

While scholars such as John Dillon consider Philo's references to other exegetes as mere rhetoric which does not point to real people or discussions, Hay's approach is convincing and deserves further consideration.[22] For the purposes of this book all of Philo's references to other interpretations have been carefully studied. The great variety of their style and content is so conspicuous that they must indeed reflect different exegetical orientations of independent Jewish exegetes. Philo's references thus provide an invaluable glimpse into the original variety of Alexandrian Judaism, which does not happen to have been fully preserved by the Church Fathers.

Philo's references to his colleagues allow us to reconstruct approaches to Scripture which have not been preserved elsewhere. Reading Philo's fragments in the context of Homeric scholarship, I shall argue that his colleagues adopted certain critical methods practised in Alexandria. It is even possible to distinguish several different approaches among Philo's colleagues: some adopted a mythological-comparative approach, analysing stories such as the Tower of Babel in light of similar material in the *Odyssey*; others adopted a historical approach, investigating the Binding of Isaac in the context of ancient child sacrifice, while still others engaged in text emendations. For Philo, all these methods were anathema and amounted to an impious violation of Scripture. When studying these fragments, we have to bear in mind that their transmitter was an outspoken opponent of them who wanted his readers to dismiss their views as silly figments of the imagination. As Dillon once put it in another context, 'it is rather like trying to piece together Conservative Party policy during an election campaign solely on the basis of scattered criticisms from Labour spokesmen'.[23] Just as Dillon himself was not deterred by such a challenge regarding fragments of Platonist philosophers, we shall proceed to recover the views of Alexandrian exegetes which lay hidden in Philo's polemics. Luckily, some of the fragments are impressively long, covering several pages of Cohn-Wendland's critical edition.

---

[20] Hay 1979–80. Hay 1991b; quotation on p. 97.   [21] Shroyer 1936.
[22] Dillon 1983, p. 84, argues that 'it is not necessary that there should be any real author for most of these *aporiai*'; Snyder 2000, pp. 122–3, adopts a more nuanced approach, admitting the great diversity of Alexandrian Judaism, which cannot, however, in his view be investigated, because of the immense loss of original books.
[23] Dillon 2003a, p. 17.

Variety characterizes not only the discussion among Alexandrian Jews reflected in Philo's work, but also Philo's own work. As has long been noticed, the many extant treatises of his writings do not convey a uniform picture. When the critical edition began to be prepared at the end of the nineteenth century, scholars investigated the nature of Philo's different works as well as their possible chronological order. Louis Massebieau and Leopold Cohn made substantial contributions, both distinguishing between the *Allegorical Commentary* and the *Questions and Answers* (*Q&A*), on the one hand, and the *Exposition of the Law* (*Exposition*) as well as the historical and 'apologetic' treatises, on the other.[24] Paul Wendland was able to demonstrate the authenticity of Philo's treatise on the Therapeutae by arguing that although it sharply differs from the *Allegorical Commentary*, it shows significant similarities to the *Exposition*.[25]

The question of Philo's different audiences, which has been taken into account since the inception of modern research, has received renewed attention in recent scholarship. Ellen Birnbaum made significant progress in this area by pointing to conspicuous differences in Philo's notions of Jews and Judaism:[26] the *Allegorical Commentary* speaks about Israel; the *Exposition* talks about Jews and appears to address a wider audience not familiar with Jewish history. Similarly, Gregory Sterling and James Royse distinguished Philo's different audiences.[27] According to their analysis, the readers of the *Q&A* require an elementary instruction in exegesis, while the *Allegorical Commentary* addresses advanced readers. The *Exposition*, on the other hand, provides a more thematic introduction to a wide audience of mainly non-Jews.[28]

Philo's attitude towards Homeric scholarship will be studied in the context of his different exegetical series. Separate chapters will be devoted to the *Allegorical Commentary*, the *Q&A* and the *Exposition*. The former two series conform to the conventions of a running commentary and will be shown to have developed in a distinctly Alexandrian environment. At the same time, however, they make rather different use of academic methods. In the *Allegorical Commentary* Philo responds to highly critical Jewish colleagues in Alexandria and develops his own, more conservative approach, which combines literal scholarship with extended allegory. This

---

[24] Massebieau 1888, pp. 10–33, 59–65, and Cohn 1899, who both argued for the priority of the *Allegorical Commentary* in comparison with the *Exposition* and the 'apologetic' works, but they differed regarding its relationship to the *Q&A*.

[25] Wendland 1896, pp. 716–19.   [26] Birnbaum 1996.

[27] Sterling 1999, pp. 148–64; Royse 2009; see also Böhm 2005, pp. 116–22, 238–52.

[28] For an analysis of characteristic themes in Philo's different writings with a view to their particular audiences, see also Birnbaum 2004.

particular synthesis was radically new and laid the foundation for many subsequent writers. The *Q&A*, by contrast, appeals to less sophisticated readers, who may have been Philo's own students. The question and answer format is no longer used as an academic tool, but rather as an organizing principle. Philo's treatise thus provides important new insights into Jewish Bible instruction in Alexandria.

The *Exposition*, on the other hand, will be shown to have emerged in a strikingly different context from the other two exegetical series. This work no longer follows Alexandrian conventions of a running commentary and is generally more removed from the concerns of textual scholarship. This treatise is crucial to understanding Philo's use of exegesis in a world where Rome and non-Jewish readers played an increasingly important role. The analysis of the *Exposition* in light of both Homeric scholarship and its implied audience suggests that this series belongs to Philo's mature period, when he was already involved in politics, travelling as the head of the Jewish embassy to Rome.

Looking at the development of Alexandrian exegesis over a span of approximately two hundred years, it is conspicuous that Philo and his colleagues as well as his predecessors held contrary positions on the question whether the Jewish Scriptures are unique or similar to other foundational texts. While Aristobulus and Philo's anonymous colleagues affirmed the congeniality of Moses' Torah and Homer's epics, Philo insisted on the uniqueness of the Jewish Scriptures. Much of his exegesis can be understood as an effort to create a separate Jewish discourse. Philo was intimately familiar with Greek hermeneutics and in a sense presents the peak of extant Jewish Bible scholarship in Alexandria, but he may also be seen to mark its end. He neither integrated the Bible any longer into the general academic discourse around Homer nor encouraged open dialogue and controversy. Philo instead turned increasingly to preaching the correct interpretation of Scripture, hoping to provide conclusive answers which would render further inquiry superfluous.[29] This 'parting of the ways' of biblical and Homeric scholarship must be appreciated in the context of rising political tensions in Alexandria, where prominent Homeric scholars such as Apion were also fervently anti-Jewish.[30]

Studying the diversity of Jewish engagements with Homeric scholarship in Alexandria, one can only regret that Leopold Cohn, a scholar truly

[29] This conclusion broadly correlates with the findings of Goldhill 2008, which focuses on the transition from the Classical to the Christian period, without, however, taking Philo into account.

[30] On Apion as scholar and historian, see Dillery 2003; on the events themselves, see esp. Harker 2008; Gambetti 2009; van der Horst 2003.

destined to make a fundamental contribution in this field and perhaps even render this book superfluous, did not address the topic. He not only edited Philo's texts and was a leading expert on his work but also wrote the entry in the *Realenzyclopaedie* on Aristarchus, the most important Homeric scholar in Alexandria. Cohn moreover wrote an enormously erudite treatise on the early scholia to Plato's writings, which still commands respect today.[31]

Furthermore, Adam Kamesar has recently produced some pioneering articles, which anticipate the present book. Kamesar interpreted Philo's literary references to Scripture, noted already by Yehoshua Amir, in the context of Greek scholarship.[32] He also noticed that Philo was less open to comparisons between Scripture and the Homeric epics than some of his predecessors, thus acknowledging the variety of Alexandrian Judaism. At the same time, however, Kamesar neither attempted a comprehensive study of Alexandrian exegesis nor took the Alexandrian scholia into account.[33]

HOMERIC SCHOLARSHIP

Some explanations about Homeric scholarship are necessary as an introduction for readers not familiar with it. Homeric scholarship in the broad sense can be traced back to very early times, reaching an important climax in Aristotle's *Aporemata Homerica* and the twenty-fifth chapter of his *Poetics*. These works responded to widely known criticisms of the epics, especially Plato's dismissal of Homer as an unphilosophical and thus misleading writer.[34] Aristotle offered a highly influential alternative to the approach of his predecessors, calling for an appreciation of the epics as literature similar to tragedy.

Alexandria subsequently became the leading Hellenistic centre of Homeric scholarship, where immensely important commentaries were produced. While none of the original works has survived, a very considerable number of fragments is extant in the scholia to the *Iliad* and the *Odyssey*.[35] As the

---

[31] Cohn 1884, who is frequently quoted by Schironi 2005.

[32] Kamesar 1997; Kamesar 2009, pp. 73–7; Amir 1984, an abbreviated English version can be found in Amir 1988, pp. 428–40; see also Amir 1974; Borgen 1997, pp. 80–101; Stein 1935, pp. 4–10; Novick 2009.

[33] Kamesar 2004 refers to the later Byzantine scholia and investigates allegorical rather than literal exegesis.

[34] On Aristotle, see Richardson 1992; Bywater 1909, pp. 323–54; Dupont-Roc and Lallot 1980, pp. 386–404; Else 1986; on Plato, see esp. Männlein-Robert 2002.

[35] Summary treatises, such as the grammar of Dionysius of Thrax's or Ps.-Plutarch's *On Homer*, reflect only indirectly the scholarly activity in Alexandria and should therefore be used with caution; on Dionysius see Dickey 2007, pp. 70, 77–8; Schenkeveld 1994, pp. 263–301; for references to Dionysius' work in the analysis of Bible exegesis, see Kamesar 1994; Sandnes 2009, pp. 40–58.

scholia are of rather daunting dimensions and have never been translated, thus not being easily accessible to a wider audience, they require some introductory explanation.[36]

The Homeric scholia are now available in critical editions and contain our main evidence of Alexandrian scholarship.[37] Having lost the original works, we have to rely on fragments in later compilations, which are based on a complex chain of transmission. By means of the scholia we gain access to the work of the most eminent Homer scholar in Alexandria, namely Aristarchus, as well as to the views of his predecessors Zenodotus and Aristophanes of Byzantium. Zenodotus, the first chief librarian of Alexandria, who probably published an edition of the *Iliad* around 275 BCE, began to develop a rudimentary system of critical signs by which he indicated his own text emendations.[38] Although his precise methods as well as the originality and academic value of his work are still debated in modern scholarship, it is clear that this figure is heavily overshadowed by Aristarchus, who preserved his arguments only for the purpose of sharply attacking them.[39]

Zenodotus' student Aristophanes grew up in Egypt and was from his youth onwards associated with the academic activities of the Museum and the Library. In the field of Homeric scholarship he made several lasting contributions, which laid the foundation for Aristarchus' work. He invented the Greek accent marks still in use today, refined the system of the critical signs indicating text emendations and also published a new edition of the Homeric text.[40] As far as can be seen in the sparse fragments, Aristophanes reached a new level of academic rigour, being far more cautious than his predecessor regarding text emendations. Whereas he did not yet compose full commentaries on Homer's epics, he began to offer explanations of literary works that took into account their historical circumstances.

Aristarchus of Samothrace, the fifth head of the Library and tutor in the royal family, set new standards of Homeric scholarship in mid-second-century BCE Alexandria. He not only produced two successive editions of the text, but also wrote treatises on specific topics as well as two running

---

[36] See also Dickey 2007; Montanari 1993; Pontani 2005b, pp. 23–103; Nünlist 2009a.
[37] Erbse 1969–99; Pontani 2007; see also the older edition by Dindorf 1855.
[38] Pfeiffer 1968, pp. 105–19; Fraser 1972, vol. I, pp. 449–51; Montanari 1993, pp. 265–56; Schmidt 1997; Montanari 1998, pp. 6–9.
[39] M. L. West 2001, pp. 33–45, rehabilitated Zenodotus by pointing to evidence of a local text version, which may explain his 'erratic' readings.
[40] Pfeiffer 1968, pp. 171–203; Fraser 1972, vol. I, pp. 459–61; Montanari 1993, pp. 268–70; Dickey 2007, pp. 92–4.

commentaries (ὑπομνήματα).[41] The critical signs in Aristarchus' edition of the Homeric text were linked to his commentaries, where he discussed the respective textual and literary problems in considerable detail. Whether or not he ever pronounced the famous principle, preserved by Porphyry, that 'Homer is to be elucidated from Homer', Aristarchus paid special attention to the internal coherence of the entire corpus.[42] Arguing that both the *Iliad* and the *Odyssey* stemmed from the same author, he inquired into his characteristic style and presentation of dramatic figures. The comparison of similar or apparently contradictory lines became a central notion; Aristarchus also considered the epics in their historical context, examining their language and ideas against the background of their supposed time of composition.

Aristarchus has been increasingly identified as a scholar of Aristotelian orientation, who must have been familiar, either directly or indirectly, with Aristotle's literary notions of the epics. While N. J. Richardson and Franco Montanari have already pointed to Aristotle's strong influence on Alexandrian and Byzantine scholarship, more recently Francesca Schironi has emphasized the similarities between Aristotle's theories and Aristarchus' philological work.[43] It has thus become clear that the latter not only interpreted numerous epic lines parallel to Aristotle but shared with him fundamental literary sensitivities. Schironi has shown that both saw the epic in the light of tragedy, paid attention to the plot as well as to the plausibility of the actions, worked with a notion of 'appropriate' character traits and carefully examined lexical issues. The increasing sophistication of Alexandrian scholarship thus corresponds to a more pronounced adoption of Aristotelian notions. It was in this form that Alexandrian scholarship became most known, being spread by Aristarchus' numerous students.

A few words must be said about the transmission of the scholia. None of the original Alexandrian works has survived. In the Augustan period, however, two scholars made extensive use of them. Aristonicus faithfully transmitted Aristarchus' work, directly relying on the latter's original commentaries, while the slightly later Didymus wrote a composite commentary with many references to Aristarchus' work and Zenodotus' views.

---

[41] For summary treatments see Fraser 1972, vol. I, pp. 462–5; Montanari 1993, pp. 270–2; Montanari 1998, pp. 10–18; contra Pfeiffer 1968, pp. 210–33; for detailed studies see Lehrs 1882; van der Valk 1963–4, vol. II, pp. 84–263.

[42] Fraser 1972, vol. I, p. 464; Porter 1992, pp. 70–80; contra Pfeiffer 1968, pp. 225–7.

[43] Richardson 1994, 1980; Montanari 1993, pp. 259–64; 1995; Schironi 2009; see also Lührs 1992, pp. 13–17; Gallavotti 1969; Podlecki 1969; Struck 2004, pp. 69–71.

Unfortunately, the works of Aristonicus and Didymus are also lost. Relatively large quantities of their treatises, however, survive in the marginal explanations (scholia) of medieval manuscripts. For the *Iliad* the most important witness is the famous Venetus A codex, preserving, via the *Viermännerkommentar*, most of the ancient Alexandrian material.[44] Following Karl Lehrs' pioneering research, scholars today rely on the A scholia for Aristarchus' work, while some have stressed that also the Byzantine bT scholia contain early Alexandrian material.[45] For the purposes of the present book I have focused on the A scholia in order to be on the safest possible grounds with regard to Alexandrian Jews.

Readers used to the Bible commentaries of Philo or the rabbis will find the Homeric scholia surprisingly familiar. They systematically follow the epic text, consisting of an initial quotation (the lemma) and a subsequent commentary. The latter often begins by raising a question and then providing one or several answers. Aristarchus characteristically refers for this purpose to other epic lines in different contexts. A scholion often refers to a variety of views by either naming the particular scholars or more generally indicating what 'some say'. The reader who is unfamiliar with scholarly Greek and who wants to look up references beyond those which I have translated may initially be puzzled by the brevity of their style.[46] It is often not easy to distinguish between the interpreter's own words and his references to the Homeric text. While modern editions of the scholia clarify the picture by using different print for the lemma and the subsequent commentary, the use of Homeric language within the commentary, as an abbreviated reference to the context under discussion, still demands particular attention. Also, much is taken for granted in the scholia. Abbreviating larger commentaries, the scholia regularly omit the initial critical sign which had been used, as well as the subject of the sentence, leaving it open whether the poet or the dramatic character is discussed.[47] In order to help the reader, the scholia quoted in this book have regularly been contextualized by a paraphrase.

---

[44] See also Dickey 2007, pp. 7, 11, 18–19; Schmidt 2002, pp. 160–77.

[45] Lehrs 1882, pp. 1–16; Lehrs' analysis was subsequently accepted and further developed by Ludwich 1884–5, vol. I, pp. 51–4, who found Didymus more reliable in his testimony of Aristarchus' readings; see also Pfeiffer 1968, pp. 213–15, 218; Fraser 1972, vol. I, pp. 463–4. The importance of the bT tradition for a reconstruction of earlier Alexandrian traditions has been stressed by Schmidt 1976, pp. 8–16; Lührs 1992, pp. 4–6.

[46] See also the very useful passages and glossary provided by Dickey 2007, pp. 141–265 as an introduction to the field.

[47] See also Nünlist 2009a, pp. 8–9.

JUDAISM, HELLENISM AND ROME

My argument for close connections between Jewish Bible exegesis and Homeric scholarship in Alexandria has significant implications for our understanding of the relationship between Judaism, Hellenism and Rome. While the degree and nature of Hellenization in the Land of Israel is still controversial, Alexandrian Judaism is usually acknowledged as a form of synthesis.[48] In this context Judaism is generally no longer seen as an antithesis to Hellenism, which made certain compromises, but rather as a creative way of expressing Jewish identity in the new forms of Greek literature. The subject of literal biblical exegesis, however, has been surprisingly eclipsed in this discussion: similarities between Philonic and Stoic allegory have often been studied, but the notion of Scripture as such and its literal interpretations have rarely been compared to their Greek counterparts.[49] This isolation of fields is all the more surprising as strategies of canonization, together with their foundation legends, have recently been studied from a comparative perspective.[50]

The persisting dichotomy of fields seems to be based on an intuition, shared by many, that literal Bible exegesis is quintessentially Jewish and thus incomparable. Some scholars believe that Jews were 'not infected by this critical spirit' of Greek scholarship, thus assuming a more fundamental dichotomy between the cultures.[51] On this view, Greeks were concerned with aesthetics, individual expression and literary considerations, which led to scholarship, while Jews and Christians were absorbed in religious thinking, relying on the prophetic inspiration of their Scriptures without producing literary or scholarly works.[52] It is time to reconsider these assumptions and study Alexandrian Bible exegesis in the historical and cultural context of its ancient practitioners. Such an approach requires attention to the ancient sources themselves as well as interdisciplinary perspectives.

My argument for close connections between Homeric and biblical scholarship also points to the integration of Alexandrian Jews in the elite culture of the city. Jewish scholars were familiar with academic methods developed and discussed at the Museum, which remained without visible impact among the broader population of Hellenistic Egypt.[53] Already Didymus

---

[48] See esp. Hengel 1974 (trans. of German original 1973); and the ensuing discussion of Hengel 2001.
[49] See esp. Buffière 1956; Pépin 1987; Amir 1971; Kamesar 2004; Liebes 2009.
[50] See esp. Finkelberg and Stroumsa 2003; Wyrick 2004.   [51] Siegert 1996, p. 164.
[52] For an influential formulation of such a view see Assmann 1992.
[53] See Marrou 1950, pp. 228–9; M. L. West 2001, pp. 50–2, 61–7; McNamee 1981; M. Finkelberg 2006.

in the Augustan period distinguished between Aristarchus' readings and those of the 'popular' editions.[54] At the same time, however, Didymus' and Aristonicus' discussions of Aristarchus' work drew new attention to him and even produced such a famous student as Philo's contemporary Apion.[55] Jewish intellectuals came into contact with the work of Aristarchus and his numerous students at the Museum. They seem to have been part of Aristarchus' original audience as well as subsequent admirers of his work.

This book will also throw new light on the nature and development of the different philosophical schools in Alexandria. As literary scholarship, both on the Greek and on the Jewish side, is pre-eminently rooted in the Aristotelian tradition, the importance of this school will come into new focus. Identifying Aristobulus as well as Philo's anonymous colleagues as Peripatetics, I propose to fill in an important gap in our picture and provide evidence which has thus far been overlooked. The Aristotelian tradition in Alexandria will emerge as more influential than has so far been recognized.

Philo's pivotal role in the development of Platonism will be recognized. The Platonic tradition remained for a long time reticent concerning Homeric scholarship, following the founder's harsh criticism of the epics.[56] Firmly committed to a Platonist approach, Philo nevertheless engaged Aristotelian methods of Homeric scholarship and responded to his Aristotelian colleagues.[57] His own exegetical approach can be understood as a new synthesis of Aristotelian and Platonic notions. He is thus a highly significant predecessor of Longinus and Porphyry. The latter, in particular, similarly used Aristotelian scholarship while also offering allegorical interpretations with Platonic themes.[58] Philo indeed marks a turning point in Alexandria, when the overwhelmingly Aristotelian orientation of the city began to change rather dramatically.

This book furthermore suggests that Stoicism was far less important in Alexandria than has often been assumed. Too readily have all non-literal interpretations been identified with this school, taking Aristobulus as a proof for the early influence of Stoicism among Alexandrian Jews. A careful study of the evidence, however, shows that the picture is far more complex, other non-literal approaches being available. The spread of Stoicism in

---

[54] Αἱ δὲ κοιναί or αἱ δημώδεις, see, e.g., Schol. *Il.* 5.797T, 5.881A, 12.382A.
[55] M. L. West 2001, pp. 46–85; Fraser 1972, vol. 1, pp. 463–5.   [56] Weinstock 1927.
[57] The Platonic aspects of Philo's philosophy have been thoroughly studied by Runia 1986, 1993b, 2001; more recently, see also Niehoff 2010b.
[58] Regarding Longinus, see Männlein-Robert 2001; regarding Porphyry, see below, Chapters 3, 4 and 8.

Alexandria was instead relatively late and had to do with the rise of Rome.[59] Accompanying Lucullus in the Second Mithridatic War, Antiochus stayed in Alexandria and received two books of philosophy from his teacher Philo in Rome, which prompted him to formulate his own, more integrationist view of the history of philosophy, which also included significant Stoic elements (Cic. *Acad.* 2:11–12). When Antiochus left Alexandria, Dion and Aristo as well as other Alexandrian intellectuals continued the discussion.[60] Following Augustus' conquest of Egypt, Alexandria began to entertain close intellectual ties with the new capital. Arius Didymus played a special role as an *amicus* of Augustus, who came to Rome under his tutelage but continued to write in Greek and retained contacts with Alexandria (Plut. *Ant.* 80). Significantly, his *Epitome of Ethics* revives and transmits many orthodox Stoic views.

Philo played a pivotal role in this context, too. Among the Jewish exegetes in Alexandria he was most exposed to Rome and Roman culture.[61] Belonging to one of the wealthiest families with close connections to the Roman administration, he himself travelled to Rome as the head of the Jewish embassy to Gaius, spending at least two years there (38–40 or 41), as the emperor was reluctant to receive them.[62] Philo also engaged in the intellectual discourse in Rome, assuming positions strikingly similar to those of his contemporary Seneca.[63] His *Exposition* indicates a significant transition from his early Aristotelian environment in Alexandria to a distinctly more Roman as well as Stoic context.

Finally, the conclusions of this book have important implications for the study of other fields of exegesis, especially Christian and rabbinic interpretations of the Bible. Thus far, the connections between Christian and Jewish exegesis have often been investigated with a view to allegory, remaining regrettably isolated from studies of the relationship between Christian exegesis and Greek scholarship.[64] It is now time to integrate

---

[59] On the connection between Alexandria and Rome, see Fraser 1972, vol. 1, pp. 485–94; Sedley 2003, pp. 20–32; Niehoff 2010c.

[60] See also Karamanolis 2006, pp. 44–85. Glucker 1978, pp. 90–7, rightly warns us not to project a clearly defined school of Antiochus onto the highly fragmentary evidence, but he goes too far in his scepticism when suggesting that Antiochus never had any time to speak with Alexandrian intellectuals as he was too busy with politics.

[61] Niehoff 2001, pp. 17–58.

[62] Philo's embassy is likely to have stayed in Rome also after Gaius' assassination in January 41 in order to take up the negotiations with his successor, Claudius; regarding the dates of the embassy, see Harker 2008, pp. 10–21.

[63] Niehoff 2010c.

[64] Connections between patristic exegesis and Homeric scholarship have been profitably studied by Neuschäfer 1987; Kamesar 1993; Villani 2008.

these different elements and examine scholarly as well as allegorical aspects of Christian exegesis in light of Greek and Jewish hermeneutics. The nature and degree of Christian engagements with Homeric scholarship need to be appreciated in the context of their Jewish predecessors. We have to ask whether Christian exegetes continued earlier integrations of Homeric and biblical studies, such as those attested among Alexandrian Jews.

  Moreover, the field of rabbinic exegesis is in need of a comprehensive re-evaluation. Thus far, pioneering studies of its relationship to Greek hermeneutics have relied mostly on Hellenistic grammar books and summaries of hermeneutic methods.[65] It is now time to consider rabbinic exegesis in light of the Alexandrian scholia as well as the important precedent of Alexandrian Bible exegesis. Such studies will significantly contribute to our understanding of the rabbinic move towards a more scholastic type of interpretation, which is not attested during the Second Temple Period.[66]

---

[65] Lieberman 1962, pp. 58–60; Daube 1953; Halevi 1973. More recently, Alexander 1998 has investigated the conditions and assumptions of exegesis in its context by comparing rabbinic Midrash to Alexandrian Homeric scholarship, thus laying the foundation for future research in the field.

[66] The question of whether the rabbis essentially continued earlier forms of exegesis or introduced new methods is still an object of lively debate, on which see the important methodological comments by Fraade 2007, 2009; for the study of some examples, see Niehoff 2008, 2006.

PART I

*Early Jewish responses to
Homeric scholarship*

CHAPTER 2

A conservative reaction to critical scholarship in the Letter of Aristeas

The author of the *Letter of Aristeas* is known as a proud Alexandrian Jew, who was well integrated into the elitist culture of his surroundings.[1] He wrote in elevated Greek style and was familiar with the Ptolemaic court as well as contemporary notions of a philosophical symposium.[2] In this chapter I shall inquire whether Aristeas' general familiarity with Alexandrian culture also included Homeric scholarship. This question is of particular importance because of the relatively early date of the *Letter*. Accepting Peter Fraser's arguments for its composition during Philometor's rule, probably during its second half (164–145 BCE), I shall argue that the *Letter* provides crucial insights into the state of biblical research during the peak of Homeric scholarship, when Aristarchus was chief librarian (*c*. 160–131 BCE).[3]

Pioneering work on the *Letter of Aristeas* was done by Günther Zuntz, who pointed to certain scholarly terms in the *Letter* which reflect the work of Alexandrian Homer scholars, without, however, being systematically applied.[4] In his view, the author of the *Letter* suggests certain parallels between Alexandrian scholarship and the production of the Greek translation but on the whole lacks clarity and even a consistent message. Sylvie Honigman accepts Zuntz's basic observation but argues that the blurring of scholarly activity and the process of translation was deliberate. In her view, it testifies to the author's conviction that the LXX was sacred precisely because its production conformed to scholarly rules.[5] While agreeing with both scholars that there is some blurring of discourses, I hope to show that the author's message is consistently conservative. Aristeas' use of scholarly terminology must be newly examined in light of his implied readers, whom he assumes to be familiar with Homeric techniques. Moreover, I shall argue that the notion of scriptural sanctity and critical scholarship were unbridgeable contrasts for the author.

---

[1] See esp. J. J. Collins 2000, pp. 192–5; Gruen 2008; Pelletier 1962, pp. 56, 59–63.
[2] See esp. Murray 2007; Barclay 1996, pp. 139–43. [3] Fraser 1972, vol. II, pp. 970–2.
[4] Zuntz 1959. [5] Honigman 2003.

Aristeas' generally conservative approach is conspicuous in his repeated insistence on the holiness of Scripture. He is the first extant writer using the expressions 'Holy Legislation' and 'Holy Law' in connection with the Torah.[6] Aristeas furthermore rejects more secular uses of the Bible. He warns his readers that Theopompus had been punished for his attempt to include biblical material in his historical narrative. His affliction was deserved, he explains, because 'he eagerly wished to expose Divine things to common men' (*Letter*, 315). Theodectus the Tragedian, who thought of using biblical material on the stage, did not fare any better (*Letter*, 316). Whether or not these stories have any historical basis at all, it is clear that the author of the *Letter* did not consider it legitimate to make secular use of biblical materials.[7] Aristeas was in this respect more conservative than other Alexandrian Jews. Ezekiel, for example, not only wrote a drama on the Exodus story but even staged God's voice.[8]

CANONIZING THE GREEK BIBLE TRANSLATION

We now have to investigate whether Aristeas' description of the translation of the Bible into Greek or its subsequent canonization reflects an awareness of Homeric scholarship practised in Alexandria. Initially, the key passage at the end of the *Letter*, where the actual translation and its acceptance by the Jewish people are discussed, deserves detailed analysis. The simplicity of the single paragraph devoted to the work of translation is still striking:

Οἱ δὲ ἐπετέλουν ἕκαστα σύμφωνα ποιοῦντες πρὸς ἑαυτοὺς ταῖς ἀντιβολαῖς· τὸ δὲ ἐκ τῆς συμφωνίας γινόμενον πρεπόντως ἀναγραφῆς οὕτως ἐτύγχανε παρὰ τοῦ Δημητρίου. (*Letter*, 302, ed. Pelletier 1962)

And they set out to accomplish this, bringing into accord each [detail] by comparing each other's work.[9] The outcome of this accord was thus appropriately registered by Demetrius.

---

[6] σεμνὴν εἶναι τὴν νομοθεσίαν καὶ διὰ θεοῦ γεγονέναι (*Letter*, 313); and similarly in *Letter*, 5; the expression 'Holy Law' is found in the letter of the High Priest Eleazar (ἡ τοῦ ἁγίου νόμου μεταγραφή, *Letter*, 45). Although the expressions 'in the Holy Laws' (ἐν τοῖς ἱεροῖς νόμοις) and 'in the Holy Books' (ἐν ταῖς ἱεραῖς βίβλοις) occur in the second fragment of Aristobulus' writings, we have to remember that these are Clement's introductory words, not the author's own formulations. Aristobulus himself rather speaks about 'the lawgiver' and 'our legislation' (Holladay 1983–96, vol. III, pp. 134–8).

[7] Lanfranchi 2006, pp. 40–1; J. J. Collins 2000, p. 191.

[8] Ezek. *Exagoge*, fr. 9 (ed. Holladay 1983–96, vol. II, p. 371), where God speaks with Moses at the Burning Bush, being heard but not seen.

[9] Unless otherwise stated, all translations are my own. Here I have adopted H. Thackeray's felicitous translation 'by comparing each other's work' (Thackeray 1903, p. 388); similarly Tramontano 1931, pp. 237–8.

The crucial expressions of this passage are ἀντιβολή and σύμφωνα ποιέω, both of which have been taken as technical terms of contemporary Alexandrian scholarship.[10] This, however, is far from self-evident. In the case of ἀντιβολή an anachronism is involved, because at the time of Aristeas the term meant comparison and discussion. Only later did it come to signify manuscript collation.[11] Eleanor Dickey in her glossary of grammatical terms in ancient Greek scholarship defines the term generally, namely as 'discussion, confrontation'.[12] The noun as well as the verb ἀντιβάλλω are significantly missing in Erbse's index to the scholia. Indeed, Martin West has warned us not to project Didymus' methods in the Augustan period back to Zenodotus and Aristarchus in the third and second centuries BCE. While Didymus regularly collated manuscripts, his predecessors generally had not done so.[13] The above passage in the *Letter of Aristeas* thus needs to be understood in the context of its time as a general comparison of the translations produced by the different translators. Too much was read into it when it was taken as a reference to a collation of manuscripts, such as that supposedly performed by contemporary Alexandrian scholars in the preparation of text editions.

Similarly, the notion of 'bringing into accord' remains general. The only two occurrences of this precise expression in the extant Greek literature before Aristeas are revealing. Plato uses it in a general philosophical context, while a fragment concerning the book of Aratus speaks of 'bringing into accord each [of the details]' by 'correcting' the text in light of what the poet himself wrote and on the assumption that his poetics 'accord with the phenomena'.[14] The technical term of Alexandrian scholarship 'correction' or 'corrected edition' (διόρθωσις) appears twice in this small fragment, whereas the *Letter of Aristeas* completely lacks such vocabulary. Its author can thus hardly have intended to present the translation as a process which included text-critical, editorial work. This conclusion is further corroborated by the fact that the copy said to be brought from Jerusalem for the

---

[10] Honigman 2003, pp. 46–7, translates the former expression as 'comparing versions' and relies only on general secondary literature for the image of Alexandrian scholarship; Zuntz 1959, pp. 122–3, takes the term ἀντιβολή in a technical sense of manuscript collation but then suggests that it has been used incompetently by Aristeas as a general reference to a comparison of views.

[11] Characteristically, the entry ἀντιβάλλω in Liddell and Scott 1996, p. 154 refers only to first-century BCE sources for the meaning 'to collate manuscripts'.

[12] Dickey 2007, p. 224.

[13] M. L. West 2001, p. 36; Slater 1982; contra Fraser 1972, vol. I, p. 464, who based his argument only on Schol. *Il.* 9.222, which, however, can also be interpreted differently (van der Valk 1963–4, vol. II, p. 89); Montanari 1998, pp. 6–9.

[14] Plat. *Resp.* 441e; the fragment is found in Attalus, *Math. et Astron.* 1.14 and Hipparchus, *Geogr. et Astron.* 1.3 τό τε τοῦ Ἀράτου βιβλίον ἐξαπεστάλκαμέν σοι διωρθωμένον ὑφ᾽ ἡμῶν; see also l.4.

purpose of translation is not described in terms of textual excellence. The High Priest Eleazar merely says that he has chosen good men, who are sent 'having the law'.[15] The corpus is important, not a particular version or its high quality.

Although scholarly terminology is lacking in the paragraph describing the process of translation, it does appear in the account of its reception by the Jewish people. In this context, however, scholarship is not praised as suitable for the Jewish Scriptures, but on the contrary condemned as a dangerous prospect which must be prevented. Victor Tcherikover and Harry Orlinsky recognized the reading aloud of the Greek translation and its acceptance by the people as an act of canonization.[16] Orlinsky in particular showed that the author of the *Letter* invoked images of foundational scenes, such as the congregation at Mount Sinai, in order to present the LXX as God's Holy Law. Pursuing this analysis further, I wish to point to significant motifs which the author of the *Letter* added to the traditional scenes. These relate to scholarly work and highlight the difference between a pious acceptance of a canonical text and independent inquiry into a literary corpus.

After the translation was completed, Demetrius is said to have assembled the Jewish community, reading to all of them the text which had just come from the hands of the translators. The crucial passage then follows:

Καθὼς δὲ ἀνεγνώσθη τὰ τεύχη, στάντες οἱ ἱερεῖς καὶ τῶν ἑρμηνέων οἱ πρεσ-βύτεροι καὶ τῶν ἀπὸ τοῦ πολιτεύματος οἵ τε ἡγούμενοι τοῦ πλήθους εἶπον· Ἐπεὶ καλῶς καὶ ὁσίως διηρμήνευται καὶ κατὰ πᾶν ἠκριβωμένως, καλῶς ἔχον ἐστὶν ἵνα διαμείνῃ ταῦθ᾽ οὕτως ἔχοντα, καὶ μὴ γένηται μηδεμία διασκευή. Πάντων δ᾽ ἐπιφωνησάντων τοῖς εἰρημένοις, ἐκέλευσαν διαράσασθαι, καθὼς ἔθος αὐτοῖς ἐστιν, εἴ τις διασκευάσει προστιθεὶς ἢ μεταφέρων τι τὸ σύνολον τῶν γεγραμμένων ἢ ποιούμενος ἀφαίρεσιν, καλῶς τοῦτο πράσσοντες, ἵνα διὰ παντὸς ἀέννα καὶ μένοντα φυλάσσηται. (*Letter*, 310–11, ed. Pelletier)

When the scrolls had been read, the priests as well as the elders of the translators and the leaders of the congregation of the people stood up and said: as [the scrolls] were translated well and in a holy manner and accurately in every respect, it is appropriate that they should remain as they are and that no interpolation (διασκευή) should be made. And when all had assented to these words, they, as was the custom among them, ordered that anybody will be cursed who will

---

[15] ἔχοντας τὸν νόμον (*Letter*, 46); similarly in *Letter*, 309 the author speaks of translating 'the whole law'.

[16] Tcherikover 1958, pp. 73–4; Orlinsky 1975, pp. 94–103; see also Hacham 2005, pp. 3–4; Wright 2006, pp. 56–7; contra N. L. Collins 2000, pp. 119–27, who suggests that the scene cannot have had any religious or canonizing function as Demetrius was not Jewish. This interpretation, however, overlooks Aristeas' emphasis on the reception of the LXX by the elders of the Jewish community.

introduce an interpolation (διασκευάσει) by either adding or generally transferring something of what is written or by making a deletion. They did this well with the intent that they [the scrolls] be preserved everlasting and standing fast for ever.

In this passage scholarly terminology is introduced, yet not in order to recommend academic practices, but, on the contrary, to reject them. The author explicitly defends the sanctity of the translation (ὁσίως διηρμήνευ-ται) against any interference with the text, which is in his eyes an impious tampering with Scripture. The main expression used here, διασκευή or διασκευάζειν, is a technical term of Alexandrian scholarship, which refers to text interpolation.[17] It appears in the fragments of Aristonicus' work, which directly reflects Aristarchus' commentaries as well as his text-critical signs used in the editions.[18] Indeed, Aristarchus, the most pre-eminent of the Alexandrian Homer scholars, seems to have been the first who used this term systematically. He thus referred to an irresponsible interpolation and used the term only with a highly derogatory connotation. His own work regularly aimed at correcting such earlier tampering with the epic texts.

Reaching the climax of his academic career during his tenure as chief librarian *c.* 160–131 BCE, Aristarchus often distinguished his own work from that of his predecessor Zenodotus, who began the work of critical scholar-ship in Alexandria. Aristarchus frequently accused him of sheer incompe-tence and suspected that he corrupted rather than emended the text. He thus complained that Zenodotus introduced a 'ridiculous' change to *Il.* 16.666, which he rewrote (διεσκεύακε γράφων) to say that Zeus addressed Apollo from the mountain of Ida (Schol. *Il.* 16.666A). Similarly, an anony-mous 'interpolator' (ὁ διασκευαστής) was accused by Aristarchus of intro-ducing an expression 'contrary to the poet's usage' (Schol. *Od.* 11.584). On another occasion he criticized an 'interpolator' (ὁ διασκευάσας), who had, according to his reconstruction, added two verses (Schol. *Il.* 11.11A).

The term διασκευή refers in these and other contexts to an addition of a verse which Homer had not originally written.[19] Aristarchus identified such interpolations on internal literary grounds and not by comparison of

---

[17] The technical significance of the word in the context of textual criticism has been noted by Meecham 1935, p. 306; van der Kooij 2008 interprets Aristeas' polemics against text revision as a reaction to deliberate and ideological changes of the Greek text in Alexandria, such as reflected in 2 Macc. 2:17; Tramontano 1931, p. 245; Pelletier 1962, p. 234–5, thinks primarily of a reaction to Samaritan recensions. Regarding the Homeric context of the term διασκευή, see esp. Lehrs 1882, pp. 328–31.

[18] For details on Aristonicus' role in transmitting Aristarchus' work, see Chapter 1; Lehrs 1882, pp. 1–16; Ludwich 1884–5, vol. 1, pp. 51–4; Pfeiffer 1968, pp. 213–15, 218; Fraser 1972, vol. 1, pp. 463–4; Lührs 1992, pp. 4–6. In Schol. *Il.* 18.356b and Schol. *Il.* 19.327A Didymus uses the term διασκευή in the context of an athetesis by Aristophanes, reflecting the usage of his own time.

[19] See also Schol. *Il.* 20.269–72A, 24.130–2A, 2.807A, 12.371A, 16.97–100A.

manuscripts. He did not point to a version of the text where the relevant verses were lacking but instead argued that they could not have been written by Homer himself, because they did not suit the overall nature of his poetics. A good example of Aristarchus' reasoning is his conclusion that twenty-three verses had been added to the description of Helen. This 'interpolation' is, according to Aristonicus, rejected by Aristarchus on three grounds: first, there is a contradiction between *Il.* 3.396–8, where Helen sees Aphrodite as beautiful, and *Il.* 3.386, where the goddess is said to appear to her in the image of an old woman; secondly, Helen's suggestion that the goddess herself become Paris' lover is blasphemous; and, thirdly, it is improper to imagine the goddess addressing Helen as a 'hard woman' (*Il.* 3.414).[20]

Moreover, Aristarchus used the term 'interpolation' to refer to a transfer of motifs from one verse to another. He argued, for example, that *Il.* 12.175 was not an original Homeric verse but had been formed on the basis of elements from *Il.* 15.414.[21] On the whole, Aristarchus pointed to interpolations which, in his view, had been added by a later writer with little understanding of Homeric poetry. Such accretions could have resulted either from meddling with the text and transferring motifs or from an attempt to explain something in the epic which looked like a lacuna but truly was not one. Aristarchus saw his role as a scholar mainly as purging the text from such later additions and uncovering its original size and beauty. A central tool in this process was the method of athetesis, namely the marking of spurious verses by a special sign in the margins of the text. It is important to note that such a marking of lines did not imply their omission from the manuscript.[22]

Aristarchus' work provides an important background for the above quoted passage in the *Letter of Aristeas* which describes the canonization of the LXX. It is initially striking that the author uses the typically Aristarchan term διασκευή to designate corruptions of the biblical text. Both reject such changes, suspecting irresponsible tampering with the canonical text. Whereas Aristarchus, however, assumes that such corruptions have already occurred, blaming especially his predecessor Zenodotus, Aristeas envisions

---

[20] Schol. *Il.* 3.395A; see also Schol. *Il.* 4.208A referring to the 'interpolation' of *Il.* 3.396–418.

[21] Schol. *Il.* 15.414a1A; an anonymous scholar, who agreed with Aristarchus, significantly paraphrased διεσκέασται as μεταπεποίηται (Schol. *Il.* 15.414a2). Similarly, students of Aristarchus noted that *Il.* 19.400 had inspired the interpolator of *Il.* 8.185, who transferred the names of the horses and constructed a new verse, which had been duly athetized by their teacher (Schol. *Il.* 19.400A, 8:185b).

[22] Nickau 1977, pp. 6–7; Nünlist 2009a, pp. 16–17.

the prospect of interpolations to the newly emerged translation and is determined to prevent them. In other words, Aristarchus presupposes the faulty nature of his Homeric text, while Aristeas points to the authentic Greek translation of the Hebrew Bible, which needs to be protected from textual manipulations.

If Aristeas' position is thus interpreted in the context of Homeric scholarship in Alexandria, it clearly emerges that he was familiar with text-critical methods. Anticipating that someone would manipulate the biblical text, he must have had fellow Jews in mind, who would introduce such changes. Moreover, he specified three kinds of interpolation, namely additions, omissions and transfers, thus indicating beyond any doubt that he was referring to text-critical methods.[23] Opposing such practices as fervently as the author of the *Letter* does, he must have known already existing biblical scholarship. Aristeas probably reacted to a dramatic increase of academic activity among Alexandrian Jews following Aristarchus' stellar career. The output of Jewish Bible scholarship in Alexandria must have been sufficiently large and impressive to provoke a conservative reaction on the part of Aristeas.

This interpretation is corroborated by recent studies of LXX Genesis, which have shown that the translation itself had already emerged in Jewish scholarly circles close to Greek scholarship. Martin Rösel has analysed the highly sophisticated style of the translator, who was not only conversant with Greek literature but also aimed at standardizing the Hebrew–Greek equivalents, harmonizing tensions between verses and stories as well as clarifying difficult passages.[24] These features, he convincingly argues, can best be explained by assuming that the Greek translator of the Book of Genesis was close to the Museum and its circle of scholars. It is this kind of scholarly activity to which Aristeas reacted, dismissing it as an impious manipulation of the canonical text.

THE CURSE OF INTERPOLATORS

Aristeas' curse of interpolators provides some important clues to the specific academic methods of his Jewish colleagues. Fervently criticizing certain techniques, Aristeas clearly assumed that they were already in use and

---

[23] Cf. Arist. *Poet.* 1451a29–34, where omissions and transfers are discussed in the context of the plot and to some extent even recommended as a means of testing whether any particular element is an essential part of the plot or rather a superfluous accretion.

[24] Rösel 1994, 2008; see also Kreuzer 2004.

suspected their application to the Greek Bible translation which he advocated in his treatise. The specific kinds of textual interference mentioned by him are adding to the text (προστίθημι), transferring motifs (μεταφέρω) and making a deletion (ποιέω ἀφαίρεσιν). These techniques are rooted in Homeric scholarship in Alexandria and reflect significant connections between Greek and Jewish scholars, rather than a general resentment of the Museum and Library by Jewish exegetes, as has sometimes been suggested.[25]

Aristeas' reference to a transfer of motifs conspicuously echoes Alexandrian scholarship, where this notion played a central role in explaining the occurrence of identical verses in different contexts.[26] Aristarchus frequently conjectured in such cases that a line or more had been transferred from one passage to another. He argued, for example, that *Il.* 5.891 had been transferred (μετενήνεκται) and added to *Il.* 1.177 (Schol. *Il.* 5.891A). Commenting on the latter, he athetized it and remarked that 'this [line] is not properly placed here'.[27] Even though our evidence is only fragmentary, Aristonicus says that Aristarchus devoted a special marginal sign to spurious verses which, in his view, had resulted from a transfer: an asterisk in addition to the obelus which usually marked a verse as spurious. Aristarchus thus marked *Il.* 16.237 also with an asterisk (ἀστερίσκος), because it was in his view 'transferred from the prayer of Chryses'.[28] Similarly, *Il.* 5.122 was marked with an asterisk, 'because it was transferred from here to the running competition between Patroclus and Odysseus' (Schol. *Il.* 5.122A). Commenting on the verse in the latter context, Aristarchus remarked 'that it was correctly placed (ὀρθῶς ἐτέτακτο) in the context of Diomedes' (Schol. *Il.* 23.772aA). Considerations of literary propriety and correctness guided Aristarchus throughout his scholarly work. In each case of repetition he decided which of the two identical verses was original and which was transferred. His comments on *Il.* 11.356 provide an illuminating summary of his overall considerations:

---

[25] N. L. Collins 2000, pp. 127–37, who argues that *Letter*, 310 and 311 represent completely different approaches, the former being a later interpolation into the text. This division, however, is highly artificial in view of the fact that both sentences refer to interpolation. It can certainly not support Collins' overall claim that the translation was initiated only by Demetrius the Librarian but deeply resented by Alexandrian Jews, who would not have tolerated the placing of their sacred Scriptures in the Alexandrian Library.

[26] For useful background information see Lührs 1992, pp. 149–67, who stresses that Aristarchus did not principally athetize all repetitions of identical verses but subjected each of them to a minute literary analysis.

[27] ὅτι ἐνταῦθα (οὐκ) ὀρθῶς κεῖται (Schol. *Il.* 1.177A).

[28] Schol. *Il.* 16.237A; see also Schol. *Il.* 1.454 ἐντεῦθεν μετενεχθείς, Schol. *Il.* 2.56bA, Schol. *Il.* 24.45aA ἐκ τῶν Ἡσιόδου μετενήνεκται.

An obelos and an asterisk, because it [this line] is correctly situated (ὀρθῶς κεῖται) in another place [*Il.* 5.310]. For [Hector] was not beaten as much as Aeneas, about whom [it says] 'he crushed the cup [and in addition broke both sinews]' [*Il.* 5.307]. How then was he [Hector] blinded? (Schol. *Il.* 11.356aA)

Given these oddities in connection with Hector, Aristarchus decided that the line originally belonged to *Il.* 5.310 and 'had been transferred from here'.[29]

Taking this background into account, we have to ask what the author of the *Letter of Aristeas* meant when putting a curse on anyone 'generally transferring something of what is written' (*Letter*, 311). Did he neatly join Aristarchus in rejecting transfers of verses, thus principally subscribing to academic methods? The situation appears to be rather more complex. As we have seen above, Aristarchus assumed that the text had already been corrupted in the past, while Aristeas points to the newly emerged translation as an unblemished and authentic text of the Bible, which needs to be protected against textual manipulations. Moreover, in Homeric scholarship the notion of transferred motifs was a scholarly device to explain redundancies. Aristarchus did not claim to have actually seen either a manuscript lacking the transferred lines or an interpolator performing such a change.

A new interpretation thus suggests itself. Aristeas' curse makes sense if it is appreciated in the context of an already existing practice of biblical scholarship among Alexandrian Jews. Aristeas' colleagues appear to have adopted Aristarchus' system of critical signs and marked certain biblical verses without deleting them from the manuscript. Aristeas' formulations specifically suggest that critical signs, such as an asterisk and an obelus, were used to indicate that certain biblical verses had been transferred from a different context. If this analysis is correct, it profoundly changes our overall understanding of the *Letter of Aristeas*. It emerges that the author reacted to the academic activity of his colleagues by offering an authentic Greek text of the Bible, which must be protected against critical work. Aristeas expressed himself somewhat imprecisely as he did not reject actual transfers of biblical verses but rather opposed the identification of repetitive verses as interpolations from another context. Such imprecision, however, suits someone speaking from the outside. For Aristeas, marking the biblical text with an asterisk and an obelos was as impious as actually transferring verses.

---

[29] μετενεχθεὶς ἐντεῦθεν (Schol. *Il.* 5.310A); see also van der Valk 1963–4, vol. II, pp. 456–61, who reads this and similar passages in the context of modern research on the correct version of the Homeric text.

While sharing the same academic terminology, Aristeas and Aristarchus thus assumed very different positions. Aristarchus endeavoured to recognize interpolations which had, in his view, already been introduced to the Homeric text, trusting his own scholarly skills to reconstruct the original epic by way of athetesis and stylistic correction. In this context Aristarchus often complained about the work of his predecessors, whom he considered to be rather incompetent. Such criticism, however, was aimed at particular conclusions and not at the fundamental idea of text-critical work. Aristarchus thus called for an improvement of scholarly methods rather than their general abandonment. Aristeas, on the other hand, faced Aristarchan scholarship among Jewish Bible critics in Alexandria and had recourse to the notion of a sacrosanct Greek text which was based on the Hebrew original. His main message was a general warning against text-critical approaches. A contemporary of Aristarchus, Aristeas thus used a precise term of Homeric scholarship (μεταφέρω) in order to prevent its future application to the Scriptures of the Jews.

Furthermore, Aristeas' curse of interpolators also included a reference to additions and omissions. These textual procedures, too, must be appreciated in the context of Alexandrian scholarship. To be sure, Deut. 4:2 had already condemned any addition to or omission from the 'word' of God. Yet the biblical writer was primarily concerned with the observance of a particular code of law, which should not be exchanged for other customs (LXX Deut. 13:1). Significantly, no Jew prior to Aristeas had ever referred to Deut. 4:2 in the context of preserving the canonical text. On the contrary, Jews living in the Land of Israel seem to have ignored this verse until well into the rabbinic period.[30] The *Letter of Aristeas* thus represents the earliest extant attempt to regulate the text of Scripture, preserving its minutest details and defending it against any future manipulations. This stringent and self-conscious position characteristically emerged in an environment where text criticism was a central feature of the intellectual culture.

It must initially be noted that Aristeas changed the Septuagint injunction 'not to subtract' anything from the Divine commandments. Instead of the verb οὐκ ἀφελεῖτε he used the noun ἀφαίρεσις, which looks like a technical term. Indeed, Aristarchus once used it as a reference to a deletion or athetesis made by Zenodotus.[31] Aristeas thus seems to have used the

---

[30] Naeh 1992, pp. 401–19 and bibliography there.

[31] Schol. *Il.* 1.400A; among later grammarians the term refers to a removal of letters especially at the beginning of a word. This use, however, is irrelevant to Aristeas because of chronological considerations as well as the fact that he clearly refers to a technique of text criticism.

term in a broad sense as a derogatory reference to the method of identifying spurious verses. He blurred the difference between a scholarly marking of a verse and its actual deletion from the text, thus stressing the sinful nature of his opponents' methods. As we have seen before, such a blurring is consistent with Aristeas' style. When condemning transfers of motifs, he had similarly referred to scholarly markings of verses as if they were actual interpolations. The same holds true for deletions. Adapting biblical vocabulary rather than using Aristarchus' technical term 'athetesis', Aristeas expressed his discontent. For him, such text-critical signs represented sacrilegious manipulations of the canonical text, which were no better than actually deleting and taking away from the Holy Scriptures.

Finally, Aristeas' curse of additions to the biblical text also echoes Alexandrian discussions. The notion of the superfluous was central to Aristarchus, who identified elements which had, in his view, been added to the Homeric text. Stylistic redundancies and apparently superfluous motifs were thus accounted for. According to Aristarchus' reconstruction, an irresponsible interpolator had added individual elements or even whole verses to the original epic. He regularly exposed such hermeneutic mistakes and marked the relevant lines as spurious.[32] Writing at a time when Aristarchus' scholarship was most influential in Alexandria, Aristeas warned his readers not to follow in his footsteps and apply his academic methods to the Scripture of the Jews. Some of his colleagues had already done so and Aristeas hoped to prevent further occurrences of such Jewish and Greek cooperation.

This interpretation of Aristeas' position as essentially conservative is further corroborated by Josephus, the first writer in antiquity explicitly referring to the *Letter*. Mentioning Aristeas by name, Josephus paraphrases its content at considerable length, while at the same time introducing significant changes.[33] After describing the scene of Demetrius assembling the Jews and reading the new translation to them, Josephus stresses the community's approval (*AJ* 12.107–8). He then insists with Aristeas that the request to preserve the text emerged from the Jewish audience. Yet precisely when paraphrasing Aristeas' injunctions against interpolators, Josephus adds his own formulations. On his reading, the biblical text must be preserved in the following way:

[32] See esp. Schol. *Il.* 1.474A '[the line] is athetized, because someone added it in the [mistaken] belief...' (ἀθετεῖται ὅτι νομίσας τις... προσέθηκεν); Schol. *Il.* 9.416A (τὸν λόγον προσέθηκεν); Schol. *Il.* 2.668A (διὸ προσέθεκε); Schol. *Il.* 1.89A.
[33] Aristeas is mentioned in Jos. *Ap.* 2.47 and *AJ* 12.17; regarding Josephus' direct familiarity with the *Letter*, see Wasserstein and Wasserstein 2006, pp. 45–50.

Should someone see either a superfluous element (περισσόν) having been added in writing to the Law or an omission (λεῖπον), he should examine it and make the correcting device (διορθοῦν) known. (*AJ* 12.109)

Elias Bickerman and Albert Baumgarten have noted that Josephus does not recommend a consultation of the authoritative Alexandrian version of the LXX, which was supposedly deposited in the Library.[34] Josephus instead refers to scholarly devices and even introduces Aristarchus' technical term 'superfluous' (περισσόν). The Greek text of the Bible translation was obviously considered to be partly corrupt, the existing deletions and additions urgently requiring a correction. Did Josephus even have in mind the standard Alexandrian system of scholarly signs when speaking about publicizing the 'correcting device' (διορθοῦν)? Whatever the case may be, it is clear that Josephus, aware of both the Hebrew and the Greek versions of Scripture, advocated a critical approach to the Septuagint. He thus rewrote the *Letter of Aristeas*, adapting its conservative message to the ideal of Alexandrian scholarship.[35] Josephus' innovative paraphrase of the *Letter of Aristeas* moreover indicates that Aristeas' curse of interpolators was already in the first century CE understood in the context of text criticism. Josephus in a way took the position of Aristeas' colleagues – a step that Aristeas himself would certainly have resented.

THE IDEOLOGY OF THE *LETTER OF ARISTEAS*

Aristeas proposes a highly innovative conception of the Septuagint as Holy Writ. Its authenticity, he insists, is guaranteed by the fact that it is an adequate translation of the Hebrew original, which was verified and accepted by the leaders of the Jewish community. This verification is clearly *bona fide*, since the reading aloud of the Torah by Demetrius hardly leaves the necessary time for scholarly examination. Aristeas' construct of a Holy Greek text on the basis of the Hebrew original is especially remarkable in light of the fact that only the Greek text was known in contemporary Alexandria. He himself as well as Aristobulus, Ezekiel and Demetrius refer only to Septuagint expressions, never taking recourse to the Hebrew.[36] Aristeas'

---

[34] Bickerman 1988, p. 106; Baumgarten 2002, pp. 18–19.
[35] In the context of *Contra Apion*, Josephus rather highlights the difference between Greek and Jewish ways of preserving the foundational text, see Wyrick 2004, pp. 111–203, 260–5. Josephus' own assertion that he neither added nor omitted anything from the Scriptures when paraphrasing them in his *Antiquities* (*AJ* 1.17) can be appreciated as an adaptation of Aristeas' expressions; cf. also Inowlocki 2005.
[36] Meecham 1935, pp. 316–20, showed Aristeas' affinity with the LXX against the Hebrew text, stressing that 'the LXX translation had superseded the Hebrew original'. Aristeas' use of Septuagint expressions is especially prominent in his description of the High Priest, where he refers to τὸ λεγόμενον λόγιον

narrative even presupposes the prior existence of the Torah in Greek. When Ptolemy hears of the completed translation and is impressed by Moses' wisdom, he asks why 'none of the historians or poets has mentioned' it before (*Letter*, 312). The answer is not that the text was hitherto unavailable to Greek speakers, but rather that it was a 'Holy Legislation'.[37] Aristeas then mentions the stories of Theopompus and Theodectus, speaking in this context of 'previously translated' passages or books (*Letter*, 314).[38]

Given the exclusive Greek environment of the author of the *Letter of Aristeas*, we have to investigate why he had recourse to the Hebrew *Urtext*, while his contemporaries seem to have forgotten all about it. His Jewish audience even needed to be reminded that the Torah was originally written in Hebrew and therefore required a translation – that its language was not Syrian, as many assumed.[39] Furthermore, Aristeas recalled the Land of Israel, whence the Hebrew Torah came to Alexandria, depicting it in the most idealizing fashion. This move is conspicuous, too, because the Land of Israel is generally not mentioned in the extant fragments of other contemporary Alexandrian Jews. Aristeas suggested not only that the magnificent Temple and its exemplary priesthood were situated in Jerusalem, but that the rural life of the country was far more healthy than in Egypt, where many left the countryside for commerce in the big city (*Letter*, 83–111).

Aristeas anticipated that his position would cause some surprise on the part of his Jewish readers, who were proud Alexandrian intellectuals. In order to avoid condescending reactions to the High Priest in Jerusalem, he virtually opens his account by praising him as someone who:

gained pre-eminent esteem for his integrity and reputation among the citizens as well as others, having achieved a very great benefit for his own citizens and others in other places. (*Letter*, 3)

Aristeas thus draws a thoroughly Hellenistic picture of the High Priest in Jerusalem, who emerges as a gentleman with a significant political role, potentially beneficial also to the Jewish citizens of Alexandria. Similarly, the translators are not presented as naturally superior on account of their

---

and τὴν λεγομένην κίδαριν (*Letter*, 97–8). Regarding Aristobulus, see esp. his quotation of whole Septuagint verses in fr. 2 (ed. Holladay 1983–96, vol. III, pp. 138, 142) and Walter 1964, pp. 32–3; for details on Demetrius, see Chapter 3 below. See also Bickerman 1976–86, vol. I, pp. 143–5, discussing further examples of LXX expressions in Ezekiel, Demetrius and Artapanus.

[37] σεμνὴν εἶναι τὴν νομοθεσίαν (*Letter*, 313); similarly in *Letter*, 31.

[38] This has been noted before by Kahle 1959, p. 213; Hadas 1951, p. 223.

[39] Tcherikover 1958 has conclusively shown that the author of the *Letter* addressed a Jewish rather than a general Greek audience. Explanations regarding the Hebrew original of the LXX can be found in *Letter*, 3 (πρὸς τὴν ἑρμηνείαν τοῦ θείου νόμου διὰ τὸ γεγράφθαι παρ' αὐτοῖς ἐν διφθέραις Ἑβραϊκοῖς γράμμασιν) and *Letter*, 11.

familiarity with the Hebrew original. They are instead dressed in Greek garb so that Alexandrian readers may be more impressed by the representatives of what probably appeared to them a rather provincial place. Aristeas' audience could thus learn that they are 'gentlemen' (ἄνδρας καλούς) and 'good elders' (ἀγαθοὺς πρεσβυτέρους), having lived a worthy life and gained experience in the things of the Law.[40] At the symposium with the king the translators generally do not mention Hebrew wisdom, let alone Hebrew expressions, but instead make every effort to impress Ptolemy – as well as Aristeas' Jewish readers – as pious intellectuals in the Alexandrian style.[41]

Aristeas thus made an innovative contribution by justifying the authenticity of the Greek Torah by recourse to its translation from the Hebrew original, which had been directly imported from the Land of Israel. It has often been remarked that he adopted a famous motif of the Alexandrian ideology. After all, the Ptolemaic kings were known to have imported books for the Library, including the notorious acquisition of the Athenian manuscripts mentioned by Galen.[42] While Galen's story, however, clearly focuses on the Alexandrian preference of the 'old' (παλαιός) over the newly copied books, Aristeas' account of the plans for the translation are more ambiguous.[43] What exactly was requested for the Alexandrian Library?

The perspective of Aristeas and Andreas in the *Letter of Aristeas* is revealing. When requesting the release of the Jewish prisoners by the king, they say:

in as much as the legislation, which we do not only plan to transcribe (μεταγράψαι), but to translate (διερμηνεῦσαι), is laid down for all the Jews. (*Letter*, 15)

The distinction between transcription and translation, echoed also in *Letter*, 9–11, complements our earlier impression that the author of the *Letter* writes in a context where the Torah was already known in Greek. What was the point of the new translation and which problem was it meant to solve? Demetrius' epistle relates to these matters. Relying on *savants* (ὑπὸ τῶν εἰδότων), he reports the following on the state of the 'books of the law of the Jews':

τυγχάνει γὰρ Ἑβραϊκοῖς γράμμασι καὶ φωνῇ λεγόμενα, ἀμελέστερον δέ, καὶ οὐχ ὡς ὑπάρχει, σεσήμανται. (*Letter*, 30)

They happen to be composed in the Hebrew letters and language, but are [now] carelessly marked, not as they should be.

---

[40] *Letter*, 46, 39 and 32; see also J. J. Collins 2000, pp. 124–5.
[41] *Letter*, 172–300; see also Tcherikover 1958, pp. 65–9; Schimanowski 2003, pp. 58–9; Charles 2009.
[42] Honigman 2003, pp. 41–53; Rajak 2005.
[43] Gal. *Comm. in Hipp. Epid.* 17a606–7 (quoted by Fraser 1972, vol. II, p. 480).

This short description has given rise to innumerable different translations and interpretations. The main cruxes are the expressions σεσήμανται and οὐχ ὡς ὑπάρχει. Zuntz rightly criticized Kahle's earlier suggestion that the former refers to translation, because the verb σημαίνω simply does not provide such a meaning.[44] This does not imply, however, that Kahle was altogether wrong. His intuition that σεσήμανται refers to the Greek text is sound.[45] Aristeas distinguishes between the composition of the Torah in Hebrew, which he associates with the former days, and the neglected state of the present Greek text.

The carelessness (ἀμελέστερον), from Aristeas' point of view, must be connected to the scholarly marking of the Greek text. This interpretation initially suggests itself because of linguistic reasons. The primary meaning of σημαίνω is 'to show by a sign'. The noun σημεῖον is the standard word for critical signs in the margins of a text. Almost every book of the *Iliad* in the A scholia closes with a remark that τὰ Ἀριστονίκου σημεῖα had been used, thus referring to Aristonicus' summary of Aristarchus' work dealing with text-critical signs.[46] Seleucus similarly wrote at least three books entitled κατὰ τῶν Ἀριστάρχου σημείων.[47] Diogenes Laertius lists the σημεῖα, attached by Alexandrian scholars to Plato's texts, including the above mentioned obelus for spurious verses (Diog. Laert. 3.65). More importantly, Aristobulus uses the verb precisely in the context of text criticism. He says σεσημάγκαμεν περιαιροῦντες τὸν διὰ τῶν ποιημάτων Δία καὶ Ζῆνα. This key sentence should be rendered as follows: 'we have marked [this], removing the divine names Δίς and Ζεύς throughout the verses'.[48] Aristobulus thus identifies interpolations in a pagan text, which, he was convinced, originally referred to the God of the Jews. It is conspicuous that the marking involves a dimension of περιαιρέω. As we saw above, Aristeas precisely inveighs against interpolators who 'make a deletion' (ποιέω ἀφαίρεσιν).

---

[44] Zuntz 1959, pp. 117–22; cf. also Howard 1971, pp. 339–40, who takes the negation οὐχ together with σεσήμανται, translating 'and they have no meaning as they now exist'. This is a response, in Howard's view, to Palestinian criticism of Alexandrian Bible recensions.

[45] Kahle 1959, pp. 212–14; cf. Zuntz, 1959, pp. 117–22, who suggests that the 'writing' of the Hebrew manuscripts was careless but admits that this interpretation creates numerous contradictions with subsequent paragraphs of the *Letter*.

[46] Cf. also Lehrs 1882, p. 2, who suggests that the expression may refer to Aristonicus' report of a work by Aristarchus entitled περὶ σημείων.

[47] Quoted by M. L. West 2001, p. 48.

[48] Aristob. *ap.* Euseb. *Praep. evang.* 13.12 (fr. 4, ed. Holladay 1983–96, vol. III, p. 172). Walter 1964, pp. 131, 140–1, already identified Aristobulus' treatment of Aratus' text as an emendation in the spirit of Alexandrian scholarship, without, however, noting the particular meaning of the expression σεσημάγκαμεν in this context. Note that Aristobulus' use of critical techniques pertains only to pagan texts. As far as the extant fragments indicate, his attitude to the Jewish Scriptures is more conservative (for details, see Chapter 4 below).

The above interpretation of *Letter*, 30 is furthermore corroborated by a comparison with *Letter*, 310, where Aristeas urges that the newly translated books should remain 'as they are'. The expression οὕτως ἔχοντα, referring to a preservation of the text without future emendations, is complementary to the expression οὐχ ὡς ὑπάρχει in *Letter*, 30, which refers to the problematic stage of text-critical work. It is thus the original, pre-critical stage of the biblical text which Aristeas hopes to recover through the notion of a new translation from the Hebrew original. The new Torah in Greek is offered as a mirror image of the Hebrew in the sense that both eclipse text criticism. Aristeas associates this Greek translation with Ptolemaios II Philadelphos, thus placing it in the third century BCE. This step is significant, too, because it reaches back to an early stage of Alexandrian Judaism, to a time before Aristarchus and other famous Homer scholars. Aristeas thus grounds his conservative approach in a long gone 'Golden Age', pointing to a Hebrew as well as pre-critical Alexandrian tradition to which he wishes to reconnect his readers.

If my interpretation is correct, a certain blurring of vocabulary and textual layers is visible in *Letter*, 30. The author addresses in one sentence the dimensions of translation and text criticism, referring to both the Hebrew letters of the original as well as the text-critical signs of the Greek translations circulating in contemporary Alexandria. I take these to refer to different historical stages, but there remains the impression that very different things have been associated in one sentence. We have to remember, however, that Aristeas, unlike Galen telling the story of the Athenian manuscripts, juggles different discourses. The reason for this blurring is the fact that he hopes to solve the problem of existing text criticism among his Jewish colleagues by recourse to the Hebrew original, which had not been blemished by scholarly research. Aristeas' answer to critical scholarship comes from a completely different quarter and therefore creates some blurring of discourses.

Furthermore, Kahle's argument that the *Letter of Aristeas* presents a legend rather than historical fact deserves to be taken seriously. The *Letter* does not describe the first Greek translation of the Torah.[49] Its author does not even appear to be primarily concerned about the translation proper.

---

[49] See also Wright 2008; Kreuzer 2004, who interprets the story of the *Letter* as an indication that the LXX was published in response to Ptolemaic cultural politics, speaks of a general atmosphere rather than of the historicity of Demetrius' initiative; Rajak 2009, pp. 38–50, rightly warns scholars not to focus on 'catching out' Aristeas and accuse him of false fiction, calling instead for an appraisal of the *Letter*'s message in terms of a 'historical myth' which significantly shaped Jewish memory in Alexandria.

Working in an exclusively Greek environment, he is interested in the preservation of an authentic Torah in face of the contemporary rise of text criticism. Rejecting the methods of Aristarchus and his Jewish colleagues, who applied them to their Scriptures, Aristeas stresses the notion of a sacred text conveying divine ideas and glorifies the legislation as 'most philosophic and unmixed' (*Letter*, 31). It is not even necessary to imagine that Aristeas supplied his readers with a specific version of the LXX. He would have been happy if his readers simply distanced themselves from Aristarchus and Jewish Bible scholars, using unmarked scrolls and dismissing the notion of the Torah as a form of literature.

Living in the capital of scholarship, both Homeric and biblical, Aristeas nevertheless wished to suggest that the Greek text of the Torah, which he recommended as authentic, was also accurate. For this purpose he introduces terminology pertaining to ἀκριβής (accurate), which sounded scholarly without committing to a particular method.[50] He even has Demetrius suggest that the translators will 'examine' the agreed upon text (*Letter*, 32). Significantly, however, they will choose the text that is 'accurate according to its meaning' rather than a text established by literary methods.[51] The vocabulary of accuracy adds to the blurring of discourses of translation and scholarship. Aristeas' position is understandable in light of his cultural context. Addressing readers living in the vicinity of the Museum and the Library, Aristeas uses some scholarly terms in order to satisfy general expectations. His readers were likely to ask about the textual quality of the Greek text proposed by Aristeas. Lest they should dismiss his overall project as unserious or even primitive, he offers certain formulations creating a scholarly ambiance. This move, however, is restricted to Demetrius' epistle and remains rather naïve.

When Aristeas reacts to the increase of biblical scholarship among Alexandrian Jews, following the monumental work of Aristarchus at the Museum, he sounds rather defensive. Unless special measures are taken, he implies, Bible critics will treat and, in his view, abuse the text of the Jewish Scriptures. We shall see throughout this book that Aristeas' proposed remedies were not widely accepted, Alexandrian Jews instead adopting an impressive variety of scholarly methods in their studies of the Bible. At the same time, however, Aristeas' story of the Greek Bible translation and his

[50] *Letter*, 31, 32, 310.
[51] *Letter*, 31, 32, 310; the expression λαβόντες τὸ κατὰ τὴν ἑρμηνείαν ἀκριβές must refer in this context to meaning, as often in the Homeric scholia (see esp. Schol. *Il.* 5.143, 5.663–4, 6.71, 10.228–31). Significantly, the element of examination is missing both in King Ptolemy's version of the translators' activity and in Eleazar's (*Letter*, 39, 46).

overall conception of the LXX are echoed in Philo's work. Writing almost two centuries later, Philo regularly applied literal scholarship in his Bible commentaries but rejected the most radical forms of text criticism, such as historical analysis and athetesis.[52] His relatively conservative position, in comparison with his contemporaries, is rooted in the approach developed in the *Letter of Aristeas.*

It is initially evident that Philo, like Aristeas before him, attached special importance to the sanctity of Scripture, often calling it 'Holy Book', 'Holy Writings' and 'Holy Law'.[53] Without explicitly mentioning the *Letter of Aristeas*, Philo preserves the main outline of the story, stressing the following motifs: Philadelphus' role in the initiative of the translation, the dispatching of the translators by the High Priest in Jerusalem, their festive reception in Alexandria and their actual work of translation on the island of Pharos (*Mos.* 2.28–40). Philo was clearly familiar with the *Letter*. This is conspicuous in passages where Philo presupposes Aristeas' narrative but abbreviates it, because the details are no longer relevant for him. He thus refers to the symposium, a central part of the *Letter*, which has no function in his own story, by merely providing a summary of the type of questions raised by the king and stressing the great wisdom of the translators' answers (*Mos.* 2.33). Had Philo not known Aristeas' account, he would hardly have introduced the motif of the symposium. Similarly, Philo considerably expands the praises of Philadelphus, while summarizing the events pertaining to the delegation to Jerusalem as well as its reception there by the High Priest (*Mos.* 2.29–31). The description of the translators precisely follows in Aristeas' footsteps: they are versed both in their native Hebrew as well as in Greek learning.[54]

Numerous scholars have noted that Philo adds a dimension of awe and Divine revelation to the process of translation.[55] While Aristeas depicted the translators' work in a highly factual manner, pointing to their comparison of the individual results, Philo insists on the miraculous element:

as if possessed by God, they wrote under inspiration, not each something else, but all [wrote] the same nouns and verbs, as if an invisible instructor was telling each of them.[56]

When Philo's account is compared with the *Letter of Aristeas*, it emerges that his concerns are rather different. Although Aristeas paid little attention

---

[52] For a detailed discussion of Philo's views, see Chapters 8 and 9 below.
[53] On these terms see esp. Burkhardt 1988.   [54] *Mos.* 2.32, cf. *Letter*, 121.
[55] Pelletier 1962, pp. 78–81; Wasserstein and Wasserstein 2006, pp. 35–45; Hadas-Lebel 2003, pp. 105–10; Collins 2000, pp. 148–53; Siegert 2004, pp. 211–12.
[56] καθάπερ ἐνθουσιῶντες προφήτευον οὐκ ἄλλα ἄλλοι τὰ δ᾽ αὐτὰ πάντες ὀνόματα καὶ ῥήματα ὥσπερ ὑποβολέως ἑκάστοις ἀοράτως ἐνηχοῦντος (*Mos.* 2.37).

to the work of the translation itself, Philo deeply worries about the accuracy of the translation. Abraham and David Wasserstein recently noted that Philo is acutely aware of the problems involved in such a process.[57] He even admits that usually a translation is not identical to the original and stresses the multivalence of words as well as the particular richness of the Greek language (*Mos.* 2.38). While Aristeas did not reflect on these problems, Philo insists that they did not apply to the project of the LXX, where perfect correspondences of words were found under Divine guidance (*Mos.* 2.38–9). The notion of a miracle involved in the translation of the Torah thus solves the problems of translation recognized by Philo.

Aristeas' curse of interpolators has been moved by Philo from the context of canonization to the translation itself. Philo still refers to the same methods of interpolation, namely 'taking away or adding or transferring' (*Mos.* 2.34), but connects them with the translators. According to Philo, they were intensely aware of their responsibility, knowing that they must not change the text in any of these ways but had to 'keep the original form and shape'. The translation, which finally emerged, could thus be trusted to reproduce the Hebrew original accurately. This has been confirmed, Philo stresses, by bilinguals, whose judgement was based on a comparison of the Greek and the Hebrew (2.40).

In glaring contrast to Aristeas, Philo no longer speaks about the preservation of the text once it has been translated. Whereas he stresses that Mosaic Law is not subject to any change (*Mos.* 2.15–17), he no longer warns his readers to abstain from scholarly approaches to the Greek text of the Bible. In this respect Philo is the direct mirror image of Aristeas: while he applies scholarly terms to the process of translation, thus ensuring its accuracy, Aristeas refrained from scholarly terms in connection with the translation but used them polemically against contemporary Bible scholars. This difference points to significant developments in the Jewish community of Alexandria. Aristeas faced a considerable increase of text-critical work among his colleagues, but Philo writes after the peak of Alexandrian scholarship, when a wide variety of academic techniques had long been accepted by many Jews.

---

[57] Wasserstein and Wasserstein 2006, pp. 43–5.

CHAPTER 3

Questions and answers in Aristotelian style: Demetrius' anonymous colleagues

In contrast to the *Letter of Aristeas*, which opposes, as we saw, the application of rigorous academic methods to the Bible, Demetrius' fragments provide early evidence of positive connections between biblical and Homeric scholarship. Some Alexandrian Jews read their Scripture as a piece of literature and applied literary techniques to its interpretation. Following Jacob Freudenthal's seminal work, scholars have generally recognized the importance of Demetrius in this context.[1] While Freudenthal's dating of Demetrius to the third century BCE can no longer be maintained, his overall interpretation of Demetrius in light of zetetic literature is certainly valid and deserves further study.[2]

Thus far, the argument has remained surprisingly general, relying for the Homeric evidence on Alfred Gudemann's famous dictionary article.[3] A comprehensive study of Demetrius' fragments in view of their immediate Alexandrian environment is still warranted. The first step in this direction must be a clear distinction between Demetrius himself and the already existing questions and answers mentioned by him. In this chapter I shall focus on Demetrius' references to the latter, using them as a basis for reconstructing the views of other, anonymous exegetes in Alexandria.

If these snippets of information are analysed in light of their cultural environment, it emerges that Demetrius' colleagues were firmly committed to the Aristotelian style of question and answer. Moreover, these fragments throw new light on the development of the genre in Alexandria, where Aristarchus was sensitive to the same kinds of question, providing strikingly similar answers. The role of Demetrius himself, I shall argue, is more marginal. He was meaningful as a bridge between the anonymous Bible scholars he mentioned and a wider Jewish audience, innovatively

---

[1] Freudenthal 1874, pp. 44–5; Gutman 1958–63, vol. I, pp. 132–47; Fraser 1972, vol. I, pp. 691–4; Gruen 1998, pp. 112–18; J. J. Collins 2000, pp. 33–5.
[2] For further details on his dates, see the last section of this chapter.
[3] Gudeman 1927; Kamesar 1994, pp. 219–21, opened new avenues in a short, but pioneering treatment.

combining the question and answer style with a continuous paraphrase of Scripture.

Central for our purposes are Demetrius' two references to questions which had already been raised before, one pertaining to a contradiction between verses and the other to a question of verisimilitude. While the general practice of raising questions concerning the biblical text is mentioned in the *Letter of Aristeas*,[4] Demetrius' fragments provide the earliest evidence in the extant Jewish literature of specific critical inquiries.

A PROBLEM OF CONTRADICTION

Inquiries into the contradictions of a text presuppose that it was authored by one writer and should thus be rather homogeneous. The text in its entirety is studied on the assumption that any line or verse can throw light on any other within the same corpus. If in the process of such studies contradictions and tensions between the different parts become visible, they demand an explanation. Principally, there are two options: either the lines can be harmonized or one of them is dismissed as inauthentic. Alexandrian Jews related to the Torah as such a unified corpus, Aristeas having already alluded to connections between the books of Genesis and Deuteronomy (*Letter*, 128–71). The Prophets and the Writings, on the other hand, never reached the same canonical status in Alexandria, as Philo's rare and more personal references to these books indicate.

Demetrius reports that the following problem of contradiction had been discussed by a colleague:[5]

Someone inquired (ἐπιζητεῖν δέ τινα) how the Israelites had weapons as they left [Egypt] unarmed, for they said that they will return again after having gone on a 'three day journey' [Exod. 5:3] and offering a sacrifice.

It seems therefore (φαίνεται οὖν) that those who did not drown [at the Red Sea] used the weapons of those who drowned. (*ap.* Euseb. *Praep. evang.* 9.29.16, ed. Holladay 1983–96, vol. 1, p. 76)

---

[4] ἐπερώτησις (*Letter*, 122). Regarding the specific question on kosher food regulations, see Chapter 4 below.

[5] This fragment belongs to Demetrius' work even though Eusebius does not explicitly identify its author. Following Freudenthal 1874, pp. 36, 46–7, there is a general scholarly consensus of attributing the fragment to Demetrius, which can be corroborated by the following considerations: at the very end of *Praep. evang.* 9.29.16, where materials from Demetrius and Ezekiel are intermittently presented, Eusebius quotes Ezekiel's lines on a wondrous bird, which he takes to be the phoenix. Subsequently, he introduces the fragment in question by the laconic phrase: 'καὶ μετὰ βραχέα'. As no other author is mentioned, we must assume that Eusebius returned to Demetrius' work quoted just before Ezekiel. The style of the fragment supports that conclusion, because it is a paraphrase in accusative + infinitive construction depending on a previous introduction 'Demetrius said'.

The starting point of this inquiry is the apparent contradiction between LXX Exod. 5:3, where the Israelites leave Egypt without military equipment, and LXX Exod. 17:8–9, mentioning the subsequent battle between the Israelites and Amalek. Demetrius' colleague partly quotes and partly paraphrases LXX Exod. 5:3, where Moses and Aaron plead before Pharaoh that 'we shall go on a three day journey into the desert in order to offer a sacrifice to our God'.[6] The Septuagint indication of purpose (ὅπως) is taken to mean that they only intended to offer a sacrifice, thus not taking with them any weapons antithetical to worship.[7] Demetrius' colleague highlights this aspect by introducing the motif of a prospective return to Egypt. On his view, Moses and Aaron promise Pharaoh that 'they will return again after having gone on a "three day journey" and offering a sacrifice.' This image of peaceful Israelites bent on worship, yet utterly unprepared for warfare, is corroborated by the biblical scene at the Red Sea, where they are said to be 'greatly afraid', taking courage from Moses' assurance that God will fight on their behalf.[8]

LXX Exod. 17:8–9, by contrast, hints at Israel's military prowess in the subsequent encounter with the Amalek. Whereas the Masoretic text has the Amalek approach and fight against Israel (ויבא עמלק וילחם עם ישראל), the LXX renders ἦλθεν δὲ Αμαληκ καὶ ἐπολέμει Ισραηλ, leaving it open whether Israel is in the dative or the nominative case. The reader of the LXX can thus imagine Israel either as being attacked by the Amalek or as actively fighting them. Moreover, according to the LXX, Moses instructs Joshua to choose 'mighty men' (ἄνδρας δυνατούς) rather than simply 'man' (אנשים).[9] The general term 'to fight' (הלחם) is rendered by the expression 'to arrange in battle order' (παράταξαι). The military know-how and strength of Israel are thus stressed, reflecting a similar tendency to Artapanus, who

---

[6] As the anonymous exegete explicitly mentions Exod. 5:3, we should accept that verse as the starting point of the inquiry rather than Exod. 13:18, which is often considered in this context (Holladay 1983–96, vol. I, pp. 89–90). The latter is unlikely to have provided a significant impetus for zetetic exegesis, because the biblical expression וחמושים had been translated by the LXX as a reference of time ('in the fifth generation'), thus excluding any military connotation for Alexandrian exegetes, who had no access to the Hebrew original. Note also that LXX interprets the *wav* in ונזבחה in Exod. 5:3 as an indication of purpose (ὅπως); see also Exod. 5:8, 17, where the theme of going out and sacrificing is repeated as the leitmotiv of the whole passage.

[7] The same assumption is echoed in *Letter*, 103, where the author stresses that he and Andreas should have been speedily admitted to the Temple in Jerusalem since they were 'unarmed'.

[8] LXX Exod. 14:10, 14.

[9] The LXX thus repeats a term used in Exod. 18:21, 25, translating אנשי חיל. Even though we deal here with a systematization of language, the choice of words is still significant as it indicates the translators' ease with the notion of Israel's military prowess.

presents Moses as a leader of the Egyptian army, and Aristeas, who speaks of the Jewish population of Egyptian fortresses.[10]

Aware of the discrepancy between the two verses in LXX Exodus, Demetrius' colleague provides a solution based on the assumption that there is a significant gap in the biblical text. He suggests that something happened between the Exodus and Israel's encounter with Amalek. Even though Moses did not explicitly say so, the reader is invited to conjecture that the Israelites equipped themselves with the weapons left behind by the drowned Egyptians. Although none of the Egyptians is said to have survived the sudden immersion of the Red Sea, nothing is actually said about the state of their equipment (LXX Exod. 14:28). Modern readers may well assume that it was ruined. Demetrius' colleague, on the other hand, suggests that it remained in good shape and thus served the Israelites later on. The problem of the contradiction is solved with emphasis on the notion that the Israelites came only accidentally into the possession of weapons and were not originally or inherently belligerent. The popularity of this solution is still visible in the writings of Philo and Josephus.[11]

This first appearance of the critical question and answer method in Jewish Bible exegesis must be understood in the context of Alexandrian culture. Demetrius' anonymous colleague belonged to the Aristotelian tradition prominent there. A significant background to his work is Aristotle's *Aporemata Homerica*.[12] While the extant fragments of Aristotle's treatise no longer allow us to judge its precise scope, Diogenes Laertius knew of six volumes, thus indicating that Aristotle addressed a very considerable number of individual lines.[13] To judge by the extant fragments, which reflect to some extent also the tastes of later writers, Aristotle distinguished between three levels, namely the text itself, the question and one or more answers.[14]

---

[10] Artapanus *ap.* Euseb. *Praep. evang.* 9.27.7–10; *Letter*, 13 speaks in connection with Alexandrian Jews of 'military equipment' (καθοπλίσας) and 'fortresses' (ἐν τοῖς φρουρίοις) and 'allied forces' (συμμαχιῶν). The manuscript evidence of the LXX, however, indicates that such images became more controversial. While CodA accepts the nominative case of the term Israel in LXX Exod. 17:8 but changed the verb to ἐπορεύθη, others identified the case as accusative, specifying τὸν Ἰσραηλ. Symmachus characteristically adapted the Greek to the Hebrew and wrote πρὸς Ισραηλ; see also Wevers 1990, p. 268.

[11] Jos. *AJ* 2.132; Philo, *Mos.* 1:214–16; on the different exegetical path taken by rabbinic exegetes in the Land of Israel, see Loewenstamm 1972, pp. 96–100.

[12] For a recent discussion of the development of the question and answer method from the Classical period to the Byzantine, see Papadoyannakis 2006; on philosophical aspects of Aristotle's aporetic treatises, see Jacob 2004, pp. 40–8.

[13] *Diog. Laert.* 5.26; the extant fragments moreover indicate a typical predilection for the *Iliad* (twenty-six fragments out of thirty-seven), on which see Cribiore 2001, pp. 194–7.

[14] The present format of the Aristotelian fragments is corroborated in its general outline by the fact that Zoilos, Homer's staunchest critic in the early period, had focused on specific verses, exposing

Aristotle thus responded to earlier critics, such as Zoilos, by transforming their attacks into particular questions and inquiring why Homer had nevertheless expressed himself in a manner which appeared unacceptable. Aristotle's answers justified the poet's style, showing that his predecessors had failed to appreciate the literary dimension of the epics.

Aristotle regularly introduced his questions with the διὰ τί formula.[15] His answers were often stylized by later writers introducing them with phrases such as λύων or φησί. Aristotle's *Aporemata Homerica* complements his more theoretical treatment of the epics in the twenty-fifth chapter of his *Poetics*. The title of the chapter, περὶ δὲ προβλημάτων καὶ λύσεων (*Poet.* 1460b6), indicates both the affinity of the two discussions as well as the importance of inquiry into the Homeric texts.

Contradictions between epic lines had already been explored by Aristotle. The two conflicting descriptions of Crete in the *Iliad* and the *Odyssey*, for example, prompted the following discussion:

'Crete of the hundred cities' [*Il.* 2.649].
Why does [the poet] say here 'and the others who dwelt in Crete of the hundred cities', while in the *Odyssey* he says that Crete is 'fair and rich and surrounded by water', adding 'and there are many men in it, past counting, and ninety cities' [*Od.* 19.173–4]? For it seems contradictory (ἐναντίον) that here he speaks of ninety, while there of a hundred.

Yet Aristotle says that it is not inappropriate if not all are depicted by him [Homer] as saying the same things, for then it would be necessary that they [people] also say to each other altogether the same things. (Arist. *Apor. Hom.* fr. 146, ed. Rose 1886)

Aristotle is concerned here with the different numbers of cities mentioned respectively in the *Iliad* and the *Odyssey*. His solution derives from a literary analysis of each passage, giving special attention to differences of perspective. Parallel to his analysis in the twenty-fifth chapter of his *Poetics*, Aristotle suggests that it is legitimate for an author to vary the description of things in different contexts.[16] In Alexandria, where the issue of the Cretan cities was hotly discussed, some taking it as evidence for the different

certain details to ridicule. Although his writings are not identified as *aporemata* but as 'treatises' (κατὰ τῆς Ὁμήρου ποιήσεως λόγους), Zoilos provided a framework of close commentary for Aristotle's subsequent discussion (*FGH* fr. 1).
[15] The διὰ τί formulation appears in the following fragments (ed. Rose 1886): 142, 145, 146, 147, 148, 149, 150, 151, 152, 153, 155, 156, 157, 158, ἠπόρησεν Ἀριστοτέλης διὰ τί (fr. 159), 163, 164, 166, 170, ζητεῖ δὲ ὁ Ἀριστοτέλης διὰ τί (fr. 171), 173, 174, 176, 178. On other occasions Aristotle directly discussed the problem, see, e.g., ἀπρεπὲς εἶναι δοκεῖ (fr. 143), φαύλη δοκεῖ (fr. 160), πῶς γάρ (fr. 161), παράδοξον (fr. 167), ἀνώμαλον (fr. 168), ζητεῖ Ἀριστοτέλης πῶς (fr. 172).
[16] See also Hintenlang 1961, pp. 67–9.

authors of the two epics, Aristarchus adopted Aristotle's approach.[17] He
provided two harmonizing arguments, saying that either the term 'a hundred cities' was meant in the sense of 'many cities' or the poet gave an
approximate, round number in the *Iliad*, but a precise calculation in the
Odyssey (Schol. *Il.* 2.649).[18]

Another problem of a contradiction, pertaining to the description of the
sun, is addressed by Aristotle in his *Aporemata Homerica*:

'[you,] sun, who see all things' [*Il.* 3.277].
Why does he [the poet] say that the sun sees all things and hears all things, while
he depicts him as requiring a messenger concerning his own cattle, [as it is written]
'swiftly then to Helios Hyperion came Lampetia of long robes, bearing tidings that
the friends had slain the cattle' [*Od.* 12.374–5].[19]

Aristotle, providing a solution, says either that the sun sees everything, but not
at the same time, or else that Lampetia was a messenger to Helios as vision is
to man, or else, he said, it is appropriate (ἁρμόττον) that Agamemnon in single
combat thus defines him as '[you,] sun, who see everything and hear everything'

---

[17] Xenon and Hellanicus, named the χωρίζοντες, used this discrepancy between the *Iliad* and the
Odyssey as yet another proof of their sensational claim that the epics had been written by two
different authors; on their general tendency, see Schol. *Il.* 2.356, where the author of the *Iliad* is said
to have depicted Helen as forcibly following Paris, while the author of the *Odyssey* suggested that
she came along willingly; Schol. *Il.* 10.476a, where the term προπάροιθεν is said to have a temporal
meaning in the *Iliad*, but a local meaning in the *Odyssey*; Schol. *Il.* 11.692, where 'those who separate'
dwell on the contradictory numbers of Nelos' sons; Schol. *Il.* 13.365, where the problem of Priam's
different daughters and their respective identification as the 'fairest' is discussed; Schol. *Il.* 16.747,
where 'those who separate' suggest that the author of the *Iliad* did not present its heroes as using
fish, while the author of the *Odyssey* did; Schol. *Il.* 21.416, where they point to the discrepancy
between the author of the *Iliad*, who lets Aphrodite join Ares, and the author of the *Odyssey*, who
depicts her as united with Hephaistos.

[18] Whereas Aristarchus' first argument was influential among the exegetical scholiasts and Porphyry
(Schol. *Od.* 19.174; Porph. *Quaestiones Il.* 649), another more creative interpretation circulated in the
Roman period. Strabo reports that Ephorus solved the problem by suggesting that 'the ten cities had
been built after the Trojan War', while others suggested that ten cities had been destroyed (Strabo
10.4.15); see also Niese 1877, pp. 283–4. Two longer versions of the latter solution are preserved in
Schol. *Od.* 19.174, where Idomeneus, the leader of the Cretans, was banished upon his return from
Troy. Idomeneus avenged the mutiny of his adopted son by destroying ten Cretan cities, which
were subsequently restored. The motif of Idomeneus' exile and the destruction of ten cities appears
independently in Apollodorus' work, indicating that these motifs were rather widely known around
the turn of the era (*Epitome Bibl.* 6.8). The author is no longer identified with Apollodorus the
Athenian grammarian. On grounds of style the former is usually dated around the turn of the era, for
details see Frazer 1921, pp. ix–xvii. In Apollodorus' story it is Nauplius who expels Idomeneus. There
are no verbatim parallels between the two stories, the scholiast stressing the motifs of the destruction
of the cities and their restoration as well as Leucus' status as adopted son, while Apollodorus is
interested in political changes. Only the key term ἐξελαύνω/ἀπελαύνω appears in both stories.
Virgil, *Aen.* 3.121 and his commentator Servius ad loc. also tell of Idomeneus' exile but offer different
explanations.

[19] Strikingly, this scholion preserves a version of the Homeric text which apparently antedates
Aristarchus, who introduced the expression ἔκταμεν ἡμεὶς (οὕτως αἱ Ἀριστάρχου, Schol. *Od.*
12.375).

and also Odysseus spoke thus to his friends [*Od.* 12:323], [but he only wished to arouse fear] for surely he does not see the things in Hades. (Arist. *Apor. Hom.*, fr. 149, ed. Rose 1886)

Aristotle treats here the discrepant images of the sun in the *Iliad* and the *Odyssey*, asking whether, according to Homer, Helios was omniscient or not. The gravity of the problem is indicated by the fact that three solutions are provided, each somewhat hesitantly. Aristotle suggests that the verses may be harmonized either if we acknowledge that Helios' omniscience was progressive over time or if we read the figure of Lampetia as an allegory of Helios' seeing organ or, finally, if we realize the different perspectives of different *dramatis personae*. The last solution corresponds to a discussion of different perspectives in *Poet.* 1461a5–9 and closely resembles the answer provided in the previous fragment.[20] In the above passage, however, Aristotle does not stress the licence of the poet in different contexts, but rather the variety of motivations attributed to different heroes in the text. This Aristotelian solution also became influential and is echoed in the later scholia.[21]

Demetrius' anonymous colleague clearly belongs in this Aristotelian tradition of *aporemata*. His query concerning the contradiction between two verses in the Book of Exodus could equally have been raised by Aristotle, had he come across the Jewish Scriptures. Demetrius' solution, on the other hand, reflects also more recent developments of the Aristotelian tradition in Alexandria. Revising Rudolf Pfeiffer's earlier argument for a significant break between Alexandrian scholarship and the Classical tradition, scholars have increasingly appreciated Aristotle's enormous influence on the literary activity of Alexandria.[22] The Library and the Museum as well as the nature of Alexandrian scholarship have been interpreted in light of Aristotelian models.[23] Aristarchus in particular emerged as a scholar of Aristotelian orientation. Francesca Schironi has recently shown that one of the similarities between him and Aristotle pertains to contradictions between epic lines. Both paid special attention to contradictions, because they admired Homer as an excellent writer who could be expected to be consistent.[24] Aristarchus

---

[20] Compare the expression πάντα μὲν οὐχ ἅμα in Schol. *Od.* 12.374 with the formulation πάντα μὲν ὁρᾷ ἥλιος ἀλλ' οὐχὶ ἅμα (Arist., *Apor. Hom.* fr. 149, ed. Rose 1886).

[21] Schol. *Od.* 12.374, where an additional Aristotelian solution is offered, suggesting that the expression 'all' really means 'most things'.

[22] Pfeiffer 1968, pp. 87–104. Pfeiffer's conclusions correspond to the ancient story about the neglect of Aristotle's work until its publication in Rome (Strabo 13.54; Plut. *Sulla* 25).

[23] Fraser 1972, pp. 312–35, 447–79; Pöhlmann 1994, pp. 26–40; Canfora 2002, pp. 167–75; Richardson 1994; Montanari 1993, pp. 259–64; Gallavotti 1969; Podlecki 1969; Struck 2004.

[24] Schironi 2009, pp. 288–90; see also van der Valk 1963–4, vol. ii, pp. 417–24; Lührs 1992, pp. 13–17, 194–202, who studied Aristarchus' atheteses based on contradictions and argued in a rather more general way for the Aristotelian background of his scholarly work.

thus rejected some readings of his predecessor Zenodotus, because in his view they created contradictions in the epic, while he justified some of his own readings by pointing to their consistency with other Homeric lines.[25] Although Aristarchus, like Aristotle, occasionally solved a contradiction with a non-literal interpretation, he also went beyond his teacher and marked certain verses as spurious (athetesis).[26]

Living at a time when the epics were increasingly examined from within themselves, Aristarchus introduced another important method of resolving contradictions. He was able to harmonize the respective verses by pointing to gaps in the text and filling them creatively. This technique became known as κατὰ τὸ σιωπώμενον, because it assumed that the poet had left something unsaid.[27] Aristarchus thus suggested that it is possible to fill in the gaps and recover the poet's unspoken intentions. Once he treated a contradiction of lines strikingly similar to that of Demetrius' anonymous colleague. Examining the puzzling appearance of Achilles' spear, Aristarchus significantly also anticipated his solution:

> 'But [Achilles] left there his spear on the bank of the river' [*Il.* 21.17].
> While he [Achilles] explicitly lays aside the spear, he does not explicitly take it up but later appears to be using it [*Il.* 21.67–70]. The reference is to Zenodotus, who does not know that it is necessary to admit that many things take place implicitly (κατὰ τὸ σιωπώμενον). (Schol. Il. 21.17A)

Aristonicus, who transmits this fragment, places Aristarchus' interpretation in the context of his arguments with Zenodotus. The latter seems to have pointed to the contradiction between *Il.* 21.17 and 21.67–70, probably identifying the former as spurious. Aristarchus rejected his predecessor's text criticism, stressing that the two verses are in perfect harmony, if we recognize that something has happened in between.[28] Achilles is thus said to have picked up his spear just as the Israelites were said to have taken the weapons of the drowned Egyptians. The brevity and highly factual character of the question and answer by Demetrius' colleague also corresponds to the spirit of Aristarchus, who filled in the gaps with no more than the essential information. Subsequent scholars, who adopted this technique, tended to provide more extensive narratives.[29]

---

[25] Schol. *Il.* 4.339A; 8.562A; 7.330A.   [26] Schol. *Il.* 2.45A, 20.269–72A.

[27] Nünlist 2009a, pp. 157–73; Meinel 1915; Kamesar 1994, pp. 58–61.

[28] Nünlist 2009a, pp. 159–60, has shown that Zenodotus also assumed that the poet had left certain things unsaid, filling in the gaps, but used this principle more sparingly than Aristarchus. The latter's harsh criticism of Zenodotus' complete ignorance of the exegetical principle can thus not be accepted.

[29] See also Meinel 1915, pp. 28–32; Kamesar 1994, pp. 220–1, who has already noted a general similarity between the principle 'from silence' and some exegetical procedures in Demetrius' fragments.

How far did the similarity between Demetrius' anonymous colleague and Aristarchus go? Did the former, too, write his comments on the foundational text in an environment where critical questions concerning contradictions had already been raised? Demetrius' colleague may thus have reacted to a previously proposed emendation by insisting on the principle 'from silence'. In this case, we would have to assume not only that Demetrius was already familiar with significant zetetic Bible exegesis before him, but also that such exegesis reached further back in Alexandrian history than has hitherto been assumed.

Furthermore, did Demetrius' colleague also raise his question on Exodus in the broader context of a running commentary, such as the ones written by Aristarchus? This question can naturally not be answered with any degree of certainty as firm evidence is lacking. It nevertheless seems likely that the fragment in Demetrius' work was part of some sort of commentary, which was available to Demetrius in written form.[30] Otherwise it is difficult to explain the very detailed reference to particular verses and their separate discussion, a procedure closely conforming to the convention of the commentary genre, which would be an obstacle to a running narrative.

A PROBLEM OF VERISIMILITUDE

Investigations into the verisimilitude of a text rest on the assumption that it should correspond to an external reality accessible by other disciplines, such as the natural sciences or history, which claim utmost objectivity and truth value. If the text is examined with a view to such external, hierarchically superior criteria and found to disagree with objective facts, its reliability is called into question. In the Classical period queries into the verisimilitude of Homer's text were paramount, while Aristotle attempted to shift the discourse towards more internal criteria. Demetrius' reference to a problem of verisimilitude allows us to gain a better understanding of the dynamics of the scholarly discourse in Alexandria.

Demetrius reports the following discussion:

The question was raised why at all (διαπορεῖσθαι δὲ διὰ τί ποτε) did Joseph at the meal give a fivefold portion to Benjamin even though he was incapable (μὴ δυναμένου αὐτοῦ) of taking in such quantities of meat?[31]

Consider especially the following Homeric examples: Schol. *Il.* 1.3, 6.266d, 8.1b, 9.239, 9.505, 14.139–41, 14.317b, 11.256c, 17.761, 22.101–2.

[30] Milikowsky 2005, pp. 23–4, also suggested that Demetrius used written sources of Jewish literal exegesis.

[31] While Demetrius relies here on the LXX expressions ἡ μέρις and πενταπλασίως, he paraphrases rather than quotes Gen. 43:34.

He did this because seven sons had been born to his father from Lea, but [only] two from his mother Rachel. Therefore he served Benjamin five portions and took himself two. Then there were seven portions corresponding to those [which] the sons of Lea received.

Just so concerning [Joseph's] giving double-folded garments to each [of the brothers], while to Benjamin he gave five [such garments] and 300 pieces of gold and 'to his father he sent accordingly (κατὰ ταύτα)'[32] so that his mother's house would be equal. (*ap.* Euseb. *Praep. evang.* 9.21.14–15, ed. Holladay 1983–96, vol. I, p. 70)

Assuming that the opening of this fragment reflects Demetrius' own words, I suggest that he refers here to another scholarly discussion which had come to his notice. Already before Demetrius someone had inquired in the Classical διὰ τί style why Benjamin was given an unlikely amount of meat. The question is clearly identified as a problem of verisimilitude, Moses apparently contradicting scientific truth when describing a character as extending beyond his natural abilities (μὴ δυναμένου αὐτοῦ). Demetrius' colleague solves this problem in two steps.[33] Initially, the biblical scene is interpreted in its larger literary context, implying that Joseph was concerned to rectify the unequal status of Jacob's sons. The unrealistic presentation is thus justified by reference to its narrative purpose in the drama of the hero's psychology. This solution became sufficiently influential to be echoed in Philo's explanation that Joseph gave a richer portion 'to his maternal brother', watching whether the other siblings still cherished animosity or envy (*Jos.* 234).

Demetrius' colleague corroborates his initial solution through a comparison with another biblical scene (ὡσαύτως), where the issue of Benjamin's preference is mentioned as well (Gen. 45:22–3). The connection between these two passages is usually interpreted as an application of the solution from Gen. 43:34 to Gen. 45:22–3.[34] Upon closer examination, however, the situation appears to be more complex. The latter passage clearly has a more active role and provides further proof for the suggested interpretation of Gen. 43:34. Initially, the expression κατὰ τὰ αὐτά

---

[32] LXX Gen. 45:23; note that in the present version of the text αὐτοῦ has dropped out after 'father'.

[33] It is theoretically possible that Demetrius himself provided the answer to the problem. Style, however, tells against it. The question and answer on Joseph and Benjamin represent a unique cluster in Demetrius' overall paraphrase of Scripture. Immediately after the above answer, he abruptly returns to the biblical narrative, summarizing Israel's sojourn in Canaan from the time of Abraham's election until Jacob (*ap.* Euseb. *Praep. evang.* 9.26.16). The move from the question and answer to the flow of the narrative lacks elegance, leaving a clearly visible seam. Given the fact that Demetrius identifies the question as a problem that had already been discussed, it is likely that the answer, too, was circulating in Alexandria.

[34] Holladay 1983–96, vol. I, p. 71, translates 'the same explanation applies to...'

(LXX Gen. 45:23) is taken out of its context and no longer read as a reference to the subsequent list of items sent to Jacob. It is instead connected to the preceding report of Benjamin's portion. Read thus, κατὰ τὰ αὐτά suggests that Joseph was concerned about the equality of his gifts to Benjamin and his father's house. This interpretation is perfectly suited to solve also the problem of Joseph's preferential treatment of Benjamin in the other context of the meal. It is less clear, however, whether it follows the discussion of Gen. 43:34 or whether, on the contrary, it originated in the context of Gen. 45:22–3 and was subsequently applied to Gen. 43:34.

This question and answer by Demetrius' colleague must also be appreciated in the context of Aristotelian scholarship and its application in Alexandria. Concern for realistic presentation was already central to Aristotle's discussion of the epics in the twenty-fifth chapter of his *Poetics*. Assuming with Plato that the poet is an 'imitator' of external referents, like a painter drawing from life, he makes the novel suggestion that the poet:

always imitates in one of three ways, namely either things as they are or were, or things as they are told or appear to be or things as they ought to be (Arist. *Poet.* 1460b5–11).

Facing the 'criticisms [involved] in the problems', Aristotle insists that poetry must not be judged by the standards of any other art (*Poet.* 1460b15–22). Presentations of 'impossible things' (ἀδύνατα) must therefore be properly appreciated in their narrative context and not taken as indications of Homer's failure, as Zoilos, for example, had taken them.[35] Aristotle stresses that unrealistic presentation must serve a poetic purpose; otherwise it is a mistake: he fully justifies it only if it renders the passage 'more astounding'.[36] This argument is furthermore illustrated by the example of the pursuit of Hector, which had already been discussed in the previous chapter (*Poet.* 1460a11–18). The impossible element of this scene is Achilles' shaking of his head, which is said to prevent the Greeks from further pursuing Hector. Aristotle does not precisely explain in what way this implausibility increases the dramatic effect but stresses that such an appeal to the irrational is suitable to the epic, while it would be unacceptable on the stage.[37]

The question and answer of Demetrius' colleague belongs in this Aristotelian tradition. The expression μὴ δυναμένου αὐτοῦ closely resembles

---

[35] Μέμφεται τῷ ποιητῇ ὅτι λίαν γελοίως πεποίηκεν, Zoilos, Schol. 5:4 (*FGH* fr. 7, p. 111) see also Zoilos, Schol. *Il.* 5.20 (*FGH* fr. 8, p. 111); Richardson 1992; Dupont-Roc and Lallot 1980, pp. 387–90; Bywater 1909, pp. 323–4; Janko 1987, pp. 145–8.
[36] ἐκπληκτικώτερον (*Poet.* 1460b16–32).
[37] *Poet.* 1460a15; see also the discussion by Dupont-Roc and Lallot 1980, pp. 390–1.

Aristotle's formulations in the *Poetics* (ἀδύνατα). The problem of verisimilitude moreover revolves around a Classical issue of physical inability, paralleling Aristotle's example of the horse with its two legs on the right side thrown forward (*Poet.* 1460b18–19). Although the solution does not explicitly refer to 'astounding' effect, it considers the dramatic and narrative function of the scene, offering a psychological perspective based on context. This solution is a direct application of Aristotle's recommendation to consider the literary context and the particular motivation of each hero (*Poet.* 1461a4–9).

The additional step taken by Demetrius' colleague, namely his interpretation of one verse by comparison with another, goes beyond Classical Aristotelian methods and reflects the more recent work of Aristarchus. Francesca Schironi has shown that, following Aristotle, Aristarchus was deeply concerned to explain unrealistic and implausible scenes, using the terms ἀπίθανος and γελοῖος instead of its Aristotelian counterpart ἀδύνατος.[38] Assuming that Homer's original epics were generally true to reality, Aristarchus rejected some of Zenodotus' readings because they violated the principle of realistic presentation, while on other occasions he athetized epic lines, insisting that 'horses do not drink wine' or arguing that 'it is implausible that horses speak'.[39] Whereas Aristotle in his Homeric scholarship hardly ever referred to parallel verses, Aristarchus regularly examined cases of implausibility in the context of other lines.[40] His commentary sometimes strikingly resembles that of Demetrius' colleague. One such example is the following:

> 'And the gates being flung wide open brought light (τεῦξαν φάος), but Apollo leapt out to face [Achilles] so that he might ward off ruin from the Trojans' [*Il.* 21.538–9].

Zenodotus athetized these lines, considering it ridiculous (γελοῖον) that the city should be enlightened through the gates, the whole place being exposed.

---

[38] Schironi 2009, pp. 284–8; see also Lührs 1992, pp. 167–94. Note also that an exegetical scholiast, probably reflecting Didymus' work, explains Aristarchus' athetesis of *Il.* 16.97–100 in terms of ἀδύνατος (Schol. *Il.* 16.97–100T). In this case the athetesis does not rely on the Classical identification of a contrast between the text and external reality, but on a contradiction between verses as well as the axiomatic assumption that erotic concerns are irrelevant to the interpretation of Ganymede's being lifted to heaven.

[39] Schol. *Il.* 1.100A, 19.416–17A, 1.129A, 2.55A, 2.76A, 2.319A, 2.667A, 3.74A, 16.666A.

[40] Arist. *Apor. Hom.* fr. 148, 151; Aristar. in Schol. *Il.* 7.130A, 1.180A, 6.71A, 6.479–80A, 5.734–6A, 5.299A, 5.684A, 8.441A, 11.636A. See also Schol. *Il.* 24.420, where Byzantine scholars identify a problem of verisimilitude as a 'paradox' and contradiction between verses. Modern scholars have debated whether Aristarchus was the originator of the method which Porphyry subsequently called Ὁμήρου ἐξ Ὁμήρου σαφηνίζειν (Porph. *Quaest. Il.* 6.201). Porter 1992, pp. 70–4, argued against Pfeiffer 1968, p. 231, for the probability of the maxim's Aristarchan origin; while Schäublin 1977 stressed that the maxim was rather widespread in the Imperial period and not confined to the *grammatikoi*.

However he [Homer] says 'brought light' in the sense that they brought deliverance to those fleeing, as in the expression (ὡς ἐν τῷ) 'he brought a light [of safety] to his comrades for he struck the man' [*Il.* 6.6–7]. (Schol. *Il.* 21:538–9A)

Aristonicus, who transmits this fragment, explains that Zenodotus read the expression τεῦξαν φάος literally and rejected the lines because of their implausibility. Aristarchus, by contrast, insisted on the metaphorical meaning of the expression, which is corroborated by an epic line from another context. The discussion here is composed of precisely the same three steps as that of Demetrius' colleague: initially a problem of verisimilitude is raised, then an innovative interpretation is offered and, finally, another verse is adduced in support of that interpretation.

The same intertextual type of question and answer later resurfaces in Porphyry's *Quaestiones*, which continues the Aristotelian tradition of literary analysis.[41] In the third century CE Porphyry's approach was to quote individual epic lines, raising a question on each of them and then providing a sophisticated answer, which was usually literal and also related to earlier discussions of the problem.[42] Porphyry also stylizes his solutions, often introducing them with a precise definition. The most frequent and clearly Aristotelian is: 'the solution [derives] from [a consideration of] linguistic expression' (ἡ λύσις ἐκ τῆς λέξεως).[43] The fragments of Porphyry's *Quaestiones* thus testify to a tradition of Aristotelian questions and answers, which remained highly influential over a long span of time.

Questions of verisimilitude were also treated by Porphyry, who significantly attributed their initial impetus to earlier scholars, such as Zoilos.[44] Following Aristarchus, Porphyry often solves such a problem by reference to a parallel epic line. An illuminating example is his discussion of Aphrodite's appearance:

They said that it is impossible (ἀδύνατον) that Aphrodite herself changes into an old woman and that Helen saw the neck of the goddess [*Il.* 3.385, 395]. Solution: in many places he [the poet] depicts demigods as grasping the forms of the gods,

---

[41] Carroll 1895; Sodano 1965.

[42] Unfortunately, Porphyry generally does not identify earlier exegetes but only provides their interpretation. His discussion of the famous crux in *Il.* 1.1, for example, opens with a review of four earlier διὰ τί questions (ζητεῖται, ζητοῦσι); see also *Quaest. Il.* 2.8ff. (ἀποροῦσι); *Quaest. Il.* 2.362, 2.484, 24.527ff. (ζητοῦσι [δέ] τινες); *Quaest. Il.* 3.98ff. (ἀποροῦσι τινες); *Quaest. Il.* 4.2 (κατηγοροῦσι); *Quaest. Il.* 4.226 (ἐζήτηται), *Quaest. Il.* 5.7 (Ζωίλος ὁ Ἐφέσιος κατηγορεῖ); references to earlier solutions can be found in *Quaest. Il.* 1.113, 2.478ff., 3.306, 5.7, 5.20, 12.175–81 (ἀθετεῖ Ἀρίσταρχος), 15.56–77, 15.147–8, 15.212–17, 15.449–51.

[43] See also Porph. *Quaest. Il.* 2.49, 3.121, 3.365, 4.105–11, 4.491, 5.7, 5.341, 13.3, 15.189; cf. Arist. *Poet.* 1461a9–10.

[44] Porph. *Quaest. Il.* 5.7, 4.105–11, 4.491.

thus when Poseidon, after having been made similar to Calchas, appeared, Aias says: 'he is not Calchas the prophet and reader of omens, for easily did I recognize the signs he left of feet and legs as he went from us, and plain to be known are the gods' [*Il.* 13.70–2]. (*Quaest. Il.* 3.396–397)

The problem of verisimilitude is presented here as an older issue which had been raised before. The solution derives from a consideration of Homer's overall work, where semi-heroes are found to have special insights. In line with Aristarchus and Demetrius' colleague, Porphyry refers to another verse in support of his solution. His appeal to πολλαχοῦ ποιεῖ-ται corresponds to the expressions ὡς and ὡσαύτως in Aristarchus' and Demetrius' fragments. Porphyry, too, uses his proof text in a rather creative manner. Just as Demetrius' colleague had taken a particular expression out of its original context in order to render it more suitable for his purposes, Porphyry gently manipulates the image of Poseidon.

The fragments of Demetrius' colleagues thus throw important new light on the development of the Aristotelian tradition in Alexandria. They show that Aristotelian scholarship was not only adopted and developed by Aristarchus, as was already known, but spread also further into circles of Jewish Bible exegetes. The latter show the characteristic Aristarchan blend of an Aristotelian question and a literary, more intertextual answer. The scholarly tradition, which resurfaces in Porphyry's commentary, clearly had a broader basis in Alexandria than has been hitherto recognized. This is especially significant if the fragment of Demetrius' anonymous colleague was part of a larger, written commentary, as is likely to have been the case.

DEMETRIUS

We now have to examine how Demetrius himself fits into the context of his scholarly colleagues. Did he belong to the same academic milieu or did he rather follow his own agenda, only marginally integrating questions and answers which had come to his notice? The difference of styles is immediately conspicuous. Demetrius wrote a continuous paraphrase of Scripture and related it only indirectly to problems arising from the text. Instead of formulating explicit questions and presenting separate answers he tended to integrate ready solutions into the flow of his narrative. Unlike his colleagues, Demetrius was not primarily a *lutikos*, adhering to the conventions of the genre, but instead an exegete with prominent interests in biblical chronology.

Echoes of the question and answer method are visible in Demetrius' own work. An illuminating example is a passage addressing the problem of Joseph's negligent attitude towards his father:

> Even though Joseph fared well for nine years, he did not send for his father, because (διὰ τό) he was a shepherd, as were his brothers, for shepherding is a disgrace in the eyes of the Egyptians. [Demetrius says] that he himself explained that this was the reason (διὰ τοῦτο) why he did not send for him. For after his family had arrived, he told them that whenever they are summoned by the king and asked what they do, they should say that they are cowherds. (*ap.* Euseb. *Praep. evang.* 9.21.13, ed. Holladay 1983–96, vol. I, pp. 69–70)

Demetrius retells the biblical story by initially presenting the solution and thus precluding explicit questions. At the same time, however, his emphasis on διὰ τοῦτο still echoes the underlying διὰ τί question. Why had Joseph not sent earlier for his father? This question reflects a rare interest in the figure of Jacob, which corresponds to Demetrius' overall tendency.[45] The question may have arisen either from a general consideration of the whole story or from an examination of a particular verse. Considering the latter possibility, one does not immediately perceive a biblical passage which may have prompted the question, because there is no verse explicitly stating that Joseph did not send for his father.

One biblical scene may nevertheless have intrigued Demetrius, namely Gen. 46:30–4, where Jacob finally arrives in Egypt, meeting Joseph after many years of separation and uncertainty. Jacob overflows with emotion, telling his son how happy he is to see him before his death. The objective of his old age has thus been fulfilled and he may now die in peace. This emotional outburst is abruptly ended by Joseph's speech. Instead of reacting to the very personal words of his father, he says that he will now inform Pharaoh of their arrival and of their profession as shepherds. Demetrius may well have been struck by the discrepancy between the verses, asking whether Joseph's words were indeed a direct response to Jacob. They may be seen either as inappropriate behaviour bespeaking a questionable character or as a text corruption. Demetrius instead chooses the path of harmonizing the verses. On his view, Joseph referred to their profession as shepherds in

---

[45] Demetrius is overwhelmingly concerned with Jacob throughout the long fragment on the family. The sibling rivalry, on the other hand, hardly receives any attention, Demetrius merely mentioning Joseph's birth and sale (*ap.* Euseb. *Praep. evang.* 9.21.5 and 11). Philo, *Jos.* 165–77, and Jos. *JA* 2.95–9, by contrast, focus on Joseph's behaviour towards his brothers, explaining why he did not reveal himself on their first encounter; for further details on ancient interpretations of the Joseph story, see Kugel 1990; Niehoff 1992, 2010a.

order to explain why he had not earlier called for his father, seeing that the latter was overwhelmed with joy at the meeting.

Demetrius thus creatively applies the question and answer method which was already used by his colleagues in the Jewish community of Alexandria. Intrigued by a discrepancy in the biblical text, he solves the problem by paying attention to context and creatively filling in the gaps. While formulated as a paraphrase of Scripture, his exegesis reflects the milieu of aporetic inquiry. At the same time, however, it is clear that Demetrius is more removed than his colleagues from academic commentary. His style is likely to have appealed to a wider Jewish audience, who did not have the leisure to immerse themselves in the study of minute commentaries but would be happy to share summary accounts of solutions.

Another, often discussed fragment provides some new insight into the nature of Demetrius' work. The subject is Moses' marriage to Zipporah:

[Demetrius says that] Moses fled to Median and there married Zipporah, Jethro's daughter, who was, as can be guessed from the names, of the descendents of Keturah and thus of the stock of Abraham, as he was a descendent from Joksan who was born to Abraham by Keturah. From Yoksan Dedan was born and from Dedan Raguel, and from Raguel Jethro and Hobab, and from Jethro Zipporah, whom Moses married.

[Demetrius says that] the generations are in agreement (συμφωνεῖν). Moses was the seventh from Abraham, while Zipporah was sixth. For Isaac, from whom Moses descended, was already married when Abraham married Keturah at the age of 140 and begot by her a second son Ishbak, from whom Zipporah traced her genealogy. There is nothing contradictory (οὐδὲν οὖν ἀντιπίπτει) therefore [in saying that] Moses and Zipporah lived at the same time. (*ap.* Euseb. *Praep. evang.* 9.29.1, ed. Holladay 1983–96, vol. 1, pp. 74–6)

Demetrius treats here the question of how Moses and Zipporah could have been contemporaries, getting married as mentioned in Exod. 2:21. This question arises in view of another tradition according to which Zipporah was closely related to Abraham and thus apparently preceding Moses by one generation. This contradictory tradition appears in LXX Gen. 25:3, where the Greek translators added the name Raguel to the genealogical list, identifying him as one of Dedan's sons. Demetrius alludes to that passage when saying that Zipporah's descent from Abraham can be 'guessed from the names'.[46] Demetrius is thus aware that LXX Gen. 25:3 does not explicitly draw a connection between Raguel and Zipporah's ancestor, but

---

[46] Contra Wacholder 1968, pp. 452–8; 1974, pp. 98–101, who interpreted the evidence precisely the other way round, arguing that Demetrius generally invented dates and chronologies in the spirit of fellow Alexandrian chronographers, ultimately influencing the rendition of the LXX.

he takes them to be identical on the basis of their common name. On this assumption there is a contradiction between Gen. 25:3 and Exod. 2:21, because Zipporah and Moses are one generation apart and could not get married. Demetrius solves the problem by stressing that Zipporah only appears to antedate Moses. In reality, however, that is not the case, because Abraham started to have children with Keturah only in his very old age, skipping a whole generation in the line descending from Isaac.

Demetrius mentions the genealogical details in order to harmonize the verses.[47] He wishes to show that 'there is nothing contradictory' (οὐδὲν οὖν ἀντιπίπτει) and 'the generations are in agreement' (συμφωνεῖν). These terms echo Aristarchan scholarship with its characteristic concern for the inner consistency of the text. The leading Homer scholar of Alexandria had stressed that the different descriptions of Olympus are consistent with each other (συμφωνήσει).[48] He moreover insisted on the consistency of grammatical features, which are shown to agree in all instances.[49] Demetrius' exegesis must thus be situated in the general vicinity of Alexandrian scholarship, while reflecting an exceptional interest in the calculation of dates which was generally foreign to Aristarchus.[50] Nevertheless, even he occasionally inquires into the precise relationship of dramatic figures. Aristarchus considers, for example, athetizing a line, because 'it is implausible' that an older woman should be Helen's servant, but then he solves the problem by suggesting that two different persons with identical names are involved (Schol. *Il.* 3.144A).

The question of Demetrius' own dates remains to be discussed, having significant implications for our overall picture of Alexandrian Bible exegesis. Following Freudenthal, scholars often place him in the third century BCE. This, however, rests purely on an assumption that fragments

---

[47] Gutman 1958–63, vol. 1, pp. 136–7, and Gruen 1998, p. 114, n. 18, suggested that Demetrius used the genealogical details in order to transform Zipporah into a Jewish woman, thus rendering her suitable for a marriage with Moses. This suggestion, however, is unlikely, because in pre-Philonic times the issue of intermarriage with foreign women does not appear to have been a problem, as patrilineal descent was assumed (following the Pentateuch); for details, see Niehoff 2001, pp. 17–33.

[48] Schol. *Il.* 8.19A, 14.174A.

[49] Schol. *Il.* 17.136A, 18.319A, 11.786A, 22.32A; Didymus subsequently used the term συμφωνεῖν in the context of comparing different text editions (Schol. *Il.* 3.259A, 11.40A, 19.365–8A).

[50] Two further fragments of Demetrius treat chronological problems which have been well discussed by Gruen 1998, p. 113; Freudenthal 1874, pp. 54–6; Gutman 1958–63, vol. 1, pp. 134–5; contra Bickerman 1975, pp. 77–9, who interprets Demetrius' calculation in light of the known competition in the Hellenistic period for the most ancient roots of one's people. Note that Homeric scholiasts, attested in the later exegetical tradition, took a similar interest in Priam's offspring, asking precisely how many children had been born, how it was possible that he fathered nineteen children from one woman, as well as who were the offspring of the other unnamed wives at Priam's court (Schol. *Il.* 24.495–7).

mentioned by Eusebius and a small fragment quoted by Clement are authored by the same writer. The Clement fragment contains a reference to Ptolemy the Fourth and establishes the date *post quem* of Eusebius' Demetrius as well, if indeed these two are the same.[51]

The identity of the authors, however, is far from self-evident, the style of Eusebius' Demetrius significantly differing from that of Clement. Instead of working on the details of the biblical text, the latter is said to have written a book concerning the kings of Judaea, referring to the captivity of the tribes under Sennacherib and Nebuchadnezzar as well as to the rule of Ptolemy the Fourth. Clement's Demetrius is a historian interested in political events ranging from late biblical times to his own period. Eusebius' Demetrius, by contrast, never places biblical material into a framework of external historical calculation.[52] Unlike his namesake, he does not follow in the footsteps of their fellow Alexandrian Eratosthenes, whose *Chronological Tables* placed the capture of Troy on the same historical plane as the conquests of Alexander the Great.[53] The historian Demetrius mentioned by Clement must thus be distinguished from the exegete Demetrius mentioned by Eusebius. Given the identity of their names, it is not surprising that scholars conflated their works. Similar mistakes occurred also with regard to Greek scholars in Alexandria. Felix Jacoby has conclusively shown that Sosibius the textual scholar must be distinguished from Sosibius the historian (*FGH* 3.635–7).

If the historical framework of Clement's fragment is no longer relevant to the dating of Eusebius' Demetrius, how can we determine the latter's time? Demetrius and his anonymous colleagues must have written their works before Alexander Polyhistor (80–40 BCE), because Eusebius quotes the material from his account. More precise dates can only be suggested on internal, literary grounds. The above analysis has shown that the anonymous Bible scholars mentioned by Demetrius were remarkably close to Aristotelian scholarship as practised and developed in Alexandria by Aristarchus. They are thus likely to have worked during the latter's *floruit*, namely between about 160 and 131 BCE, when he was chief librarian. Demetrius himself probably worked a little later in the second century BCE.

By way of conclusion the value of Demetrius' fragments must be emphasized. They provide the earliest evidence of positive interactions between biblical and Homeric scholars in Alexandria. Some Jewish intellectuals in

---

[51] Clem. *Strom.* 1.21.141.1–2. [52] Gutman 1958–63, vol. 1, p. 134.
[53] On Eratosthenes' chronological work, see Fraser 1972, vol. 1, pp. 456–8.

the second century BCE began to interpret their Scriptures as a piece of literature, submitting it to a detailed and critical literary analysis. Demetrius' anonymous colleagues are of special interest, because they closely adhered to the Aristotelian method of question and answer, addressing problems of contradictions and verisimilitude. Moreover, their answers closely resemble Aristarchus' highly intertextual techniques in his commentary on the *Iliad*. The evidence from Demetrius' colleagues indicates the influence of both Aristotle and Aristarchus throughout Alexandrian scholarship, including biblical research.

The significance of Demetrius' fragments must also be stressed in view of the overall development of Jewish Bible exegesis. While his successors in Alexandria frequently used the question and answer method, as we shall see below, in the Land of Israel the method of raising explicit questions and treating textual problems made an appearance only several centuries later.[54] Rabbinic literature is characterized by a significant move towards a more scholastic approach to Scripture than had hitherto been customary in the Land of Israel.[55] The Midrash *Genesis Rabbah*, which was redacted probably around 400 CE, played an especially prominent role in this process. It is based on a close reading of the literal text and provides a running commentary on the Book of Genesis.[56]

This Midrash contains many questions concerning contradictions and problems of verisimilitude. The biblical story of Abraham and Sarah, for example, who took with them 'the persons they had made' (הנפש אשר עשו ואת) is problematized. Rabbi Leazar said in the name of R. Jose b. Zimra: 'if all the nations assembled to create one insect, they would be unable (אין יכולין) to endow it with life'.[57] On another occasion, a question concerning unrealistic representation is attributed to a Roman *matrona*. Using Classical Aristotelian terminology, she asks whether it is indeed likely that Joseph resisted the advances of Potiphar's wife. In her view, it is hardly 'possible (איפשר)' that a 17-year-old youth would overcome sexual desire, as narrated in Scripture.[58] The solution to this problem relies, in line with the style in

---

[54] The difference between the Midrash called 'Rewritten Bible', which sometimes indirectly solves textual questions, and the form of an explicit commentary has rightly been stressed by Fraade 2006.

[55] The *Pesher Habakkuk* from Qumran, which has often been adduced as a congenial forerunner of rabbinic exegesis, belongs to the altogether different field of prophetic exegesis and employs oneirocritical methods, as shown by Nitzan 2009.

[56] In this context the argument by Lerner 1882 that *Genesis Rabbah* initially emerged as a rather short commentary and was later embellished by *aggadic* material is still highly relevant.

[57] *Gen. Rab.* 39:14 (ed. Theodor and Albeck 1965, pp. 378–9); a useful English translation is available in Freedman 1939, referring to Gen. 12:5.

[58] *Gen. Rab.* 77:10 (ed. Theodor and Albeck 1965, pp. 1070–1); for a similar discussion of a problem of verisimilitude, see *Gen. Rab.* 74:55 (ed. Theodor and Albeck 1965, p. 1021).

Demetrius' fragments, on a reference to another Scriptural context. Rabbi Yose responds to the *matrona* by insisting that the account is plausible in light of the fact that Scripture admits Yehuda's and Reuben's sexual lapses (Gen. 38:16–18, 35:22).

Similarly, *Genesis Rabbah* addresses an apparent contradiction between Gen. 37:36, where the Midianites are said to sell Joseph to the Egyptians, and Gen. 39:1, where the Ishmaelites do so. An anonymous exegete asks 'how many bills of sale were written for him [Joseph]?'[59] The solution assumes the method of κατὰ τὸ σιωπώμενον: the exegete points to a significant gap in the text, not all of the sales having been explicitly mentioned. Following in the steps of Demetrius' anonymous colleagues, the rabbinic exegete proposes to reconstruct Scripture's unspoken intention and lists a chain of sales, ranging from the brothers through the Ishmaelites to the Midianites and ultimately to the Egyptians.

---

[59] *Gen. Rab.* 74:22 (ed. Theodor and Albeck 1965, p. 1028); see also Halevi 1973.

CHAPTER 4

Aristobulus' questions and answers as a tool for philosophical instruction

Aristobulus is known as the first Jewish author who clearly defined himself as a philosopher.[1] Writing in Alexandria between 155 and 145 BCE, he must be interpreted in the context of the *Letter of Aristeas* and Demetrius.[2] In comparison with these two, it is conspicuous that Aristobulus produced a unique, yet distinctly Alexandrian blend of critical scholarship and philosophy. While his Bible exegesis has been prematurely identified as a Stoic type of allegory, a systematic study of his work in its original, cultural environment is still warranted.[3] When Aristobulus is interpreted in the context of contemporary Alexandria, he emerges as an Aristotelian scholar, who offers metaphorical solutions to textual problems.[4] In the field of hermeneutics he throws important new light on the development of the Aristotelian tradition in the city.

The interpretation of Aristobulus as a Stoic allegorist has already been challenged by Peter Fraser and Nicolaus Walter. The former questioned

---

[1] Euseb. *Praep. evang.* 13.12.8 (= fr. 4; ed. Holladay 1983–96, vol. III, p. 174), where Aristobulus presents the Jewish tradition in terms of 'our philosophical school'; Aristobulus' self-definition has been accepted by Eusebius, who called him a philosopher (*Praep. evang.* 8.938 = fr. 2; ed. Holladay 1983–96, vol. III, p. 134), *Praep. evang.* 13.113b (= fr. 3; ed. Holladay 1983–96, vol. III, p. 150); see also: Yarbro Collins 1983–5, pp. 832–4; Barclay 1996, pp. 152–3; J. J. Collins 2000, pp. 186–90.

[2] Aristobulus' reference to the translation of Scripture into Greek is too brief to prove his familiarity with the text of the *Letter of Aristeas*, but at least it indicates that he knew its main story line (Euseb. *Praep. evang.* 13.12.1–2 = fr. 3; ed. Holladay 1983–96, vol. III, pp. 152–6); regarding Aristobulus' dates, see Yarbro Collins 1983–5, pp. 832–3; Holladay 1983–96, vol. III, pp. 45–75 (with a detailed review of the scholarship on this subject).

[3] Following Long 1992, it has been questioned whether the Stoics were indeed allegorists or rather etymologists, who uncovered early religious thought in poetic texts. Long's argument, however, seems to overemphasize the difference between etymology and allegory as well as that between strong and weak allegory. In my view, the Stoics must be identified as allegorists, because they took the epics to say something other than their author had intended. See also Brisson 2004, pp. 44–9.

[4] Clement was the first writer to identify him as a Peripatetic (*Strom.* 1.15.72.4), yet this designation has usually been dismissed as an ill-informed or manipulative reference; for a good overview of the discussion in modern scholarship, see Holladay 1983–96, vol. III, pp. 204–5, n. 24; Rajak 2009, p. 78, by contrast, takes the Aristotelian label seriously.

whether an Alexandrian writer is likely to have adopted the methods of the rivaling school of Pergamum, while the latter stressed that Aristobulus used neither the terminology nor the motifs of Stoic allegorists.[5] Moreover, it is significant that Aristobulus mentions in the few extant fragments a number of philosophers, especially 'the Peripatetic school', but not even one Stoic thinker.[6] To the early Christian transmitters of his work, however, it was self-evident that Aristobulus' non-literal readings are a form of (Stoic) allegory. Clement and Eusebius introduced the term 'allegory' into their own comments on the fragments.[7] For Aristobulus himself an exclusive choice between either myth and Stoic allegory was anything but warranted. Indeed, assuming such an alternative in Alexandria at the time of Aristobulus is anachronistic.

A few words need to be said first about the genre of Aristobulus' work. The available excerpts from his 'commentary works' (βίβλοι ἐξηγητικαί) indicate that he raised 'questions' on the biblical text and solved them by extended answers.[8] The setting is described in terms recalling the *Letter of Aristeas*, namely as a conversation between a teacher and a lay person. In the case of Aristobulus it is the Ptolemaic king who raises questions and is instructed in the 'proper explanation', while in the *Letter of Aristeas* the author himself and Andreas addressed a question regarding Scripture to the High Priest in Jerusalem.[9] In contrast to Demetrius' anonymous colleague the method of question and answer is not used by Aristobulus for the strictly academic purpose of a commentary but is rather applied to a fictive classroom situation. In comparison with the *Letter of Aristeas*, however, where only one rather general question is treated, Aristobulus is far more focused on the details of the text itself, exploring several verses in the few extant fragments.

---

[5] Fraser 1972, vol. I, p. 695; Walter 1964, pp. 124–48; the Stoic interpretation has nevertheless been repeated by Barclay 1996, pp. 153–4; Holladay 1983–96, vol. III, p. 73; and, more hesitantly, by Yarbro Collins 1983–5, pp. 832–4. Note that the image of difference and rivalry between Alexandria and Pergamum has been challenged in certain areas of linguistic inquiry, especially with regard to the distinction of analogy or anomaly in grammar (Porter 1992). The difference, however, between the cities in their overall hermeneutic approach remains visible: Alexandrian scholarship was overwhelmingly literal, while scholars in Pergamum engaged predominantly in allegory, see Blank and Atherton 2003; Schenkeveld and Barnes 1999, pp. 224–5.

[6] The Peripatetic αἵρεσις is mentioned by Aristobulus in Euseb. *Praep. evang.* 13.12.10 (= fr. 5; ed. Holladay 1983–96, vol. III, p. 180).

[7] *Strom.* 6.3.32.4 (= fr. 2a; ed. Holladay 1983–96, vol. III, p. 142). Clement's tendency to modernize Aristobulus' work in light of his own Christian theology is further conspicuous in his quotation of *Timothy* 6:16 (*ibid*). Similarly, Apollodorus' interpretation of Athene was identified by a later transmitter as allegory (*FGH*, vol. II, p. 1124).

[8] Anatolius *ap.* Euseb. *Hist. eccl.* 7.32.26–7 (= fr. 1; ed. Holladay 1983–96, vol. III, p. 130).

[9] Euseb. *Praep. evang.* 8.10.1 (= fr. 2; ed. Holladay 1983–96, vol. III, p. 134); cf. *Letter*, 129.

Aristobulus stresses overall themes, providing answers which are more elaborate and prominent than their very concise parallels in Demetrius' fragments.[10] He wishes to convey a general message, linked to what he said in earlier contexts.[11] It is his declared aim to 'demonstrate that God's power is everywhere' and his belief that a proper appreciation of Scripture leads to 'holy opinions about God'.[12] In line with Aristeas, he expects his readers to recognize Scripture's overall orientation towards 'piety, justice and self-control'.[13]

This blend of textual inquiry and thematic discussion is typical of some less well-known Alexandrian writers in the vicinity of Aristarchus. Foremost among them is Apollodorus, who is in the ancient sources unanimously described as a γραμματικός.[14] He 'studied a long time with Aristarchus' before attending Diogenes' and Panaitios' lectures in Athens.[15] His biography thus associates his text-critical training with Alexandria, while his philosophical interests are identified at a later stage with prominent Stoic thinkers in Athens. Apollodorus' works addressed general themes, such as 'Concerning the Gods' and 'Chronology'. The extant fragments indicate that he participated in discussions of specific Homeric lines, taking positions with a view to Aristarchus as well as the Alexandrian scientist and scholar Eratosthenes.[16] His adoption of the latter's historical calculation according to Olympiads shows that his work initially emerged in the context of Alexandrian scholarship.[17] Of special interest for us is his treatise *Concerning the Gods*. Following Homer's descriptions, which he prefers to those of Hesiod, Apollodorus provides rather systematic interpretations of the different gods.[18] His work became known and influential through his numerous students. Heraclitus at the beginning of the second century CE

[10] For details on Demetrius and his colleagues, see Chapter 3.
[11] Euseb. *Praep. evang.* 8.10.1 (= fr. 2; ed. Holladay 1983–96, vol. III, p. 136); *Praep. evang.* 13.12.4b (= fr. 4; ed. Holladay 1983–96, vol. III, p. 172); *Praep. evang.* 13.12.11 and 15 (= fr. 5; ed. Holladay 1983–96, vol. III, pp. 180, 190).
[12] *Ap.* Euseb. *Praep. evang.* 13.12. 7–8 (= fr. 4; ed. Holladay 1983–96, vol. III, pp. 172–4).
[13] *Ap.* Euseb. *Praep. evang.* 13.12.8 (= fr. 4, ed. Holladay 1983–96, vol. III, p. 174); cf. *Letter*, 168–71, where Aristeas insists that Scripture contains nothing 'mythical' (οὐδὲ μυθωδῶς) but aims at the practice of justice. General exegetical similarities between Aristobulus and Aristeas have already been noted by Dawson 1992, pp. 74–8.
[14] *Testimonia* 1, 4, 5, 11, 19 (*FGH*, vol. II, pp. 1022–5); note that Heraclitus the Allegorist speaks of his 'scholarly exposition' (*Homeric Problems* 7.1 = T10).
[15] συνεσχολακὼς δὲ πολὺν Ἀριστάρχῳ χρόνον (*Testimonia* 2, *FGH*, vol. II, p. 1022, which also mentions his listening to Diogenes); his connection with Panaitios is mentioned in *Test.* 1 and 5.
[16] See esp. fr. 63 (*FGH*, vol. II, p. 1038), where the opinion of Apollodorus' followers (οἱ δὲ περὶ Ἀπολλόδωρον) is compared with that of Eratosthenes' and Aristarchus' followers; see also frs. 32, 64, 67, 73.
[17] F. Jacoby, *FGH*, vol. II, pp. 753–61 (with a useful review of earlier scholarship).
[18] See esp. fr. 353 (*FGH*, vol. II, pp. 1123–4).

still relied on him and acknowledged the considerable following he had commanded.[19]

Similar examples of combining textual analysis with thematic studies are provided by the Alexandrian Dioscorides and the earlier Athenian writer Palaephatus, an author who possibly had Egyptian connections.[20] The former wrote a treatise *Concerning the Customs [preserved by] Homer*, which discusses significant epic passages dealing with dining customs. Dioscorides' main interest is stated at the very beginning: he wishes to show that Homer regarded 'prudence as the foremost virtue' and gave instructions for a proper life of self-restraint.[21] Treating the details of epic meals, especially the modesty of its heroes, Dioscorides shows some familiarity with Aristarchus' interpretations.[22] Similarly, Palaephatus wrote a treatise *Concerning Incredible Things*, which aimed to convince its readers that certain fabulous stories are true, albeit not in the simple sense taken for granted by naïve people.[23] In his discussions of particular examples Palaephatus relied, where possible, on Homeric motifs, harmonizing them with more recent stories.[24]

GOD'S DESCENT AS AN ARISTOTELIAN PARADOX

Having appreciated the genre of Aristobulus' work as well as its cultural context, we have to examine specific examples of his exegesis. Our attention will be focused on the question of how he combined critical literary analysis with his overall philosophical argumentation. More importantly, did he follow in this respect any particular school or did he adapt certain models to his own needs?

The first problem which deserves our attention is Aristobulus' discussion of God's descent on Mount Sinai. According to the extant fragments, he opens his exegesis with the following statement:

[19] Heracl. *Hom. Prob.* 7.1; regarding the latter's dates, see Buffière 1962, pp. ix–x; Pontani 2005a, pp. 9–13; Russell and Konstan 2005, pp. xi–xiii.

[20] Concerning both writers, see Susemihl 1891–2, vol. II, pp. 54–7, 347–51; Palaephatus' Egyptian connection is mentioned in T4 (the *Suda* saying that he is either Egyptian or Athenian, having written an 'Egyptian Theology', quoted by Nünlist 2009b); regarding his dates and the nature of his work, see T2–3; Nünlist 2009b; Fornaro 2007; J. Stern 1996, pp. 1–10; Brodersen 2002, pp. 13–14.

[21] Fr. 5 (*FGH*, vol. II, p. 193), see esp. his insistence that the 'poet inveighs against drunkenness' (p. 195).

[22] Weber 1888, pp. 124–39.   [23] Prologue, Περὶ ἀπίστων, ed. Festa 1902.

[24] See, e.g., chap. 1, where Palaephatus explains in the spirit of Homer (*Il.* 11.832, *Od.* 21.295ff.) that the Centaurs were a savage and courageous kind of people, who were later, as a result of an optic mistake, imagined as possessing a body composed of human and horse elements, as related by Pindar (*Pyth.* 2.39–88). Some elements of Palaephatus' explanations are parallel to the scholia on *Od.* 21.303, while his overall approach is independent and more rationalistic.

It is said throughout the writing of the Law that a Divine descent took place on the mountain, at the time when the Law was given, so that all [the Israelites] should see the active power of God.[25]

The fact that Aristobulus identifies a problem which appears 'throughout the writing of the Law' (διὰ τῆς γραφῆς τοῦ νόμου) distinguishes him as a literal scholar, who adopted the widely known principle of studying a canonical text in its entirety and from within itself. We have been already that Aristarchus regularly applied it in his Homeric scholarship and, following him, Demetrius' anonymous colleague used it in relation to the Jewish Scriptures.[26] Aristobulus summarily refers to the problematic issue with the expression 'Divine descent', implying that he studies different occurrences of Divine anthropomorphism.[27] In the passage quoted above he provides already a brief answer by tacitly translating the anthropomorphic notion of the Divine descent into the more ethereal image of God's 'active power' (ἐνέργεια).[28] This interpretation resonates with Apollodorus' Homeric exegesis, which frequently refers to the gods' δύναμις or ἐνέργεια.[29] Whereas Apollodorus, however, adopted distinctly Stoic notions, identifying the power of each god on the basis of etymology with his or her individual character traits, Aristobulus remains far more general and speaks only of God's 'active power'.[30]

Having assured his readers that there is a proper philosophical solution to the problem of God's descent, Aristobulus indicates what is at stake:

Κατάβασις γὰρ αὕτη σαφής ἐστι. Καὶ περὶ τούτων οὖν οὕτως ἄν τις ἐξηγήσαιτο βουλόμενος συντηρεῖν τὸν περὶ θεοῦ λόγον. (*ap.* Euseb. *Praep. evang.* 8.10.12 = fr. 2; ed. Holladay 1983–96, vol. III, p. 142)

For this descent is manifest. Whoever wishes to retain the phrase about God, should offer the following explanation about these things.

We saw in Chapter 2 that Aristobulus was familiar with text-critical methods and applied them to a line from Aratus. Referring to critical marks, he admitted that he had excised the word Zeus and replaced it with θεός,

---

[25] Λέγεται δὲ καὶ κατάβασις ἐπὶ τὸ ὄρος θεία γεγονέναι διὰ τῆς γραφῆς τοῦ νόμου καθ᾽ ὃν ἐνομοθέτει ἵνα πάντες θεωρήσωσι τὴν ἐνέργειαν τοῦ θεοῦ (*ap.* Euseb. *Praep. evang.* 8.10.12 = fr. 2; ed. Holladay 1983–96, vol. III, p. 142). Yarbro Collins' translations are especially precise and have often been consulted.

[26] For details, see Chapters 1 and 3.   [27] See esp. LXX Exod. 19:16–25, 20:18–21, 24:15–8.

[28] See also Euseb. *Praep. evang.* 8.10.17 (= fr. 2; ed. Holladay 1983–96, vol. III, p. 148), where Aristobulus further explains his solution.

[29] Fr. 352–3 (*FGH*, vol. II, pp. 1123–4); Apollodorus' interpretation echoes Stoic notions, Zeno already having suggested that Aphrodite is 'the power of bringing together' (*SVF* 1.168); Algra 2003.

[30] Algra 2003.

assuming that Aratus had really intended the latter.[31] Given Aristobulus' general background in Alexandrian scholarship, it is not surprising that he considers the possibility of athetizing the biblical verses where the Divine descent is mentioned.[32] He decides against it, supporting anyone 'wishing to retain (συντηρεῖν) the phrase about God'. The motif appears to have been too self-evident and too frequent to be solved by an emendation. Aristobulus' readers, who are expected to share his basically conservative attitude towards the biblical text, are thus invited to give attention to the exegetical solution he will propose.

Aristobulus' explanation of God's descent is highly complex, drawing on a verse from a different context and ultimately relying on the Aristotelian notion of the 'perplexing' effect. Initially, Aristobulus introduces a motif from a different context, namely the burning of Mount Sinai (Deut. 5:23):[33]

It is set forth (δηλοῦται) that 'the mountain was burning with fire' (Deut. 5:23), as the Law says, because of the Divine descent, while there were the voices of the trumpets and the fire irresistibly burning.[34]

Aristobulus uses the verb δηλόω to introduce a meaning from another context, namely from the *Book of Deuteronomy*. He wishes to show that the meaning of Scripture is clear, even if not always apparent to all readers. God's descent onto Mount Sinai can thus be properly understood by a comparison of verses, which allows a transfer of meaning from one context to another. It is suggested that the Divine descent materialized in the form of a fire that lit up the whole mountain. This exegetical move on the part of Aristobulus reflects a standard technique of Alexandrian scholarship, both Homeric and biblical, which we have already encountered in the context of Aristarchus and Demetrius. Aristobulus, too, was familiar with this method, creatively using it for his own philosophical purposes. It must be emphasized that Aristobulus remained remarkably faithful to the literal text. He neither adopts the language of secrecy nor implies that Moses has intentionally hidden his message; and he certainly refrains from the kind of dramatic interpretation found in the Derveny Papyrus, which also uses the term δηλόω as a hermeneutic key.[35]

---

[31] *Ap.* Euseb. *Praep. evang.* 13.12.7 (= fr. 4; ed. Holladay 1983–96, vol. III, p. 172).
[32] On the method of athetesis, the marking of a spurious verse without actually omitting it from the text, see Chapters 1 and 2.
[33] Cf. Exod. 19:18, where the smoke is mentioned.
[34] *Ap.* Euseb. *Praep. evang.* 8.10.13 (= fr. 2; ed. Holladay 1983–96, vol. III, p. 142).
[35] See esp. Derv. Pap. col. XIII, lines 5–6; col. IX, ll. 10–13; col. VII, ll. 5–7; regarding the use of δηλόω, see Derv. Pap. cols. XIII, XXI, col. XVI. ll. 9–11, where the author explains the Orphic verse 'and he himself became the sole one' as follows: 'by saying this, he [Orpheus] makes it clear (τοῦτο δὲ

Aristobulus continues his explanations in a scholarly fashion, devoting a long paragraph to show that the Divine descent cannot have been meant in a spatial sense (τὴν κατάβασιν μὴ τοπικὴν εἶναι).[36] He aims at scientific standards, initially providing precise information about the setting. The mountain is said to have a 'circuit of five days', and the Israelites present at the site are estimated to be 'no fewer than a million', even though only approximately half of this number is recorded in Scripture.[37] Aristobulus provides an exaggerated picture in order to highlight the enormity of the event. If indeed the mountain was as huge as he suggests and the Israelites as numerous, then the conclusion can be drawn (ὥστε) that 'the descent does not pertain to space, as God is everywhere' (*ap.* Euseb. *Praep. evang.* 8.10.15 = fr. 2; ed. Holladay 1983–96, vol. III, p. 144).

Aristobulus then urges his readers to appreciate the paradox of the Divine appearance:

But concerning the power of the fire, which is exceedingly marvellous (παρὰ πάντα θαυμάσιον), because it consumes everything, he [Moses] has shown (ἔδειξε) that while burning irresistibly, it does not consume anything entirely – and if it were not from God, [such a power] would itself be unavailable (προσείη). For none of the plants growing on the mountain were burnt up, even though the place burnt intensely, but the green sprouts of all the plants remained untouched, while the voices of the trumpets were heard even more loudly together with the lightning-like manifestation of the fire, even though no such instruments were at hand nor anyone playing them, but everything happened by Divine device. (*ap.* Euseb. *Praep. evang.* 8.10.16 = fr. 2; ed. Holladay 1983–96, vol. III, p. 146)

Aristobulus' argument is based on the fact that the biblical scene is scientifically impossible. The image of a fire, which does not consume everything while continuously burning, is as unlikely as the sound of trumpets with nobody to play them. This problem of verisimilitude, however, is not solved by allegory but instead used to point to the reality of God's supernatural powers. The term θαυμάσιον conveys this positive meaning of the marvellous and indicates Aristobulus' exegetical context. It immediately recalls

λέγων δηλοῖ) that Mind, being alone, is always worth everything, as if the rest were nothing' (text and translation in Kouremenos *et al.* 2006). It is remarkable that Aristobulus did not adopt this kind of exegesis, because he himself was familiar with Orphic literature and quotes an Orphic passage (*Praep. evang.* 13.12.5 = fr. 4; ed. Holladay 1983–96, vol. III, pp. 164–70), the authenticity of which has been discussed by Walter 1964, pp. 202–59; Holladay 1983–96, vol. III, pp. 219–20. Aristobulus' faithfulness to the literal text can also be seen on the two other occasions where he uses the verb δηλόω, namely in Euseb. *Praep. evang.* 8.10.8 and 13.12.12 (= fr. 2 and 5; ed. Holladay 1983–96, vol. III, pp. 138, 184).

[36] *Ap.* Euseb. *Praep. evang.* 8.10.14 (= fr. 2; ed. Holladay 1983–96, vol. III, p. 144).
[37] *Ap.* Euseb. *Praep. evang.* 8.10.14 (= fr. 2; ed. Holladay 1983–96, vol. III, p. 144); regarding the number of Israelites mentioned in Scripture, see LXX Exod. 12:37, Num. 1:46, 11:21.

Aristotle's justification of 'impossible' presentations on condition that they render the narrative 'more perplexing' (ἐκπληκτικώτερον).[38] Aristotle had thus offered a solution to the problem of epic scenes, which had been severely criticized as offending scientific standards of truth.[39] Moreover, the element of the 'amazing' (τὸ θαυμαστόν) was in Aristotle's view an acceptable device in literature, while it would be more problematic on the stage.[40]

Aristotle's literary notions were adopted in Alexandria by Aristarchus, who also justified 'unbelievable' lines, if they could be shown to be dramatically plausible.[41] At the same time, however, he developed his own approach by athetizing numerous verses and, as far as the extant fragments show, no longer using the terms θαυμάσιον and ἐκπληκτικός.[42] The development and reception of the Aristotelian tradition is furthermore illuminated by Palaephatus.[43] The following explanations, which introduce his book, illustrate his faithfulness to Aristotelian notions and provide an important background for Aristobulus:

poets and prose-writers rendered some of the things which happened more incredible and marvellous (εἰς τὸ ἀπιστότερον καὶ θαυμασιώτερον) for the sake of men's amazement.[44]

Both Palaephatus and Aristarchus adopted the notion of dramatic effect from Aristotle's poetic theory, each applying it for his own specific purposes. Whereas Palaephatus offered rationalistic explanations of 'unbelievable' stories, Aristarchus justified certain controversial lines of the epics. Aristobulus, too, started with a detailed text analysis, considering the emendation of problematic lines. Following Aristotle more closely than Aristarchus, he stressed the perplexing nature of the biblical scene and then used it independently for his own theological purposes. It served him to point to a miraculous Divine reality conveyed in the text. For him the paradoxical nature of the fire descending on Mount Sinai was an important indication of God's superhuman presence. Aristobulus thus used a classical Aristotelian

---

[38] Arist. *Poet.* 1460b25.
[39] For details on Aristotle's discussion of 'impossible' scenes, see above, Chapter 3.
[40] Arist. *Poet.* 1460a11. [41] Schironi 2009, pp. 284–8.
[42] Note an exception to Aristarchus' normal usage in Schol. *Il.* 24.164a, where the term θαυμαστικῶς is, however, applied to the explanation of a particular word form.
[43] Palaephatus' Aristotelian orientation was already noted in antiquity by Theon in his *Progymnasmata* (T3b quoted by Nünlist 2009b); see Fornaro 2007, col. 376).
[44] Prologue (ed. Festa 1902, p. 2); the importance of this introductory statement has been played down by J. Stern 1996, pp. 16–17, who suggests that Palaephatus generally thought more negatively about myth, namely as a subsequent distortion of a historical event; cf. also Schol. *Il.* 17.314–15, 15.97a.

category along the same lines as Palaephatus, but with considerably more textual and theological sophistication.

The nature of Aristobulus' commitment to Aristotle's approach can further be appreciated by comparing it with Porphyry's discussion of a similar problem in the *Iliad*, namely the burning of Diomedes' shoulders and head. Porphyry admits that this epic scene is 'impossible' as the fire would have been fatal for the hero. His own preferred solution derives from the *double entendre* of the text: 'either he [the poet] does not literally mean fire (οὐ κυριολογεῖ) but speaks about an illumination, or else he speaks metonymically about power as "shoulders"' (Porph. *Quaest. Il.* 5.7). Although Porphyry clearly uses Aristotelian literary notions, he neither stresses the marvellous effect of the scene nor uses it for theological purposes, as Aristobulus would have done.

GOD'S LIMBS READ AS ARISTOTELIAN METAPHORS

Another important aspect of Divine anthropomorphism which Aristobulus singles out for discussion is the biblical description of God as possessing limbs. Eusebius prepares the reader by introducing this issue with an emphasis on the non-literal dimension of such biblical images, insisting that biblical references to Divine limbs are nothing but names or literary presentations.[45] Aristobulus himself records in a similar vein the initial question of the Egyptian king:

Why throughout our Law hands, an arm and a face as well as feet and walking around are signifiers (σημαίνεται) of God's power? (*ap.* Euseb. *Praep. evang.* 8.10.1 = fr. 2; ed. Holladay 1983–96, vol. III, p. 134)

This question is already formulated in a way that implies the solution of the problem. Aristobulus goes on to suggest that there is a difference between the signifier and the signified. The former, he insists, must be appreciated with a view to the 'suitable explanation (λόγου καθήκοντος)' of the concrete images. He stresses that such images must not be understood as contradicting 'the [philosophical] things I said before'. Unlike Aristeas, who spoke in a similar context about the 'deeper meaning' of the text (λόγον βαθύν), Aristobulus is concerned with the appropriate sense and the overall consistency of his message, which exposes Moses' teaching of 'piety, justice and self-control'.[46]

---

[45] Euseb. *Praep. evang.* 8.9.38 (= fr. 2; ed. Holladay 1983–96, vol. III, p. 134).
[46] *Ap.* Euseb. *Praep. evang.* 13.12.8 (= fr. 4; ed. Holladay 1983–96, vol. III, p. 174); cf. *Letter*, 143, 150 (τροπολογῶν); on the latter, see Tramontano 1931, pp. 129–32.

In a famous statement Aristobulus then explains his hermeneutic assumptions, which deserve careful attention:

Παρακαλέσαι δέ σε βούλομαι πρὸς τὸ φυσικῶς λαμβάνειν τὰς ἐκδοχὰς καὶ τὴν ἁρμόζουσαν ἔννοιαν περὶ θεοῦ κρατεῖν καὶ μὴ ἐκπίπτειν εἰς τὸ μυθῶδες καὶ ἀνθρώπινον κατάστημα. Πολλαχῶς γὰρ ὃ βούλεται λέγειν ὁ νομοθέτης ἡμῶν Μωσῆς ἐφ᾽ ἑτέρων πραγμάτων λόγους ποιούμενος (λέγω δὲ τῶν κατὰ τὴν ἐπιφάνειαν) φυσικὰς διαθέσεις ἀπαγγέλλει καὶ μεγάλων πραγμάτων κατασκευάς. (*ap.* Euseb. *Praep. evang.* 8.10.2–3 = fr. 2; ed. Holladay 1983–96, vol. III, p. 136)

I want to urge you to receive the interpretations in their natural sense and to get hold of suitable notions about God, and not to lapse into a mythical and human way of thinking. For the things which Moses our lawgiver wishes to say he represents in many ways using words regarding other matters (I mean matters pertaining to appearance) and [thus] conveys natural dispositions and preparations of great deeds.

The expression πρὸς τὸ φυσικῶς has often been interpreted in light of Stoic philosophy.[47] This approach indeed suggests itself, because Nature is such a central notion in Stoic philosophy and hermeneutics.[48] Zeno had stressed the connection between divine forces and Nature. According to Cicero, he insisted that 'natural law is divine' and in some contexts identified 'ether with god' or expressed the view that 'a reason which pervades all Nature is possessed of divine power'.[49] This philosophical position had immediate hermeneutic implications, as Zeno had already interpreted the gods in Hesiod's *Theogony* as signifiers of cosmic elements.[50]

Zeno's followers Cleanthes and Chrysippus seem to have debated whether either the world itself or its reason or all-embracing Nature should be identified with god.[51] Chrysippus is accused of depriving the traditional gods of their personal features, interpreting 'the god whom men call Jupiter' as ether or everlasting law (Cic. *Nat. D.* 1.40). Cicero moreover indicates that the interpretation of the poets was started by Zeno, who applied himself to Hesiod; he was later given particular attention by

---

[47] See review by Walter 1964, pp. 135–6; see also Gutman 1958–63, vol. I, pp. 213–16; Holladay 1983–96, vol. III, pp. 206–7, n. 31; Yarbro Collins 1983–5, p. 838; Barclay 1996, p. 154.

[48] See esp. Ierodiakonou 1999; Inwood and Donini 1999, pp. 682–90; White 2003, pp. 124–52; Algra 2003.

[49] 'aliis autem libris rationem quandam per omnem naturam rerum pertinentem vi divina esse adfectatam putat' (Cic. *Nat. D.* 1.36 = *SVF* 1.162, 165).

[50] Cic. *Nat. D.* 1.36 = *SVF* 1.167; *SVF* 1.100; see also Steinmetz 1986, pp. 19–21, who stressed that Zeno allegorized only Hesiod's works, not Homer's.

[51] Cic. *Nat. D.* 1.39. The testimony here is extremely hostile, referring to the Stoic philosophical tradition as 'dreams', thus making it difficult to decide to what extent the debate was real or only imagined by later onlookers.

Chrysippus and Diogenes of Babylon, who interpreted Homer in comparison with a wealth of other literature.[52] While the term 'allegory' is not used in this context, it emerges that Chrysippus and Diogenes were concerned to 'accommodate fables' (*fabellas accommodare*) to their own theological conceptions, thus 'converting [them] into physiological terms' (*ad physiologiam traducens*). Holding that even 'impious fables' include 'scientific theory' (*physica ratio*), these thinkers extrapolated principles of natural science from ancient poetry, giving special attention to the names of the gods as a hermeneutic key.[53]

Aristobulus obviously confronts a similar contrast between myth and more ethereal conceptions about God. He, too, sees his role as an interpreter who bridges a hermeneutic gap, addressing more sophisticated readers who are able to grasp a meaning beyond the literal face value of the text. The difference between him and Stoic exegetes, however, remains vast. Initially, it must be stressed that Aristobulus does not provide explanations relating to natural science. His God remains the historical God of Israel, who is 'metaphorically' described as having hands.[54] No reference is made to cosmic elements, nature in general or the etymology of names.[55] Aristobulus' distinction between μυθῶδες and φυσικῶς refers to a contrast between anthropomorphic images and their true or solemn meaning appropriate to the historical God of Israel.

More importantly, Aristobulus invests considerable efforts in explaining Moses' authorial intention, while the Stoics ignored the deliberate meaning of the ancient poets, assuming that they transmitted earlier scientific ideas without themselves being aware of it.[56] Aristobulus refers to Moses as a highly self-conscious author who chose different ways of communicating his message, which is still valuable and accurate, thus requiring no reconstruction of its original outlines by means of allegory. In this context he even speaks of Moses' 'Divine spirit' (τὸ θεῖν πνεῦμα) and emphasizes

---

[52] Cic. *Nat. D.* 1.40–1, 2.63–4. Long 1992, pp. 49–53, stressed the hostile perspective of *Nat. D.* 1.36–41, contrasting it with 2.63–73, where a Stoic spokesman explains the exegetical methods of his school. The difference between the two sources, however, is overstated. They essentially point to the same technique, once from a favourable and once from a critical point of view.

[53] The last quotations are to be found in Cic. *Nat. D.* 1.41, 2.64; see also: Buffière 1956, pp. 149–52; Pépin 1958, pp. 128–31; similarly also Cornutus, on whom see Most 1989, esp. pp. 2018–29.

[54] μεταφέροντας, Euseb. *Praep. evang.* 8.10.8 (= fr. 2, ed. Holladay 1983–96, vol. III, p. 138); see also Walter 1964, pp. 135–6.

[55] Compare, by contrast, Byzantine exegetes, who associate the 'natural' meaning of the text precisely with such an allegorization of the gods (Schol. *Il.* 1.399–406).

[56] On the Stoics' being oblivious to authorial intention, see esp. Boys-Stones 2003; regarding the overall philosophical background of their approach, with its assumptions that ancient meanings and traditions had been forgotten or corrupted over time, see Boys-Stones 2001.

that he 'has been declared a prophet'.[57] The meanings which Moses himself had 'intended' (νενοημένα) are the declared object of Aristobulus' exposition.[58]

Aristobulus' explanation of 'what is signified' (σημαινόμενον) can now be properly appreciated. He himself describes it as follows:

As to the hands, then, we obviously perceive them in a more ordinary way (κοινότερον). Whenever you, as king, send out forces to accomplish something, we say 'the king has a mighty hand', the audience taking it as a reference to the power which you have.

Moses indicates (ἐπισημαίνεται) this when speaking throughout our legislation thus: 'with a mighty hand God led you out of Egypt' [LXX Exod. 13:9] and again 'I will extend my hand and smite the Egyptians' [LXX Exod. 3:20]. Moreover, Moses said to the king of Egypt at the death of the cattle and other beasts: 'Behold, the hand of the Lord will be upon your cattle and death will be widespread in your fields' [LXX Exod. 9:3] so that it is manifest (δηλοῦσθαι) that the hands refer to God's power. For one should metaphorically think (καὶ γὰρ ἔστι μεταφέροντας νοῆσαι) of all men's power and activity as being in his hands. (*ap.* Euseb. *Praep. evang.* 8.10.7–8 = fr. 2; ed. Holladay 1983–96, vol. III, pp. 136–8)

It is initially important to acknowledge that Aristobulus himself identifies his method as a metaphorical reading (μεταφέροντας), subsequently praising Moses for having 'metaphorically spoken about the elevated' (*Praep. evang.* 8.10. 9). It is furthermore remarkable that Aristobulus argues from the common usage of language (κοινότερον) rather than assuming with the Stoics that there is an inherent meaning of each word which has been lost but can be rediscovered by recourse to etymology.[59]

Aristobulus' method directly echoes literary notions of Aristotle, who solved problems in the epic text by recourse to language (λέξις). In contrast to the Stoics, Aristotle stressed that the meaning of a particular word (σημαίνειν) is not given or self-evident, but needs to be explored from various perspectives (*Poet.* 1461a31–3). Hesitation and search rather than certainty characterize such an investigation. Not surprisingly, Aristotle's discussion abounds with optatives and expressions of tentativeness, such as ἴσως. Aristobulus embraces this groping approach, stating that he will explain 'what is signified' by Scripture 'as much as possible' (*Praep. evang.* 8.10.6).

Aristobulus' reference to metaphor as an analogous, commonsense meaning closely resembles Aristotle's notion of 'the custom of language'

---

[57] *Ap.* Euseb. *Praep. evang.* 8.10.4 (= fr. 2; ed. Holladay 1983–96, vol. III, p. 136).
[58] *Ap.* Euseb. *Praep. evang.* 8.10.6 (= fr. 2; ed. Holladay 1983–96, vol. III, p. 136).
[59] On this aspect of Stoic linguistics, see Schenkeveld and Barnes 1999, pp. 180–2, 221–2.

(τὸ ἔθος τῆς λέξεως), which overlaps in some cases with metaphor.[60] Aristotle generally defines metaphor as 'a transfer of a name that belongs to something else' (*Poet.* 1457b6). Such transference is either based on analogy or derived from an exchange of words belonging respectively to general and specific categories. While both kinds of metaphor are invoked by Aristotle to solve problems in the epics, the analogical metaphor is especially relevant to our understanding of Aristobulus.[61] A metaphorical reading by analogy needs to be applied when the poet can be shown to rely on the resemblance of different elements (*Poet.* 1457b16–19). An example is the image of Ganymede as the 'wine-server' of Zeus, which is problematic because the gods 'do not drink wine'.[62] Aristotle considers two related solutions which suggest that the notion of wine is not meant literally: either the poet used the term wine in a very broad sense, since people commonly refer by 'wine' to a mixed drink, or else the poet spoke metaphorically, that is, relying on the analogy of serving wine and serving other things (*Poet.* 1461a27–31). The reader is thus invited to envision Ganymede either as serving a kind of drink which can no longer be identified as true wine, or as generally serving Zeus. Aristotle corroborates the former meaning by recalling that the worker in iron is commonly called 'brazier' even though he does not literally deal with brass.

Closely following Aristotle, Aristobulus identifies a problematic motif in his foundational text and suggests a metaphorical solution. Amalgamating two related Aristotelian categories, namely common usage of language and analogous metaphor, he interprets the biblical motif of the Divine hands as signifiers of His power. Aristobulus thus suggests that the term 'hand' has been shifted to a different, yet sufficiently similar object. This transferred meaning is confirmed in typically Aristotelian fashion by appealing to the common usage of language, namely by reference to the description of the king as 'having a mighty hand'. Aristobulus furthermore adds in typically Alexandrian fashion a few more biblical verses with similar issues

---

[60] Arist. *Poet.* 1461a27–31; see also Arist. *Poet.* 1457b2–3, where Aristotle explains that by an 'ordinary word' (κύριον) he means a word 'which everyone uses'.

[61] For examples in which Aristotle explains Homeric expressions by arguing that the poet metaphorically denoted the general by mentioning the specific, see *Poet.* 1461a16–21. In the extant fragments of Aristotle's *Aporemata Homerica* there is one example where he offered a metaphorical solution to a contradiction between Homeric lines. Treating the conflicting descriptions of the sun, once as omniscient and once as relying on a messenger, Aristotle proposes three solutions. One of them suggests that 'Lampetia was a messenger to Helios as vision is to man' (Arist. *Apor. Hom.*, fr. 149; ed. Rose 1886). See also Aristotle's interpretation of Helios' cattle, taking it as a reference to the amount of days in the lunar year (Arist. *Apor. Hom.* fr. 175; ed. Rose 1886).

[62] *Il.* 20.234 discussed in *Poet.* 1461a30.

of anthropomorphism, thus pointing to the customary usage of Moses as author.[63]

How common was Aristobulus' approach to metaphor as an exegetical device among Alexandrian scholars in the second century BCE? In comparison with the extant fragments of Aristarchus' and Apollodorus' works, Aristobulus emerges as exceptionally close to Aristotle, formulating his hermeneutics in terms directly echoing the *Poetics*. Apollodorus gives the impression of a different, more Stoic type of interpretation, regularly deriving the 'signified meaning' from the supposed etymologies of the names.[64] Aristarchus is comparatively more Aristotelian, assuming that Homer expressed himself 'clearly' by generally using 'common' words.[65] Aristarchus is concerned with the meaning 'signified' by the Homeric text, which he seeks to establish especially on internal textual grounds, namely by recourse to the context of each epic scene.[66] Sometimes he accuses Zenodotus or an anonymous emendator of misunderstanding the meaning of the text (σημαινόμενον), which led to additions and textual corruptions.[67] Aristarchus is also aware of Homer's metaphorical usage of language.[68] In none of these cases, however, does Aristarchus offer such an Aristotelian explanation as Aristobulus in his interpretation of biblical anthropomorphisms.

Within the Jewish community of Alexandria Aristobulus' approach to some extent resembles that of Aristeas. The latter explained that some animals are forbidden by Scripture, because they exhibit certain, generally recognized characteristics (*Letter*, 148). Here, too, a transfer of name is presupposed. Moses' legislation regarding the animals does not literally refer to them, but to their commonly recognized significance. Aristeas thus offered his readers 'the most solemn and natural conception of the Law' (*Letter*, 171), exposing its ethical dimension beyond the literal sense.

THE CREATION OF THE WORLD IN ARISTOTELIAN GARB

The creation of the world was a hotly debated subject of philosophy, not only among Jews. Plato's *Timaeus* presented the notion of a Demiurge,

---

[63] Regarding the Alexandrian context of comparing verses and establishing the poet's characteristic usage, see Chapters 3 and 8.

[64] See, e.g., fr. 353 (*FGH*, vol. II, p. 1123), where Apollodorus derives the σημαινόμενον of Aphrodite's epithet ἡ Κύπρις from κύω Κυόπορις, pointing to her characteristic force of bringing about conception and pregnancy; see also Brisson 2004, pp. 47–8.

[65] Schironi 2009, pp. 300–2; see esp. Schol. *Il.* 4.141A, 7.146A, 7.255A, 10.75A.

[66] See esp. Schol. *Il.* 1.525–7A, 2.341A, 10.127A, 13.25A, 22.143A. [67] See esp. Schol. *Il.* 2.668A, 10.98A.

[68] See esp. Schol. *Il.* 2.670A, 5.21A, 5.299A, 11.390A, 13.420A, 22.356A.

who created the world from pre-existing material and subsequently took care of it with fatherly concern.[69] On this view, the world was eternal from the moment of its creation onwards, thus breaking the regular laws of nature, according to which everything composed must also be dissolved. Plato's student Aristotle rejected this approach, insisting that there are no exceptions and thus an eternal world cannot have had a beginning or point of composition.[70] In contrast to Plato he thus developed the theory of a Divine, unmoved mover, who never changes, but actively sustains an eternal world.[71] Aristotle's arguments gained such prominence that Plato's immediate followers began to interpret the *Timaeus* metaphorically, namely as a story which does not literally advocate creation but rather uses the image of creation as an analogy for structure and form.[72] According to Plutarch, this approach continued to enjoy wide success later on as well (*De anima procreatione* 1012D). Some of Aristotle's arguments even resurface in the attack on Plato's cosmology by the Epicurean Velleius, who stressed that nothing created can be eternal.[73]

While it is not at all clear whether Aristobulus was familiar with Plato's *Timaeus*, he certainly accepted the biblical account and assumed a literal creation of the world. Using Septuagint vocabulary, he stresses that God 'formed (κατεσκεύακε) the whole cosmos' and 'made (ἐποίησε) heaven and earth'.[74] How could this view be dressed in Aristotelian garb? Aristobulus introduces Aristotelian notions when treating the problem of God's rest, mentioned in Gen. 2:3, which contradicts Aristotle's definition of god as an unmoved mover. In a characteristically scholarly manner Aristobulus initially acknowledges that the motif of God's 'pausing' is 'clear throughout the legislation' (*ap.* Euseb. *Praep. evang.* 13.12.11). He moreover warns his

---

[69] Modern scholars have debated whether Plato's *Timaeus* must be understood literally or rather metaphorically; for a literal reading, see Vlastos 1965; Hackforth 1959; for a metaphorical reading, see Cornford 1937, pp. 24–7; A. E. Taylor 1937, pp. 59–63; A. Finkelberg 1996.

[70] Arist. *De caelo* 279b18–280a35; Baltes 1998, pp. 377–84, and bibliography there.

[71] Arist. *Metaph.* 1063b36–1064b14, 1072b2–15; Jaeger 1948, pp. 342–67.

[72] Arist. *De caelo* 279b34–280a2. These anonymous interpreters of Plato's *Timaeus* can be variously identified on the basis of the extant fragmentary evidence. Xenocrates, for example, who was Plato's disciple and head of the Academy for more than twenty years, is known as a metaphorical reader of Plato's *Timaeus*; see Heinze 1892, fr. 54, p. 180; Dillon 2003b. Plutarch and Proclus mention in this context also Crantor, Xenocrates' student and, according to Proclus, the 'first interpreter of Plato' (Plut. *De anima procreatione* 1012D–F and 1013A–C; Procl. *In Plat. Tim.* 1.277 (ed. Diehl 1903–6). One anonymous scholiast identifies Speusippus, the first head of the Academy after Plato, as a metaphorical reader of the *Timaeus*; see Taran 1981, fr. 61a–b.

[73] Cic. *Nat. D.* 1.20.

[74] *Ap.* Euseb. *Praep. evang.* 13.12.9 (= fr. 5, ed. Holladay 1983–96, vol. III, p. 176); the term ἀκατασκεύαστος is first used in LXX Gen. 1:2 as a translation of ובהו; the verb κατασκευάζω later became a standard term for God's creative act (LXX Isa. 40:28, 43:7; Wis. 9:1–2); see also Rösel 1994, pp. 31–2; Harl 1986, p. 87. Regarding the verb ποιέω, see *Praep. evang.* 13.12.12 (ed. Holladay 1983–96, vol. III, p. 182), echoing LXX Gen. 1:1 and Exod. 20:11.

readers not to follow 'some' exegetes, who have concluded that after the creation 'God no longer does anything'.[75] It is highly significant that the creation of the world was debated among Alexandrian Jews with a view to Aristotle's notion of the unmoved mover. Stoic ideas, such as the periodic conflagration of the world, which subsequently engaged Philo's attention, do not yet seem to have been relevant in Alexandria at the time of Aristobulus.[76]

Aristobulus provides a literal solution to the biblical problem, integrating the Aristotelian idea of an unchanging god with the biblical creation story. The Divine rest, he argues, was only partial and did not pertain to every aspect of God's activity. While He indeed ceased arranging the cosmos, He continues to 'order [the elements] for all times' and 'maintains and alters them [in accordance with that order]'.[77] This interpretation resonates with LXX Gen. 2:3, which translates the phrase 'He rested from all his work, which God had done in creation' (שבת מכל מלאכתו אשר ברא אלהים לעשות) as 'He rested from all his works, which God had begun to create' (ὧν ἤρξατο ὁ θεὸς ποιῆσαι).

Finally, the relevance of the Aristotelian school for Aristobulus can be gathered from his explicit reference to it at the end of the fragment on the creation of the world. Interpreting the meaning of the Shabbat, Aristobulus relies on a Peripatetic tradition:

Some members of the Peripatetic school (τινες τῶν ἐκ τῆς αἱρέσεως ὄντες ἐκ τοῦ Περιπάτου) have said that it [wisdom] occupies the position of a lamp, for following it continually, they will remain imperturbable their entire life. But Solomon, one of our ancestors, said more clearly and more eloquently that it was there before the heaven and earth [Prov. 8:22]. And this is actually in harmony with what has been said before. (*ap*. Euseb. *Praep. evang*. 7.13.10, ed. Holladay 1983–96, vol. III, 180–1, 196–7)

In this passage Aristobulus distinguishes the Peripatetic school in order to suggest a significant correspondence between the biblical creation account, wisdom literature and philosophy. He suggests that they all imply that wisdom is metaphorically presented as light, which can be followed throughout life. It is this underlying synthesis, which enables Aristobulus to pronounce that 'properly' (φυσικῶς) the seventh day may also be called 'the first, that is the beginning of light by which all things are contemplated'.[78]

---

[75] *Ap*. Euseb. *Praep. evang*. 13.12.11 (= fr. 5; ed. Holladay 1983–96, vol. III, p. 182).

[76] For Philo's critical discussion of Stoic ideas of creation, see especially his treatise *On the Eternity of the World*; Runia 1981.

[77] *Ap*. Euseb. *Praep. evang*. 13.12.11–12 (= fr. 5; ed. Holladay 1983–96, vol. III, pp. 182, 184).

[78] *Ap*. Euseb. *Praep. evang*. 13.12.9 (= fr. 5; ed. Holladay 1983–96, vol. III, p. 178).

The overall significance of Aristobulus' fragment on the creation of the world is considerable. It emerged that some Alexandrian Jews had already applied a rigorous Aristotelian perspective to the biblical story and criticized the notion of God's rest. Aristobulus' report is our earliest evidence of this kind of criticism brought to bear on demiurges. A similar argument resurfaces much later in Velleius' polemic against Plato's creator god, who is ridiculed on account of his inactivity before the creation.[79] Indeed, the positions of both Aristobulus himself and his colleagues indicate the centrality of Aristotelian notions among Alexandrian Bible exegetes. They took his thought as their point of reference when approaching their Scriptures.

Aristobulus moreover emerged as an Aristotelian scholar, who read problematic verses metaphorically and used them for his own theological purposes. His approach fits well into his immediate Alexandrian environment, being rooted in the academic methods developed in that city, especially under Aristarchus. Occasionally, Aristobulus even takes a position more faithful to Aristotle's literary theories than does Aristarchus, thus providing important new information about the Aristotelian tradition in the city. Aristotle's thought was not only widespread and influential, but also visible in diverse circles. It reached from prominent scholars at the Museum to Jewish exegetes, some of them more academic, such as Demetrius' colleagues, while others were more philosophical, such as Aristobulus.

Looking at the early reactions to Homeric scholarship among Jewish Bible exegetes in Alexandria, we have discovered a close correlation between allegiance to Aristotle and approval of Homeric methods. Aristobulus and Demetrius' colleagues as well as Demetrius himself all embraced the literary approach developed at the Museum, applying its methods in a variety of ways to the Jewish Scriptures. At the same time they were close to Aristotle, either indirectly by following Aristarchus or directly by applying Aristotelian notions, as was especially the case with Aristobulus. Aristeas, on the other hand, combined a greater distance from Aristotle with a strong disapproval of rigorous academic methods. As we saw above, he warned his colleagues of the dangers of applying Homeric critical signs to the Bible and insisted on its uniqueness. Aristobulus, the most Aristotelian of the Ptolemaic Bible exegetes, by contrast, explicitly compared the Bible to the ideas of the Peripatetic school, accepted athetesis for pagan texts and applied literary notions to solve biblical problems.

---

[79] Cic. *Nat. D.* 1.21; Effe 1970, pp. 27–31.

PART II

Critical Homeric scholarship in the fragments of Philo's anonymous colleagues

CHAPTER 5

Comparative mythology

In this section of the book we turn to the writings of Philo, not, however, for his own sake, but rather for the purpose of gleaning evidence about his colleagues and predecessors. We will thus be able to fill in a conspicuous gap in our picture of Alexandrian Judaism, which is created by the lack of independent exegetical sources between the mid second century BCE and Philo. David Hay has already stressed that Philo did not write in an intellectual vacuum but conceived of 'exegesis as a kind of dialogical enterprise that involves debate partners and opponents', and we now face the challenge of reconstructing his intellectual environment.[1]

Following the direction of Hay's own work, we shall focus on Philo's references to other interpreters. For the purposes of this book all of Philo's references have been carefully studied. The great variety of their style and content is so conspicuous that they must reflect different exegetical orientations of independent Jewish exegetes. They certainly cannot be reduced to rhetorical figures, which do not point to real people or discussions, as has sometimes been suggested.[2] Philo's references thus provide an invaluable glimpse into the original variety of Alexandrian Judaism, which does not happen to have been fully preserved by the Church Fathers. The identity and precise historical circumstances of these exegetes can no longer be known, but Philo speaks of them as if they were contemporaries. Their work must have been relevant in his time, as he would otherwise not have paid much attention to it.

JEWISH INTERPRETERS OF THE TOWER OF BABEL

In this chapter we shall focus on an extraordinarily long and rich fragment treating the story of the Tower of Babel in the context of a similar story in the *Odyssey*. Philo must have had access to a treatise written by his

---

[1] Hay 1991b, p. 97.   [2] Dillon 1983, p. 84; for further details, see Chapter 1.

colleagues, because he refers to 'those who have written such things'.[3] The impression of a written *Vorlage* is further corroborated by the fact that Philo opens his treatise on the *Confusion of Tongues* with a quotation of the entire biblical story, while he himself usually quotes only one or two verses which are studied in detail before the next few verses are quoted and examined. Philo's unusual procedure must reflect his colleagues' work. They seem to have written a treatise which started with a quotation of the whole biblical story and then provided a literary analysis of its main themes.

Philo's introductory remarks about his colleagues leave no doubt about his general attitude. He intensely dislikes them, offering the following tendentious description:

[they] feel annoyance at the ancestral constitution (τῇ πατρίῳ πολιτείᾳ), always engaging in the censure and accusation of the laws, these impious ones (οἱ δυσσε-βεῖς), they use these and similar passages as stepping-stones as it were for their godlessness (ὡς ἂν ἐπιβάθραις τῆς ἀθεότητος αὐτῶν). (*Conf.* 2)

These critics must have been Jews, because only they would have been accused by Philo of impiety and annoyance at the 'ancestral constitution'.[4] Greeks would not be expected to adhere to the Mosaic Law and believe in the Jewish God. Philo's complaints about Greek writers significantly differ in style. In the introduction of his *Life of Moses*, for example, he accuses 'the learned among the Greeks' of a general neglect of the Jewish Scriptures and points to their reservations regarding a law code contrary to theirs (*Mos.* 1.2). Moreover, before the advent of Christianity only Jews showed such a detailed interest in Scripture as Philo's colleagues. Contemporary pagans, even those specializing in Jewish history, such as Lysimachus, did not open the Bible scrolls.[5]

In the passage quoted above, Philo provides the first glimpse into the exegetical approach of his Jewish colleagues. He says that they 'use this and similar passages' to support their 'impious' claims. This means that they not only interpreted the story of the Tower of Babel but also engaged in a more systematic study of similarly mythological stories throughout Scripture. They emerge as exegetes who share the well-known maxim of Alexandrian scholarship according to which a foundational text is examined in its entirety and from within itself. We saw in previous chapters

---

[3] τοὺς δὴ ταῦτα συντιθέντας (*Conf.* 14).

[4] These exegetes have previously been identified as Jewish by Pépin 1967, pp. 143–5; and Goulet 1987, pp. 228–42, who mistakenly interpreted these exegetes as allegorists, assuming that Philo's allegorical interpretation is based on their previous efforts.

[5] M. Stern 1974–84; Gruen 1998, pp. 41–72; Schäfer 1997, pp. 15–33, 163–9.

that Aristarchus played a central role in this context, basing his running commentaries on Homer's epics on an internal analysis of the text. Moreover, Demetrius' anonymous colleagues as well as Aristobulus and Demetrius himself accepted this hermeneutic principle and interpreted the Jewish Scriptures in the same comprehensive manner.[6]

The following report by Philo throws further light upon his colleagues' approach and suggests a profound conflict of views in Alexandria:

They say (φάσκοντες): now do you still speak solemnly about the ordinances as if they contain the canons of Truth herself? For behold, the books called holy by you contain also myths about which you regularly laugh whenever you hear others relating them.[7] Furthermore, why is it necessary to gather [examples] scattered all over the legislation, as if we had the spare time and were engaging in quarrels, rather than just recalling those close at hand and near our feet? (*Conf.* 3)

The issue at stake in this lively dispute between different exegetes in Alexandria is the overall conception of the Jewish Scriptures. Philo and his followers are criticized for attributing too much holiness to the entire corpus and rejecting the notion of myth in Scripture. Following Aristeas, Philo indeed spoke of the Greek Bible as holy and true.[8] To his colleagues this position seemed hypocritical, because it rests on a categorical distinction between Scripture and non-Jewish literature, which contains strikingly similar material. Philo's colleagues advocate the notion of a composite text of the Bible, which in their view contains also mythological passages. Even Philo, their opponent, does not accuse them of altogether rejecting the Bible or dismissing all of it as mythical.

Philo's anonymous colleagues compare the biblical story of the Tower of Babel to two Greek myths, one contained in the *Odyssey* and dealing with a similar attempt to reach heaven, the other preserved by Callimachus and narrating the confusion of tongues among animals. This double comparison indicates that Philo's colleagues identified two main themes in the biblical story. One pertains to a problem of verisimilitude regarding the possibility of reaching heaven, while the other deals with the theological and social implications of the confusion of tongues.

THE BUILDERS OF THE TOWER AND THE SONS OF ALOEUS

Addressing the theme of man's *hybris*, Philo's anonymous colleagues initially analyse the biblical story of the Tower of Babel in light of a similar

---

[6] For details, see Chapters 1, 3 and 4.

[7] ἰδοὺ γὰρ αἱ ἱεραὶ λεγόμεναι βίβλοι παρ' ὑμῖν καὶ μύθους περιέχουσιν ἐφ' οἷς εἰώθατε γελᾶν, ὅταν ἄλλων διεξιόντων ἀκούητε.

[8] For details, see Chapter 2; Niehoff 1998a and in press, e.

attempt to reach heaven narrated in the *Odyssey*. They provide the following, highly scholarly analysis:

One [example] then certainly is the story that resembles (ὁ ἐοικώς) what is narrated about the Aloeidae, whom Homer, the greatest and most esteemed of the poets presented as intending to pile up three of the tallest mountains, heaping them up in the hope that the road to heaven would become easily accessible for those who wish to climb, once these [mountains] have been fastened to the highest sky. These are the words about them:

> They yearned to pile Ossa on Olympus, and moreover Pelion with its waving forest on Ossa so that heaven might be easily mounted [*Od.* 11:315–16].

Olympus as well as Ossa and Pelion are names of mountains. But instead of these the lawgiver introduces a tower (πύργον δὲ ὁ νομοθέτης ἀντὶ τούτων εἰσάγει) with a view to [presenting it as] constructed by men of that day who wished in their folly and arrogance to touch heaven.

Is this not terrible madness? For even if the parts of the whole world were raised upon a narrow foundation previously built and were lifted up in the form of a single pillar, they would still be distanced from the sphere of ether by thousands of intervals, especially according to the inquiring philosophers (καὶ μάλιστα κατὰ τοὺς ζητητικοὺς τῶν φιλοσόφων), who agreed that the earth is the centre of the universe. (*Conf.* 4–5)

Philo's anonymous colleagues quote two lines from Homer's *Odyssey*, explaining that 'Olympus as well as Ossa and Pelion are names of mountains'. Greek writers would undoubtedly have expected their audience to be familiar with Homer's story, and they would instead have provided some explanation about the biblical account. Philo's colleagues thus address a Jewish audience, referring to Moses simply as 'the lawgiver', as was common among Jews, rather than as 'the lawgiver of the Jews', as he was often identified by Greek writers. The starting point of Philo's colleagues is the biblical story, which they wish to explain by comparison to the less well-known story of Homer.

Philo's colleagues point to a problem of verisimilitude, stressing that a human construction can never reach heaven. For this purpose they refer to the generally accepted view of 'inquiring philosophers', who can be identified as Aristotelian thinkers.[9] Taking natural science as their starting point, these Jewish Bible scholars insist that it is impossible to reach heaven. As we have seen in previous chapters, this kind of problem had already been addressed in the second century BCE by Aristobulus and Demetrius' anonymous colleagues. Whereas the former solved such difficulties by means of

---

[9] Arist. *De caelo* 239a15–296a24.

metaphorical readings, the latter offered a literary solution, referring to the psychology of the biblical character involved. Philo's anonymous colleagues follow the approach attested in Demetrius' work. They, too, solve a problem of verisimilitude by reference to the dramatis personae involved, accusing the builders of the tower of 'terrible madness'. This implies that only they imagined that they could reach heaven, whereas Moses, as the author of the story, did not entertain such foolish thoughts.

Philo's colleagues stress that the builders of the tower as well as the Aloeidae were oblivious to scientific truth when arrogantly striving to reach heaven. Their wickedness is identified as the cause of the problem. Moses and Homer, on the other hand, are not said to have violated the truth. Philo's colleagues even imply that Moses was well aware of science and adapted the known Homeric myth to the truth by replacing the motif of piling up hills with the more reasonable scenario of constructing a tower. When stressing the builders' madness, they significantly focus on the Homeric motif of 'heaping up' all the 'parts of the earth' and thus put the main blame on them rather than on the biblical heroes (*Conf.* 5). A clear distinction is thus drawn between the *hybris* of the dramatis personae and the attitude of the authors themselves. While the former arrogantly ignore scientific truth and imagine that it would be possible to reach heaven, Moses and Homer were well aware of the limitations of human possibilities. In their view, Moses even expressed his own commitment to the truth by rendering the Homeric story more reasonable.

These reflections of Philo's colleagues are deeply rooted in Homeric scholarship practised in Alexandria. It must initially be noted that they enthusiastically admire Homer, praising him as 'the greatest and most esteemed of the poets'.[10] More importantly, Philo's colleagues participate in the Alexandrian discussion of the Homeric lines on the Aloeidae. A fragment preserved in the *Venetus Codex* illuminates the lively dispute between Aristarchus and other scholars:[11]

'Ossa on Olympus' [*Od.* 11.315], so that they would fight [the gods] from equal height. [These lines] are athetized as they are impossible (ἀθετοῦνται δὲ ὡς ἀδύνατοι).

However (ἀλλά), they 'yearned', he [the poet] says, but did not accomplish. (Schol. *Od.* 11.315v, ed. Dindorf 1855)

---

[10] *Conf.* 4; cf. Philo's more restrained formulation in *Abr.* 10.

[11] For an appreciation of the dates and nature of the V scholia on the Odyssey, see Pontani 2007, pp. x–xi; 2005b, p. 21; Dindorf 1855, vol. I, pp. xv–xvii.

This complex scholion shows that Greek readers of the *Odyssey* were as much concerned with the problem of verisimilitude as were Philo's anonymous colleagues. The anonymous first interpreter, who has been identified as Aristarchus, offered a radical solution to the problem.[12] Insisting on the 'impossible' dimension of the Homeric lines, he marked them as spurious and athetized them.[13] A subsequent scholar reacted to Aristarchus' athetesis with a close reading of the Homeric text. He stressed that Homer did not present an impossible scenario but merely depicted the mistaken ambitions of the Aloeidae. This interpreter provided the same solution as Philo's anonymous colleagues, insisting on the gap between the author himself and the dramatis personae.

This literary approach is further reflected in a scholion from the Byzantine period:

'And now they would have accomplished' [*Od.* 11.317].
How then is it not silly (πῶς οὐ ληρῶδες) that the poet at all expresses doubt concerning this [the possibility of their accomplishment]?
But it seems that the poet, plaiting together impossible things with impossible things (ὁ ποιητὴς τὰ ἀδύνατα τοῖς ἀδυνάτοις συμπλέκων), refutes by a necessary confutation at first in this way: just as if you said that they were flying and therefore had wings. But truly they had no wings and therefore were not flying.
In the same way, he [the poet] concludes here, they would have accomplished if they were in the prime of youth. But as it is impossible (ἀλλ' ὥσπερ ἀδύνατον) that fighters of god should reach maturity, thus [it is impossible] that they perform this kind of war. (Schol. *Od.* 11.317, ed. Dindorf 1855)

This scholiast preserves the Homeric text despite its initial appearance as 'silly' and 'impossible'. The problem of verisimilitude is solved by insisting that Homer himself did not present impossible things as a reality. Following the earlier literary critic, who rejected Aristarchus' athetesis, this scholiast stresses the hypothetical nature of Homer's account.

In light of these scholia Philo's anonymous colleagues emerge as active participants in the general discussion of *Od.* 11.315–17. They took a position in the dispute, sharing the approach of the scholiasts who rejected Aristarchus' athetesis by stressing the literary complexity of the Homeric text. Moreover, Philo's colleagues compared the Homeric and the biblical stories, applying the same solution and treating both as literary works which can be studied by critical methods. Their broad comparative approach and their extreme openness to non-Jewish literature were not shared by more

[12] Lehrs 1882, p. 170; Schironi 2009, p. 285.
[13] For details on athetesis, a technique which identifies spurious lines by marking them in the margins, without, however, omitting them from the text, see Chapters 1 and 2.

conservative members of the Jewish community in Alexandria, such as Philo.

The LXX, on the other hand, anticipates the literary solution of Philo's colleagues and thus reflects their broader cultural context. An often noted, deviation from the Hebrew text of Gen. 11:4 can be explained in light of similar scholarly concerns. While the Hebrew *Vorlage* reads נפוץ פן שם לנו על פני כל הארץ ונעשה, the LXX renders the expression 'lest' (we will be spread) by 'before' (πρὸ τοῦ διασπαρῆναι). The builders in the Hebrew text thus considered the possibility that they may be dispersed, whereas the LXX builders knew already at the outset that they were only trying to make a name for themselves before they would definitely be dispersed. This translation not only vilifies the builders, as Martin Rösel has suggested, but also solves the problem of verisimilitude.[14] In line with the Homeric scholiasts and Philo's anonymous colleagues, the Greek translators of the Bible stress the impossibility of the builders' enterprise, which is from the beginning doomed to failure. The author, Moses, never entertained the idea of their success.[15]

The notion of myth used by Philo's colleagues reflects a distinctly Aristotelian perspective, which was popular in Alexandrian scholarly circles. We have already seen that Aristotle paid special attention to the problem of verisimilitude.[16] One way of solving it was to read certain passages as traditional stories which had been transmitted rather than originally written by Homer. Such stories are said to reflect what 'people thus say' (ὅτι οὕτω φασίν).[17] In these terse lines Aristotle introduces an important, new dimension of Homeric scholarship, which has not yet been sufficiently appreciated. Identifying certain passages as popular rather than truly Homeric, Aristotle argues for the composite nature of the epic texts. This is often the case with regard to stories concerning the immoral behaviour of the gods. In contrast to Plato, Aristotle did not altogether dismiss them but insisted that they derived from Homer's pen, not from his mind. Homer is thus understood to have included in his epics popular ideas in which he himself did not believe. According to Aristotle, Homer in a way shared Xenophanes' low view of these materials[18] but, in contrast to him,

---

[14] Rösel 1994, pp. 216–17.

[15] The LXX further highlights the hypothetical nature of the builders' aspirations by translating the Hebrew expression ועתה לא יבצר מהם כל אשר יזמו לעשות (Gen. 11:6) with a construction in the subjunctive καὶ νῦν οὐκ ἐκλείψει ἐξ αὐτῶν πάντα ὅσα ἂν ἐπιθῶνται ποιεῖν. Philo also adopted this overall line of interpretation, stressing that the builders 'ceased building the city and the tower' (LXX Gen. 11:8) and thus never achieved their goal (*Conf.* 158).

[16] For details, see Chapter 3.   [17] Arist. *Poet.* 1460b35–37 (ed. Kassel 1966).

[18] Regarding Xenophanes' criticism of Homer's epics, see Diels 1903–7, vol. I, p. 115 (fr. 12).

cherished the people's opinion for its own sake. In Aristotle's view, Homer must therefore not be judged by purely philosophical standards of truth foreign to his literary enterprise.

A fragment of Aristotle's *Aporemata Homerica* throws further light on his approach. Aristotle discusses here the scene where Agamemnon tells his audience that Hera, under Fate's guidance, reacted to Zeus's proud prophecies concerning Heracles by soliciting a vow that the child born on that day would indeed 'be lord of all those who dwell about' (*Il.* 19.109). Hera cheated Zeus in order to gain his blessing for another offspring. The problem that arises for Aristotle is the fact that Hera asked for a vow as a token of security:

> 'But come now and swear to me...' [*Il.* 19.108].
> Why does Hera induce Zeus to swear, as it is clear that he does not do the things which he promises [by oath]? If this is the case, why did she not prefer [the sign of] nodding with the head over an oath, as if he were lying whenever he does not swear? But the poet says that he [Zeus] speaks the truth 'once I bow my head to it' [*Il.* 1.527].
> At all events all this is mythical (τὸ μὲν οὖν ὅλον μυθῶδες). Homer neither says these things of himself nor does he introduce things that happened, but he mentions the things concerning the birth of Heracles as a tradition (ὡς διαδεδομένων).[19] (Schol. *Il.* 19.108A = fr. 163, Arist. *Apor. Hom.*, ed. Rose 1886)

Aristotle's discussion is initially prompted by a contradiction between two similar verses. When Hera in the above passage solicits an oath from Zeus, she says εἰ δ' ἄγε νῦν μοι ὄμοσσον (*Il.* 19.108). The same introductory expression is used by Zeus, when indicating that nodding with his head is the surest token of his commitment: εἰ δ' ἄγε τοι κεφαλῇ κατανεύσομαι (*Il.* 1.524). Given this contradiction between two linguistically similar verses, Aristotle questions why Hera demands an oath. Her behaviour is implausible and unreasonable given the earlier information about Zeus. Aristotle's solution is striking. He admits that the verse reflects neither Homer's own view nor historical reality. Hera never behaved in that way nor did Homer ever think she did. He nevertheless incorporated the scene, because it was traditional material familiar to his readers. In contrast to Plato, who categorically rejected the 'false myths' put together by Homer and Hesiod (*Resp.* 377d), Aristotle looked favourably upon

---

[19] καὶ γὰρ οὐδ' ἀφ' ἑαυτοῦ ταῦτά φησιν Ὅμηρος οὐδὲ γινόμενα εἰσάγει, ἀλλ' ὡς διαδεδομένων περὶ τὴν Ἡρακλέους γένεσιν μέμνηται; see also Hintenlang 1961, pp. 46–8, who argued for the unity of this scholion and placed it in the context of Aristotle's discussion of verisimilitude in the *Poetics*.

popular stories about the gods, which he knew were not true.[20] It is clear that Philo's anonymous colleagues follow Aristotle's approach, adopting the same hermeneutic term (μυθῶδες) as well as the same attitude to their foundational text. They must be appreciated in the context of those Greek scholiasts who transmitted Aristotle's interpretations either *verbatim* or in a more general way.[21]

Furthermore, the emphasis of Philo's colleagues on both a comparative perspective and the contrast between myth and truth echoes more recent Alexandrian discussions. The Alexandrian scientist and scholar Eratosthenes is known to have taken Aristotle's position to an extreme, arguing that Homer wrote only for the purpose of entertainment and appeal to the soul (ψυχαγωγία).[22] Measuring Homer by the new standards of scientific truth, especially in the field of geography, he often accused him of expressing foolish ideas and babbling 'in all things' without reflecting the truth.[23] In an influential statement Eratosthenes even compared Homer to an old lady engaged in myth-making (γραώδη μυθολογίαν).[24] In the scholia inquiries into myths are rather frequent. René Nünlist has recently shown that the scholiasts regularly compared Homeric passages with stories in other Classical Greek literature, often merely stating the similarities or differences between the versions.[25] Aristarchus, in particular, embarked on a systematic inquiry, distinguishing between Homer and the mythological material of the νεώτεροι. Aristarchus followed Eratosthenes in this respect, working with a negative notion of myth, but insisted in contrast to him that Homer had not relied on any of the imaginary motifs later found in the Epic Cycle and the tragedies.[26]

---

[20] Aristotle's positive notion of myth has also been noted by Calame 2003, pp. 12–13.

[21] The influence of Aristotle's solution can be seen in the bT scholia on *Il.* 19.108, where the allegiance of the scholiasts is so clear that the editor H. Erbse has commented: 'hoc scholio doctrina Aristotelis continetur'. Lacking Aristotle's theoretical sophistication, one scholiast asks: 'why did she not ask him to nod his head?', while another answers: 'fearing that he might change [his mind], she went for the strongest [means of coercion]' (Schol. *Il.* 19.108a). This popular version of Aristotle's solution shows that his ideas spread even if his successors were apparently no longer aware of their original author and the profound hermeneutic implications of his approach. For other examples, see Schol. *Il.* 20.234d, 5.385a, 8.429.

[22] Strabo 1.2.12; Eratosthenes wrote a commentary on the *Iliad*, about which nothing certain is known (Geus 2002, pp. 302–3). On Eratosthenes' activities in Alexandria and Strabo's stay in Egypt for several years as well as his special familiarity with the cultural life of the city, see Fraser 1972, vol. 1, pp. 308–10, 330–3, 315–25; Engels 1999, pp. 32–3.

[23] Strabo 1.2.12; see also Fraser 1972, vol. 1, pp. 525–9; Biraschi 2005, pp. 76–7, stressing the immense influence and authority of Eratosthenes; contra Geus 2002, pp. 264–6, who regards Eratosthenes' remarks as strictly limited to geographical facts and concludes that his theory of poetry is nothing but an 'empty formula'.

[24] Strabo 1.2.3, see also 1.2.7, 1.2.12, 1.2.14–15, 1.2.19. [25] Nünlist 2009a, pp. 257–64.

[26] Nünlist 2009a, pp. 258–9; Lehrs 1882, pp. 174–91; Severyns 1928, pp. 31–100; Roemer 1911–12.

Strabo, on the other hand, assumed a more positive and literary notion of myth, admitting that there are some stories in the epics which contradict the truth, while Homer himself was generally regarded as rational and knowledgeable.[27] Strabo also explains that such myths are not purely 'fictitious' inventions (πλάσματα), but stories with 'traces of real persons and events'.[28] His view is summarily formulated thus:

Accordingly, the poet, using some resources (τισιν ἀφορμαῖς), tells the things, either conforming to matters of history or adding myth to them (προσμυθεύει δὲ τούτοις), thus maintaining a custom both common [among poets] and his own. (Strabo 1.2.40)

Homer's description of the island of Pharos is a representative example. Facing sharp criticisms of Homer as ignorant of its precise geographical situation, Strabo solves the problem of verisimilitude by recourse to a fine source analysis. He suggests that Homer received a correct report about the island, either from a particular man or from common knowledge, but then 'added by himself a distance many times as great for the sake of the mythical element'.[29] Myth thus emerges as a purposeful literary addition to an originally true story, which serves the entertainment of the audience.

Philo's anonymous colleagues must be understood in this context of Alexandrian discussions of myth. Reflecting the scientific spirit of the city, they, too, distinguished between myth and truth. Yet they did not on this account dismiss the truth value of the whole foundational text, as Eratosthenes had done, but rather adopted the more lenient, literary approach of Aristotle and Strabo, regarding the text as a composite which contains also some myths. In typical Alexandrian fashion Philo's colleagues offer a comparative analysis and point to the story originally available to Moses. Regarding the story of the Tower of Babel they suggest a development from a more blatantly mythological story to one closer to the truth. The remaining problem of verisimilitude is solved by the Classical Aristotelian device, adopted also by Strabo, of distinguishing clearly between an author committed to the truth and his dramatis personae, who may ignore it.

---

[27] Strabo's interpretation is usually not discussed in terms of myth, but rather as an intermediate position between Eratosthenes' literalism and Crates' allegorical approach; for details, see Schenkeveld 1976; Kahles 1976, pp. 19–25; Dueck 2000, p. 34, who stresses the difference between Strabo and Eratosthenes.

[28] ἀλλὰ γεγενημένων ἴχνη καὶ προσώπων καὶ πράξεων (Strabo 1.2.14).

[29] τοῦ μυθώδους χάριν (Strabo 1.2.30).

THE CONFUSION OF TONGUES AMONG MEN AND ANIMALS

Philo's colleagues also inquired into the theological and social significance of the biblical story of the Tower of Babel. They discussed these aspects in a comparison with a fable 'mentioned by the mythologists' (*Conf.* 6). At stake is the question whether God's punishment of the builders, who lost their common language as a result of their *hybris*, was indeed justified. In this context Philo's colleagues offer extremely interesting views on the value of a united humanity and their common language, which allow us to place them more precisely within the context of a lively Alexandrian discussion on these topics.

Philo's colleagues open their comparison between the biblical and the Greek story by offering the following remarks:

> Another story similar to this is the one mentioned by myth writers (πρὸς μυθο-πλαστῶν) concerning the common language of the animals. For it is told that in former days all the animals in as much as they are on the land or in the water or winged shared one language – and in the same way among humans, while Greeks [speak] with Greeks, barbarians, who nowadays share a common language, speak with barbarians[30] – thus all [the creatures] conversed with all about the things they happened to do or experience so that they were even aggrieved together at misfortunes and rejoiced together if something advantageous happened. (*Conf.* 6)

The story of the animals' common language is otherwise only attested in the work of the Alexandrian poet Callimachus, who presented it as an Aesopic fable.[31] It is not surprising that Philo's colleagues refer to the fable as a myth, because that was rather common during the Hellenistic period.[32] The original Aesopic version of the fable, if it ever existed, is no longer extant.[33] The reference in *Conf.* 6 to more than one myth writer mentioning it indicates that by the time of Philo's colleagues the story was widely known in different literary works. The opening of the story, as reported by Philo's colleagues, closely parallels Callimachus' version and thus probably reflects the fable which circulated in Alexandria.[34] The lines

[30] καὶ ὅνπερ τρόπον ἀνθρώπων Ἕλληνες μὲν Ἕλλησι, βαρβάροις δὲ βάρβαροι νῦν οἱ ὁμόγλωττοι διαλέγονται.
[31] Callim. *Ia.* 2, fr. 11, lines 15–16 ταῦτα δ᾽ Α[ἴσιω]πος ὁ Σαρδιηνὸς εἶπεν (ed. Pfeiffer 1949–53, vol. 1, p. 173); Callimachus' fragmentary version is complemented by the summary of the lost lines in the *Diegesis*.
[32] Perry 1962, pp. 301–7.
[33] Contra Perry 1962, pp. 312–14, who conjectured that Demetrius of Phalerum preserved the original version. This argument, however, is highly speculative, because it is assumed that there must have been only one written source from which all the later versions of Aesop's fable have derived. That source is then identified as Demetrius' no longer extant work.
[34] *Conf.* 6; Callim. *Ia.* 2 lines 1–3 and *Dieg.* 6.22–3.

concerning the communication 'nowadays' among Greeks and barbarians, by contrast, must be a comment by Philo's colleagues, which even obstructs the flow of the fable. Philo's colleagues thus emerge from the beginning of the fragment as having a conspicuous, topical interest in the story.

A detailed scholarly analysis of the Greek story in relation to its biblical counterpart is then offered by Philo's colleagues:

For imparting to each other their pleasures and discomforts by means of their community of language, they rejoiced together and experienced together discomfort. And as a result of this they [the animals] obtained a similarity of conduct and experience until they became sated with the abundance of goods ready at hand and, as often tends to happen, drifted into a love for unattainable [goods]. They sent an embassy concerning immortality (περὶ ἀθανασίας ἐπρεσβεύετο), demanding deliverance from old age (γήρως ἔκλυσιν) and the flower of youth for ever, saying that one of the animals among them, that reptile, the serpent, had already attained this gift. For by shedding old age, it grows again from the beginning. It is odd [they claimed] that the superior creatures are left behind by the inferior or all by one. Yet they received a suitable punishment for their adventure and immediately became polyglot, so that they were no longer able to understand each other because of the distinction of dialects into which the one and common [language] of all had been split.

But bringing this story closer to the truth (ὁ δ' ἐγγυτέρω τἀληθοῦς προσάγων τὸν λόγον), he [Moses] distinguished between creatures lacking speech and creatures endowed with speech, so that he gave evidence of a community of language only with regard to men. And yet, they say, this is still mythical (καὶ τοῦτο μυθῶδες). (*Conf.* 7–9)

The fable quoted in this passage closely resembles the version preserved by Callimachus. In the latter's poem, too, the different animals originally spoke one common language but then grew dissatisfied and sent an embassy to demand 'release from old age'.[35] In both versions they were punished for their audacity. While Philo's colleagues speak of a fragmentation of their language (*Conf.* 8), Callimachus has Zeus 'transfer their voices to men' with the result that the latter 'became chatterboxes', each of them reproducing a specific animal voice (*Dieg.* 6.27–9).

---

[35] Callimachus describes the animals as ἐφθέγγεθ', which primarily refers to human language, but secondarily also to animal voices, while the *Diegesis* specifies ὡμοφώνει ἀν[θ]ρώποις (*Dieg.* 6.23), thus using virtually the same expression as Philo's colleagues (ὁμόφωνα ἦν, καὶ ὅνπερ τρόπον ἀνθρώπων, *Conf.* 6). The motif of the embassy is preserved only in Philo's fragment and the *Diegesis*, where almost identical vocabulary is used: κατὰ λύσιν γήρως ἐπ[ρέ]σβευσεν (*Dieg.* 6.24). In addition, the animals complain in both versions about Zeus's injustice. Yet in Philo's fragment they speak about the preference of the serpent, which has already attained a release from old age (*Conf.* 7), while in the *Diegesis* the fox accuses Zeus of ruling unjustly (*Dieg.* 6.26–7).

Recently, some scholars have identified Callimachus' version as closer to the original, assuming that the Jewish version is a modification in light of the biblical plot.[36] Arguments for the opposite view, initially proposed by Leopold Früchtel, must nevertheless still be taken seriously.[37] In Callimachus' poem there is a significant gap between the beginning of the fable and Zeus's punishment, from which Callimachus draws the conclusion that his colleagues are nothing but barking dogs or neighing horses. This moral does not really suit the fable, where the animals originally 'speak as humans'. A transfer of their language to men could thus only result in human speech. The author of the *Diegesis* seems to have been aware of this tension and sought to alleviate it by using the more general verb φθέγγομαι, which can also imply animal voices, in reference to the animals' original speech. Callimachus' moral emerges as a parody making liberal use of popular material.

Philo's colleagues, on the other hand, seem to have discussed the fable as it was known in Alexandria. Their version is congruent, focusing on the subject of unity which is disrupted by envy. The animals' complaint about the limits of equality thus resulted in a complete loss of their privileges and community. Furthermore, the Alexandrian context of their story is reflected in the motif of the rejuvenating serpent. Eusebius mentions a cult of such a serpent in Egypt. Relying on an Egyptian source, he explains the process of the serpent's rejuvenation, stressing that it was considered immortal and divine (*Praep. evang.* 1.10.47–9). The version of the fable circulating in Alexandria is likely to have included a reference to this well-known Egyptian motif.

Philo's colleagues discuss the relationship between the known Greek fable and the biblical story in a scholarly manner. Considering the motif of speaking animals to be more mythological than that of humans sharing a common language, they suggest once more that the primitive preceded the rational. Moses was in their view more enlightened than the mythologists, because he attributed a human voice only to men, thus accepting the scientific distinction 'between creatures lacking speech and creatures endowed with speech' (*Conf.* 9). It is interesting that Philo's colleagues attributed the same rationality to Moses as Aristarchus did to Homer, when athetizing a verse depicting animals as speaking with a human voice.[38] In contrast to Callimachus, Philo's colleagues did not use the Greek fable creatively in

---

[36] Acosta-Hughes 2002, pp. 178–84; Perry 1962, pp. 312–13; Kerkhecker 1999, p. 58; Gera 2003, pp. 31–32.
[37] Früchtel 1950.   [38] Schol. *Il.* 19.416–17A.

a poetic context but carefully compared it with the biblical account and offered a scholarly analysis of their historical relationship.[39] The academic level of their analysis is remarkable, anticipating modern text criticism by roughly two thousand years.[40]

Philo's colleagues conclude that the biblical story is ultimately 'mythical', because it ignores the obvious advantages of a community of language. In their view, the confusion of tongues 'does not seem to have happened for any benefit';[41] indeed they criticize the Divine punishment as both ineffective and misguided. A confusion of tongues can evidently not prevent wickedness, since people can easily communicate by 'movements of the body', such as nods and glances (*Conf.* 10). The position of Philo's colleagues is remarkably critical. They cannot find any educational message in the biblical story and judge the Divine punishment to be gravely mistaken. Their notion of myth is highly negative in this context, corresponding to Eratosthenes' position.[42]

Moreover, Philo's anonymous colleagues express their own views, which are contrary to the biblical myth but directly echo a lively Alexandrian discussion:

Should, however, any man learn additional languages, he is immediately well renowned among those who know it so that he quickly is considered a friend. He brings no small token of partnership (γνώρισμα κοινωνίας) in his familiarity with their vocabulary, from which, it seems, comes the certainty that [they] will incur nothing harmful [from him].

Why then did He remove community of language from men as if this was the cause of evil, while it should rightly be established as something most useful? (*Conf.* 13)

Philo's colleagues offer in this passage a remarkably universalistic vision of humanity united by a common language. They do not differentiate between Greeks and barbarians, instead speaking in tolerant and egalitarian terms about learning more languages in order to communicate with others. Even tensions and mistrust can be overcome by showing a 'token of partnership', namely by acquiring the other's language. The views of Philo's colleagues on these issues of cultural politics closely resemble those of Eratosthenes, who demanded that the ethnic dichotomy of 'Greek' and

---

[39] The innovative aspect of Callimachus' work has been stressed by Acosta-Hughes 2002, pp. 174–8.

[40] See, e.g., Skinner 1910, pp. 223–31, who identified the story of the Tower of Babel as a myth and investigated ancient Near Eastern parallels.

[41] Τὸ δὲ οὐκ ἐπ' ὠφελείᾳ φαίνεται συμβῆναι (*Conf.* 10).

[42] See the controversy on the issue of myth between Eratosthenes and Strabo in Strabo 1.2.3–8; cf. Philo's arguments for a positive educational message in the biblical story in *Conf.* 162–7, 191–8.

'barbarian' be altogether abandoned. He considered such distinctions to be artificial, because moral behaviour can be found among all nations (Strabo 1.4.9). A community of moral individuals was instead advocated with no regard for the respective ethnic origin of its members.[43] Eratosthenes' ideal was Alexander the Great, who disregarded his advisors and 'welcomed as many as possible of the men of good repute and did them favours'. Indians and Romans were positively appreciated in this context and not presented as some lower kind of Greeks.[44]

The novelty of Eratosthenes' views at a time when the tension between Greeks and Egyptians began to rise can especially be appreciated in light of Strabo's subsequent comments. The latter reintroduced more traditional Greek criteria to the evaluation of Others, such as adherence to the law, political instinct, education and power of speech.[45] Strabo translated Eratosthenes' ideal into the well-known notions of integrating barbarians on condition that they adopt a Greek way of life. Strabo linked the spread of the Greek language to 'living in Greek fashion' (Ἑλληνικῶς ζῆν).[46] Learning Greek thus became a one-directional means of overcoming cultural and ethnic distinctions, while correct Greek remained the marker of born Greeks. While Strabo mentions some Greeks 'conversing in their [the barbarians'] languages', he shows that such Greeks also retain their accent and never properly learn other tongues (Strabo 14.2.28).

Philo's colleagues participate in this lively Alexandrian discussion about the unity of humanity and the possibility of their sharing a common language. Apparently familiar with the influential opinions of Eratosthenes and Strabo, they incline towards the radical universalism of the former. They, too, believe in a community of humanity transcending ethnic boundaries. Philo's colleagues stress mutuality and directly address the issue of trust between people from different backgrounds. Speaking the same language, they suggest, will create a sense of mutual trust and empathy. Philo's colleagues stress the element of creating confidence, thus probably reacting to an aggravation of the political tension in Alexandria. As Jews they supported a melting-pot policy, suspecting that the biblical story of the confusion of tongues, with its emphasis on the irreversible nature of the Divine punishment, may undermine their cultural vision.

---

[43] See also Fraser 1972, vol. I, pp. 530–1, vol. II, p. 761, n. 87.

[44] Baldry 1965, pp. 168–71; Dauge 1981, p. 515.

[45] Strabo 1.4.9; regarding the limit of Eratosthenes' words in Strabo's fragment, see Baldry 1965, p. 70; Almagor 2005, pp. 48–50.

[46] Strabo 14.2.28; Almagor 2005, pp. 44–51.

The significance of Philo's anonymous colleagues can hardly be overemphasized. Providing an academic analysis of the story of the Tower of Babel in light of two Greek myths, they have emerged as careful scholars, who applied Aristotelian and Alexandrian notions of scholarship to the Jewish Scriptures. Their hermeneutic assumptions were comparative and universalistic, holding the Bible and Homer's epic to be the same kind of literary work. Culturally, Philo's colleagues were firmly embedded in the Alexandrian context, engaging in contemporary discussions and expressing their own views in dialogue with their Homeric colleagues. They can be firmly placed in the Aristotelian, rationalist camp, which held high scientific standards and advocated a melting-pot policy in Alexandria. In Philo's eyes, however, these Jewish Bible scholars had gone too far in their research and appeared to him to be impious scoffers. Nonetheless they seem to have gained sufficient respect in Alexandria to warrant his attention. It is possible that they represent a rather influential approach among Alexandrian Jews, having offered similar interpretations of other biblical stories as well.

OTHER MYTHS IN COMPARATIVE PERSPECTIVE

No other fragment of Philo's colleagues has survived, but there are some indications of their further work, which can be found in scattered references by Philo. We have already observed that he himself assumed that they engaged in a comprehensive study of Scripture, accusing them of using 'similar passages as stepping-stones for their ungodliness' (*Conf.* 2). His colleagues conversely stressed that they could have adduced many other examples (*Conf.* 3). Can such examples be recovered from Philo's polemics?

Philo's references to other exegetes who interpreted the biblical story about the sons of God and their human wives may have implied the same colleagues. In this context, too, Philo opposes an alternative interpretation, which relied on the literal sense of Gen. 6:1–4 and identified it as a myth. While Philo does not quote his colleagues' interpretation, he provides crucial bits of information about their approach.[47] Warning his readers that 'nobody may suppose that the story is a myth', Philo anticipates precisely such a reading (*Gig.* 7). He moreover raises the possibility that 'perhaps someone thinks that the lawgiver alluded to the myths of the poets

---

[47] It is possible that Philo did not quote his colleagues' views because he found their arguments too threatening. His own interpretation of the biblical story is so defensive that he even changes the LXX expression υἱοὶ τοῦ θεοῦ to οἱ ἄγγελοι τοῦ θεοῦ, thus reducing the mythological dimension of the biblical text; contra Harl 1986, p. 125, who argues that the meaning 'anges de Dieu' is the 'leçon primitive du grec'.

concerning the giants'.[48] In another context Philo assumes his reader's awareness of the similarity between the biblical story and the tale of 'the poets' about the giants, who were 'earth-born, children of the earth' (*Q.G.* 1.92). The latter expression is a double Armenian translation of the Greek term γηγενέτης, which directly echoes the Classical description of the giants as earth-born.[49] Hesiod and Aeschylus had thus spoken about the giants.[50] The motif of giants having sex with human women was so well known in antiquity that it became a leitmotiv in the pseudo-Hesiodic *Catalogue of Women*.[51] Did Philo's colleagues compare Gen. 6:1–4 to such stories, highlighting both their similarities and the mythological nature of each? This prospect is very likely, because the LXX had already adapted the biblical narrative to its Greek counterparts by translating the term 'heroes' (גברים) as 'giants'.[52] Philo's colleagues probably explored this nuance of the Greek text and discussed parallels in Greek literature.

Another biblical motif which was identified as mythological is the serpent speaking in a human voice. Philo frequently refers to someone who may regard it as a myth and even admits that, taken literally, this image indeed appears mythical (*Agr.* 96–7). He insists, however, that the story is 'no mythical fiction', because the serpent only 'appeared to utter a human voice' (*Opif.* 163). Philo's apologetic tone is conspicuous in these passages and suggests that he responds to colleagues who adopted the approach of comparative mythology. These colleagues are likely to have belonged to the same circle as the exegetes interpreting the Tower of Babel, because the latter criticized Hellenistic fables about speaking animals as blurring the essential distinction between 'creatures lacking speech and creatures endowed with speech' (*Conf.* 9).

The approach of Philo's colleagues may have been so prominent in Alexandria that it came to the attention of Celsus, the Greek philosopher and critic of Christianity. Celsus frequently referred to a Jewish treatise against Christianity and knew that some Jews allegorized Scripture.[53] In

---

[48] Ἴσως τις τὰ παρὰ τοῖς ποιηταῖς μεμυθευμένα περὶ τῶν γιγάντων οἴεται τὸν νομοθέτην αἰνίττεσθαι (*Gig.* 58).

[49] γίγαντι γηγενέται (Eur. *Phoen.* 128). Double translations of Greek terms are frequent in the Armenian translation literature; see Terian 1980.

[50] Hes. *Theog.* 185; Aesch. *Pers.* 351.

[51] See M. L. West 1997, p. 117, who also compares the *Catalogue of Women* to Gen. 6:1–4.

[52] On the tendency of the LXX regarding this story, see Rösel 1994, pp. 145–58. Note that the Hebrew is ambiguous, suggesting that the *Nephilim* were not identical to the 'heroes'.

[53] On Celsus' use of a Jewish treatise see Blumell 2007; Niehoff in press, f. Celsus' references to Jewish allegorists can be found in *C. Cels.* 4.38, 4.51. Origen suggested that Celsus could not have read the books of Philo and Aristobulus, because in that case he would have been convinced by their arguments (*C. Cels.* 4.51). This is, of course, a polemical statement, which

light of his general familiarity with Jewish writings, it is striking that he, too, compared, the story of the Tower of Babel to 'the things told about the sons of Aloeus'.[54] The motif of the speaking serpent was also in his view completely mythological.[55] The dichotomy of approaches which we observed in the context of Philo and his colleagues is thus repeated two centuries later, Celsus adopting a literal approach with emphasis on myth, while Origen continued Philo's allegorical method. Even the situation of the sources is similar. Origen's work, like Philo's, is largely extant, whereas Celsus' voice, parallel to that of his Jewish predecessors, is only heard fragmentarily through the polemics against him.

One important difference, however, is obvious between Philo's colleagues and Celsus. The latter wrote from the point of view of a proud Greek, who dismissed the Jewish Scriptures as the basis of Christianity and argued that Moses' story about the Tower of Babel was only a cheap imitation of its Homeric counterpart. Philo's colleagues, by contrast, wrote their treatises on the Bible as proud and compassionate Jews, convinced that Moses had improved the Homeric tale and brought it closer to the truth. While Celsus refers only in passing to the mythological nature of some biblical stories, Philo's colleagues offer a highly sophisticated and innovative analysis of the biblical text in light of contemporary scholarship.

---

cannot be taken as historical evidence, and corresponds to his claim that Celsus did not properly read the Scriptures but relied only on hearsay (*C. Cels.* 5.6); see also Sterling 2004, pp. 39–40, who took *C. Cels.* 4.51 as an indication of Celsus' familiarity with Philo and Aristobulus; see also Wilken 1984, pp. 94–125. Following Rosenbaum 1972, pp. 102–4, Celsus' work must be dated to the mid second century CE; contra Rokeah 1991, p. 45; and Lona 2005, pp. 54–5, who suggest slightly later dates.

[54] *C. Cels.* 4.21, see also 4.36, 5.25.   [55] μῦθόν τινα (*C. Cels.* 4.36, ed. Marcovich 2001).

CHAPTER 6

Historical perspectives on Scripture

In this chapter we continue to investigate traces of Philo's colleagues and predecessors, whose work is reflected in his reactions to them. A fragment of considerable size is preserved in Philo's biography of Abraham. Philo seems to quote here from a written source, reporting at length what 'they say' (φασί).[1] This fragment from a lost work of Philo's colleagues throws further light on the diversity of Alexandrian Judaism and enables us to reconstruct one additional aspect of the general picture. While the exegetes quoted in *De Abrahamo* will be shown to belong to an Aristotelian milieu, they must not on this account be identified with the interpreters of the story of the Tower of Babel whom we have encountered in the previous chapter. The fragment discussed in this chapter will rather illuminate the rich diversity of the Aristotelian scholarly tradition among Jewish Bible exegetes in Alexandria.

The fragment in *De Abrahamo* points to a lively discussion among Alexandrian Jews concerning the legitimacy of historical approaches to Scripture. The question arises whether Scripture evolved over time and implies a development of the religion or instead reflects an eternal, unchanging truth. I shall argue that the above mentioned fragment is of the utmost significance in this context. When analysed with a view to contemporary Alexandrian scholarship, it emerges as a highly academic interpretation of the Binding of Isaac in the context of ancient practices of child sacrifice. Philo's colleagues shared their historical perspectives with Greek scholars, such as Aristotle and Aristarchus, while differing considerably from a more traditional exegete such as Philo. Their surprisingly modern position is based on the understanding that Moses revised the more primitive stages of the Jewish religion and introduced important reforms.

---

[1] Note that Philo uses accusative constructions, which depend on φασί, thus allowing us to identify the boundaries of the fragment. In this respect he proceeds in the same way as Eusebius did with regard to Demetrius' fragments, on the boundaries of which see above Chapter 3.

HISTORY VERSUS NATURE

The *De Abrahamo*, in which the fragment on the Binding of Isaac is preserved, is a treatise which belongs to the *Exposition of the Law* and was
probably written at a later stage of Philo's career.[2] Philo mentioned the
work of his colleagues in this context because their historical perspective
directly challenged his own strategy of anchoring Scripture in Nature and
thus required treatment lest his readers follow the views of his opponents.[3]
Philo's interpretation of Nature (φύσις) in terms of Scripture was itself
the result of a considerable intellectual development and had not always
characterized him. In the treatises of the *Allegorical Commentary* Philo
primarily used the term 'Nature' as a reference to the individual characteristics of persons, things or God Himself.[4] He also spoke of Nature as
providing man with useful and necessary organs.[5] It is striking that in
these writings Philo even expressed views which are at odds with Stoic
philosophy. He insisted, for example, that Nature wrought the body as
a receptacle of pleasures and identified man's natural tendencies with his
bodily needs.[6]

Philo's two extant treatises *On Dreams* represent a transitional phase in
his career. They no longer conform to the genre of a running commentary but anticipate the thematic and philosophical orientation of his later
writings.[7] Philo states here that he intends to devote a separate treatise to
Abraham, which will show that the earliest patriarch had teaching as his
guide to virtue (*Somn.* 1.168). Whereas Abraham is still spoken of as an
immigrant and stranger rather than as the paradigmatic follower of the law
of Nature (*Somn.* 1.160), Philo already points in the direction of his future
concepts. He does so most conspicuously in a passage which links the 'laws

---

[2] On the *Exposition*, see below Chapter 10; on the chronology of Philo's works, see Niehoff in press, c.
[3] The section of Philo's *Q.G.* on chap. 22 of the Book of Genesis is no longer extant so that we cannot
know whether Philo referred to his colleagues' interpretation of the Binding of Isaac in this earlier
context, too.
[4] See esp. *All.* 1.92, 2.23, 2.42, 2.47, 2.99, 3.53, 3.61, 3.84, 3.115, 3.130, 3.157, *Cher.* 19, 38, 86, *Sacr.* 114,
Post. 13, 16.
[5] See esp. *Cher.* 39, *Post.* 4, 103–6, *Sacr.* 75, 102–3, *All.* 3.210.
[6] *Post.* 27, *Det.* 30, *All.* 3:145; cf. more Stoic views in *Cher.* 43 (men and women come together for
procreation by the call of Nature), *Cher.* 76 (the enemy of the Logos is also an enemy of Nature),
Cher. 93 (Nature prompts restraint and thus opposes drunkenness); on the background of Stoic
natural philosophy, see esp. White 2003; Schofield 2003.
[7] This transitional role of *On Dreams* emerged also in a recent study of the figure of Joseph by Niehoff
2010a. Note also that this treatise mentions serious political tensions between the Jews and 'one of
the ruling class' (*Somn.* 2.123), thus foreshadowing the violent events described in the *Embassy to
Gaius* and *Against Flaccus*.

of Nature' with the Divine commandments mentioned in Deut. 30:9–
10. Philo stresses that God delights when men turn away from their sins,
reverting to righteousness and Nature, thus embracing the ways of their
forefathers, who had kept God's laws (*Somn.* 2.174–5). It is implied that
keeping the Divine commandments and living in accordance with Nature
are virtually identical. Nature is moreover identified now in typically Stoic
fashion with righteousness.[8]

In the *Exposition* references to Nature and her laws assume a central role.
These terms are no longer used in the Classical Greek sense of a contrast
between man's inherent rights and the laws of the city, which is still echoed
in the *Allegorical Commentary*, but rather in the new sense of Scripture as
a universal, unchanging constitution.[9] I have argued elsewhere that Philo's
views in the *Exposition* are similar to Cicero's notion of Roman law.[10] In
the present context the implications for Philo's interpretation of biblical
history have to be explored. The moment Philo insists on an intrinsic
connection between Nature, Mosaic Law and the lives of the patriarchs,
he confronts a rather fundamental challenge: he has to show that all these
different layers of Scripture are harmonious, containing no contradictions
or indications of significant change.[11]

Philo addresses the question of Scripture's unity in his biography of
Abraham, which he introduces as a bridge between the creation of the
world and the revelation of Mosaic Law on Mount Sinai.[12] The connection
between these central events is drawn by pointing to the law of Nature,
which underlies everything. It is initially embedded in the creation, then
implemented by the early biblical heroes and subsequently also expressed
in the details of Mosaic Law.[13] Philo thus insists on an unchanging unity of
Judaism throughout its history. His recourse to Nature enables him to trace
the different aspects of the tradition back to one organizing principle and

---

[8] On Stoic notions of Nature in the context of their ethics, see Inwood and Donini 1999, pp. 675–84.

[9] For examples of the Classical Greek connotation, see esp. *Sobr.* 25, *Ebr.* 34, 37, 47, *Agr.* 43, 66;
contra Cohen 1985, 1987, who suggested, on highly speculative grounds, that Philo was dependent
on proto-rabbinic notions of oral law.

[10] Niehoff 2001, pp. 247–66; Runia 2001, pp. 106–8; cf. Martens 2003; Najman 2002, pp. 70–107,
who both argue for Philo's more general inversion of Hellenistic concepts.

[11] Formulations of an inherent connection between Nature, Mosaic Law and the lives of the patriarchs
can be found in *Opif.* 3, *Mos.* 2:14, *Abr.* 1–8.

[12] *Abr.* 3–4; see also Sandmel 1956, pp. 107–10; Runia 2008; Sterling 2008; Böhm 2005, pp. 125–7.

[13] See also Martens 2003, pp. 103–39; note moreover that Philo is the first extant writer who conceives
of the Ten Commandments not only as specific injunctions, but also as general categories or 'heads',
which form the basis of all the specific laws. His discussion of the specific laws under the headings
of the Ten Commandments thus corroborates his effort to create unity between the different layers
of Jewish history.

to contrast it to the constitutions of other nations, which have developed over time according to changing circumstances of history.

Philo stresses that the early biblical heroes 'lived blameless and good lives' and have thus become 'laws endowed with life and reason' (*Abr.* 4–5), but he is acutely aware of ruptures in the overall picture. Not all of the characters were equally perfect. Philo admits that even though they 'did not commit anything blameworthy on account of their deliberate judgement', some sinned 'by chance' (*Abr.* 6). Moreover, the triad Enos, Enoch and Noah strove for a life of virtue but never fully achieved it (*Abr.* 47–8). Reviewing their lives, Philo can only insist on their relative merits.[14]

Abraham plays a special role in Philo's reconstruction of biblical history, being exceptionally elevated in the latter's view. He not only became the father of the nation but was also the first whose name was joined to God in the expression 'the God of Abraham, Isaac and Jacob'.[15] Indeed, Abraham's life was so perfect that Philo entitled his biography of him 'The Life of the Wise . . . or the First Book of Unwritten Law'. The patriarchs were in his opinion no longer regular human beings, but 'symbols of virtue' or virtues, which were only nominally men (*Abr.* 52–4). This view of Abraham provided Philo with a hermeneutic key for all the different biblical stories about him (*Abr.* 60). Conforming to Nature and thus unable to sin, Abraham was shown to be superior in his merits and to implement the eternal laws of virtue.[16]

Philo wrote his idealizing *Life of Abraham* in response to rather harsh criticism of this figure. Clearly, not all Alexandrian Jews thought highly of him. His character even seems to have been questioned more than that of other biblical heroes. Philo consequently sounds rather apologetic when presenting his own interpretations. The story of Abraham's descent to Egypt, for example, with the notorious scene of his wife, Sarah, being passed off to Pharaoh as his sister (Gen. 12:10–20), provoked controversy. Anticipating criticism, Philo insists that Abraham's deeds 'call for anything

---

[14] Enos is thus 'worthy of a written memorial . . . in the everlasting [record] of nature' (*Abr.* 11), because he represents hope, the quintessential prerequisite for any form of virtue (*Abr.* 8–16). Enoch is interpreted as an example of repentance and improvement of character. His achievement is judged as secondary to perfection, just as health is preferable to recovery from sickness (*Abr.* 26). Finally, Noah is presented as righteous only in comparison to his generation (*Abr.* 36). He deserves admiration, Philo explains, but not to the same degree as the patriarchs, whose virtue was 'unchallenged' (*Abr.* 37).

[15] *Abr.* 51 referring to Exod. 3:15.

[16] Note that Philo allowed for some developments of Abraham's character (*Abr.* 70, 77, 82–4, 88), but insisted that he never sinned and instead moved from lower degrees of virtue to higher ones.

but contempt', while admitting that 'their greatness is not obvious to all' (*Abr.* 88).[17] He also recalls that some exegetes had directly accused Abraham of 'betraying the laws of marriage' and acting 'customarily out of levity of character'.[18] Philo attacks such colleagues with characteristic fervour, claiming that 'they are unable to think' and properly appreciate the patriarch's virtue (*Q.G.* 4.60). This rhetoric notwithstanding, Philo's colleagues were not impious simpletons, but rather sophisticated readers of Scripture. I shall argue that their perspectives were based on profound scholarly insights and a firm commitment to history.

THE BINDING OF ISAAC IN THE CONTEXT OF ANCIENT CHILD SACRIFICE

The biblical story of Isaac's Binding does not break with ancient notions of child sacrifice, as has often been assumed, but rather embraces them. Jon Levenson has rightly pointed in this context to the fact that the angel praises Abraham as 'God-fearing', precisely because he 'did not withhold' his only son from Him.[19] Abraham's total obedience to God's wishes is the focus of the story. The replacement of the child by a ram is not presented as a fundamental turning point, which prevents further sacrifices or bindings, but rather as a reward for the father's willingness to actually kill his son. Later biblical stories occasionally still mention child sacrifices, such as that of Yiftach's daughter (Judg. 11:29–40).

Anticipating such modern research by more than two thousand years, some of Philo's colleagues interpreted the Binding of Isaac in the context of ancient child sacrifice. Philo, who praised Abraham for his mastery of paternal love as well as his devotion to God, did not approve of their views.[20] He offered the following tendentious introduction:

But to the lovers of quarrel, who slander everything (πάντα διαβάλλουσιν) and are accustomed to value censure above praise, the committed deed does not appear great and wonderful, as we assume it to be. (*Abr.* 178)

---

[17] The Greek translators of this story also seem to have been embarrassed by the fact that Abraham twice presented his wife as his sister and twice passed her off to a foreign ruler, initially to Pharaoh (Gen. 12:1–10) and then to Abimelech (Gen. 20:1–18). The translators sought to alleviate the problem by adding the following explanation to the second story: 'he feared to say: she is my wife, lest the men of the city should kill him on her account' (LXX Gen. 20:2).

[18] *Q.G.* 4.60–1; note that similar criticism was voiced in rabbinic Midrash, on which see Niehoff 1993.

[19] Gen. 22:12 (כי ירא אלהים אתה ולא חשכת את בנך / ὅτι φοβῇ τὸν θεὸν σὺ καὶ οὐκ ἐφείσω τοῦ υἱοῦ σου); see also Levenson 1993; Bauks 2007; contra de Vaux 1964, p. 71; Simon 1973, who interpreted the biblical story as putting an end to a ritual known in the pagan surroundings.

[20] *Abr.* 170, 196, 199.

Philo's rhetoric, repeated on other occasions, invites the reader to dismiss his colleagues' views as mere slander.[21] Scholars have debated who these other exegetes may have been. Some have recognized that they must have been Jews rather than hostile Greeks, who cannot be expected to have known this biblical story.[22] Samuel Sandmel suggested that Philo's colleagues were Jews of an 'assimilationist' character and therefore more critical of Scripture.[23] Today the term assimilation is hardly used any more in connection with Alexandrian Judaism, because it implies judgemental notions about ancient Jews, who, according to the onlooker, at least partially abandoned their Judaism.[24] Regarding the above quoted passage the term is certainly inappropriate, because Philo's colleagues clearly identified themselves as Jews and were proud of the Mosaic tradition. They subsequently referred, from a distance, to both Greeks and barbarians while praising Moses as a lawgiver who set standards of excellence still authoritative in their own time.[25]

Interpreting Philo's colleagues as serious Jewish scholars, we have to search in his polemics for specific indications of how they read the Binding of Isaac. Initially, it is conspicuous that while Philo identified the Akedah as Abraham's 'greatest deed worthy of hearing', they doubted its value (*Abr.* 167). Philo moreover accuses them of customarily (ἐθίζονται) expressing criticism (*Abr.* 178). This remark implies that they not only studied the story of Isaac's Binding but approached Scripture from a more comprehensive perspective, judging the biblical heroes by their own criteria rather than idealizing them. A first glimpse into their hermeneutics is provided in the following report by Philo:

They say that many others of those who exceedingly love their family and offspring offered their own children, some of whom were sacrificed (σφαγιασθησομένους) for the sake of their fatherlands, becoming atonements either for wars or droughts or a flood or pestilential diseases, while others [were sacrificed] for the sake of what was considered reverence towards the gods, even though it is not true reverence (τοὺς δ᾽ ὑπὲρ νενομισμένης εὐσεβείας εἰ καὶ μὴ πρὸς ἀλήθειαν οὔσης). (*Abr.* 179)

---

[21] Philo's rhetoric is repeated in *Abr.* 191, where he criticizes their 'evil-speaking mouths', envy of virtue and lack of praise for Abraham's good life; see also *Abr.* 199, where Philo summarily refers to their malignant and envious disposition.

[22] See esp. Sandmel 1956, p. 128; Goulet 1987, pp. 542–4; Runia 2008, p. 141; cf. Feldman 2002, who suggests that these exegetes may have been either Jews or pagans, but more likely the latter. See also my comments on the pagans' lack of familiarity with the Jewish Scriptures in the previous chapter.

[23] Sandmel 1956, p. 128.

[24] See also G. Schimanowski's valuable remarks in this context (Schimanowski 2007).

[25] *Abr.* 180–1; Sandmel read the reference to Moses as a statement by Philo (Sandmel 1956, p. 129). The accusative and infinitive construction (μεμνῆσθαι... τὸν ἱερώτατον Μωυσῆν), indicates, however, that this sentence is dependent on the preceding φασί in *Abr.* 179 and thus forms part of his colleagues' statement.

Philo's colleagues place the story of Isaac's Binding into the context of ancient child sacrifice of which they strongly disapprove. It is significant that they do not use the LXX term for the offering (ὁλοκάρπωσις), which reflects the Hebrew *Vorlage* עלה and is connected to the regular animal offerings in the Jerusalem Temple.[26] Instead, the verb σφαγιάζομαι, with its more general and gruesome connotation of slaying a victim, is employed. Philo's colleagues thus stress the aspect of killing, insisting that Abraham's willingness to offer his son is comparable to the actual practice of child sacrifice known in the ancient world. Furthermore, they make a special point of rejecting such a sacrifice as a false form of worship, directly subverting the message of the biblical story, where Abraham is praised for his willingness to surrender his 'beloved' son.[27] Did Philo's colleagues adopt the view of the prophet Ezekiel, who condemned child sacrifice in ancient Israel as 'bad laws' by which God had 'stained' his people?[28]

Philo's colleagues explored the full implications of their critical approach and offered a historical interpretation of Isaac's Binding. They went much further than Josephus, who similarly asked whether God had been motivated by a 'craving for human blood' (*AJ* 1.233). While Josephus, however, insisted that Abraham's planned sacrifice must be appreciated in its uniqueness, Philo's colleagues stressed its similarity to pagan practices:

At any rate [they say] that the most esteemed of the Greeks, not only commoners, but even kings, giving little thought about their offspring, put them to death and saved armed forces of great size and number, when they were arrayed as allies, but destroyed them by a mere shout when they were in the camp of the enemies.

[They moreover say] that barbarian nations, on the other hand, have for long admitted child murder as a holy and god-pleasing practice, the abomination of which the most holy Moses recorded (ὧν μεμνῆσθαι τοῦ ἄγους καὶ τὸν ἱερώτατον Μωυσῆν). Charging them with defilement (μιάσματος), he says that 'they burn their sons and daughters for their gods' [Deut. 12:31]. (*Abr.* 179–81)

---

[26] LXX Gen. 22:2–3, 13; LXX Lev. 5:10. Note that Philo reintroduces the sacrificial terminology of the LXX, speaking of Abraham as a priest who acted according 'to the law of burnt offering' (νόμῳ τῶν ὁλοκαυτωμάτων, Abr. 198); cf. LXX Exod. 10:25.

[27] LXX Gen. 22:12, 16. The expression 'your beloved son whom you have loved' in LXX Gen. 22:2, 16 (τὸν ἀγαπητόν ὃν ἠγάπησας) translates the Hebrew expression את יחידך אשר אהבת, thus leaving it open whether Isaac is literally Abraham's only son or the only one of the two sons who is loved by Abraham. Philo dissolves the ambiguity by writing ἀγαπητὸς καὶ μόνος (*Abr.* 168). The basis for his interpretation is the assumption of matrilineal law, according to which the status of the child is dependent also on his mother's status. On this view, Ishmael's mother, an Egyptian servant, prevented her son from inheriting from Abraham, leaving Isaac as the only legitimate heir; on Philo's notion of matrilineality, see Niehoff 2001, pp. 17–33.

[28] LXX Ezod. 20.25–31 προστάγματα οὐ καλά and μιανῶ translating respectively חוקים לא טובים and אטמא; see also Levenson 1993, pp. 5–8, 43–4.

In this passage Philo's colleagues suggest a continuum from Abraham's Binding of Isaac to Greek as well as barbarian practices of child sacrifice. They distinguish between Greeks and barbarians, obviously preferring the former, because they turned to child sacrifice only in cases of national emergency rather than as a regular form of worship. Greek practices are not illustrated by reference to specific historical incidents. Philo's colleagues instead refer to famous literary motifs.[29] Aeschylus' and Euripides' dramatic treatments of Iphigenia's sacrifice are likely to have been on their minds.[30] This motif was so well known in Alexandria that Clement mentioned it in his list of child sacrifices, which epitomized in his view the cruelty of paganism (*Protr.* 3). Barbarian forms of child sacrifice, on the other hand, must have been associated by Philo's colleagues with Abraham's binding of Isaac. They were likely to note the fact that his willingness to sacrifice his son did not respond to any emergency situation but was instead presented as a proper form of devotion to God.

Philo's colleagues distinguish all of these early forms of child sacrifice – whether biblical, Greek or barbarian – from Moses' subsequent legislation. They point to a fundamental gap between archaic practices and Moses' emphatic rejection of them in the context of the cult of Molech. Philo's colleagues identify to such an extent with the discontinuation of child sacrifice that they even avoid the more lenient terminology of LXX Deut. 12:31. They replace the word βδέλυγμα, with its general ritual connotation, with the term μίασμα, which implies defilement by murder and was also used by Ezekiel.[31] Philo's colleagues thus emerge as scholars who point to a significant development within Judaism. In their view, the religion started with rather more primitive practices and even approved of child sacrifice, while it subsequently reached the highest level of moral excellence in the legislation of Deut. 12:31. In this scenario Abraham did not yet live up to the later standards of religiosity established by Moses. Philo's colleagues admitted that this patriarch still relied on notions which had been shared by the barbarians and to some extent also by the Greeks but were entirely unacceptable in Judaism from Moses onwards until their own time.

Moses was held in such high regard by Philo's colleagues that he, in the present form of the fragment, is called 'most holy' (*Abr.* 181). This

---

[29] The different occasions for child sacrifice are documented in Greek literature, on which see Weiler 2007; the historical reality of child sacrifice in ancient Greece has been questioned by a number of scholars who regard it merely as a literary motif, see esp. Hughes 1991.

[30] See also Feldman 2002, p. 68; Kyriakou 2006, pp. 13–15.

[31] For the use of βδέλυγμα, see esp. LXX Gen. 43:32, which refers to defilement by violating kosher food regulations.

epithet may seem too pious to derive from their own mouths and one may instead wonder whether it came from Philo, who often refers thus to Moses.[32] Whether or not the epithet belongs to the original fragment or is the result of Philo's editing, it is clear that Moses was highly esteemed by Philo's colleagues. In their view he set the proper standards of religiosity and condemned child sacrifice in no uncertain terms. It was he who broke with primitive or barbarian forms of worship. Philo's colleagues looked proudly on Moses, the legislator of the Jews, who had introduced proper laws long before Greeks and barbarians abandoned their archaic ways.

HISTORICAL PERSPECTIVES AMONG HOMERIC SCHOLARS

The historical approach of Philo's colleagues to the Binding of Isaac must be appreciated in the wider context of Homeric scholarship. While Philo wished to portray them as isolated simpletons, they were in reality scholars who shared significant methodological assumptions with their Homeric colleagues. I shall argue that they were particularly close to the Aristotelian tradition practised in Alexandria.

Although Aristotle is mainly known for his literary appreciation of the epics, it must be stressed that he had introduced significant historical perspectives in this context. He did so by suggesting that some problems can be solved by considering that a particular Homeric line or story reflects neither scientific truth nor the poet's ideals, but instead the historical reality of his time. In the twenty-fifth chapter of his *Poetics* Aristotle programmatically states that some Homeric images contradict contemporary values and must be recognized as reflecting a situation as 'it was thus at the time' (οὕτως εἶχεν).[33] In his *Aporemata Homerica* Aristotle moreover deals with specific examples. A famous crux which he investigates is Achilles' cruelty when dragging Hector's corpse at the end of the Trojan War:

Why did Achilles drag Hector around Patroclus' tomb [*Il.* 24.15], thus treating the dead contrary to custom (παρὰ τὰ νενομισμένα)? . . .
Aristotle said that [this problem] can be solved by tracing [Achilles' action] to the existing customs, because they were such at the time (ὅτι τοιαῦτα ἦν), since even now in Thessaly they drag [the corpse] around the tomb. (Arist. *Apor. Hom.* fr. 166, ed. Rose 1886 = Porph. *Quaest. Il.* 24.15, ed. Schrader 1880)

---

[32] Philo calls Moses 'most holy' sixteen times, often using the phrase κατὰ τὸν ἱερώτατον Μωυσέα; see esp. *Gig.* 67, *Agr.* 85, *Plant.* 86, *Migr.* 131, *Mut.* 30 and 189.

[33] Arist. *Poet.* 1461a2; see also Hintenlang 1961, pp. 17–22, who stresses Aristotle's generally more historical orientation in comparison to Plato; Bywater 1909, p. 332.

Aristotle frankly admitted that Achilles' behaviour contradicted accepted funerary customs, but he did not on this account dismiss this scene as his teacher had done. Plato wished to protect his students from the image of the foremost Greek hero dragging the corpse of his dead Trojan opponent, fearing that this story would encourage them similarly to give vent to their feelings of revenge. In Plato's view, it was unacceptable to depict Achilles as driven by an irrational impulse. Such a story could only cause damage to the minds of young intellectuals destined to lead the state (*Resp.* 391b–c). Therefore it was declared to be untrue and inappropriate for use in the classroom.

Aristotle, by contrast, creates a hermeneutic space which allowed him to appreciate the gap between archaic and contemporary values without altogether dismissing Homer's text. His solution introduces a new historical dimension and suggests that Achilles' behaviour conformed to primitive customs. On this view, Achilles was not primarily driven by a personal impulse, being overwhelmed by his sorrow over Patroclus' death (*Il.* 24.6–9), but instead followed the norms of ancient times. Such norms can be recovered, Aristotle argues, by studying contemporary barbarians who have preserved them, while they were discontinued among the more civilized Greeks.[34] The Alexandrian poet Callimachus, who accepted Aristotle's solution, adds an interesting explanation: 'it was an ancestral custom of the Thessalians to drag the murderer of their nearest around the tomb of the murdered'.[35] Callimachus can thus confirm that Achilles acted 'as a Thessalian' (ὡς Θετταλός).

A similar, yet morally less disturbing example is discussed by Aristotle in the context of the spears described in *Il.* 10.152–3:

But of other statements in poetry one may perhaps say not that they are better than the truth, but that it was thus at the time (ἀλλ' οὕτως εἶχεν), such as the description of the arms: 'their spears were [driven into the ground] upright on their butt-end' [*Il.* 10.152–3].

For thus they used to do at that time, as the Illyrians still do now (οὕτω γὰρ τότ' ἐνόμιζον ὥσπερ καὶ νῦν Ἰλλυριοί). (Arist. *Poet.* 1461a1–4, ed. Kassel 1966)

---

[34] The source of his knowledge of barbarian customs is not indicated, Aristotle apparently relying on some written records and perhaps also on general knowledge. The extant fragments of his ethnographic work are of a similarly general character. According to Varro, *De Ling. Lat.* 7.70, he wrote a treatise entitled νόμιμα βαρβαρικά, the fragments of which are preserved in Rose 1886, fr. 604–10. Ancient writers quoting Aristotle's fragments use the term ἱστορέω, but also φησίν as well as 'tradit' (Plut. *Ira* 11, *Quaest. Rom.* 6; Dion. Hal. *Ant. Rom.* 1.72; Antigonus, *Hist. mirab.* 16; Plin. *HN* 8.229).

[35] Porph. *Quaest. Il.* 24.15 (ed. Schrader 1880, p. 268); Callimachus' familiarity with Aristotle's solution has already been noted by Richardson 1994, p. 15.

Porphyry provides an insightful explanation of the difficulty, which Aristotle confronted in the fragment quoted above:

The upright position of the spears on their butt-end seems to be problematic (φαύλη), for even the falling down of one of them provokes widespread noise at night. (Arist. *Apor. Hom.* fr. 166, ed. Rose 1886)

Aristotle solves the problem of the spears by interpreting the text in its historical context. He suggests a significant gap between Homer's world and his own, implying that the odd position of the spears reflects primitive customs, which are no longer observed in Classical Greece. This historical reading of the Homeric lines is corroborated by reference to contemporary customs among barbarians who are found to preserve the practices from the time of Homer. The Illyrians, mentioned in this context, were known as a people in the neighbourhood of Macedonia and the Adriatic coast who had come into contact with Greek customs but retained many of their own.[36] Aristotle argues that Homer's description of the weapons is not true in a contemporary Greek context but faithfully reflects primitive Greek as well as present-day barbarian practices. According to Porphyry, he stresses in this context that:

Homer always presents such things as they were at the time (τοιαῦτα ἀεὶ ποιεῖ Ὅμηρος οἷα ἦν τότε). Ancient customs were thus (ἦν δὲ τοιαῦτα τὰ παλαιά), just as they are now among the barbarians. (Arist. *Apor. Hom.*, fr. 160, ed. Rose 1886 = Porph. *Quaest. Il.* 10.153, ed. Schrader 1880)

Now that we have appreciated Aristotle's historical considerations in his study of Homer's epics, it must be emphasized that his attitude was remarkably open and tolerant vis-à-vis other cultures. While defending the Greek foundational text in its historical context and thus rendering even problematic scenes readable in Classical Athens, Aristotle also associated it with barbarian cultures. He did not shrink from the conclusion that the barbarians of his own time were in some respects closer to Homer than he and his fellow Greeks.

How influential was Aristotle's approach among Alexandrian scholars? On the whole, Hellenistic and especially Byzantine scholars tended to be

---

[36] In *Hist. an.* 499b, 606b Aristotle discusses the peculiarities of climate, which produce in each country a particular kind and size of animal. In Illyria, he says, there exists an un-cloven kind of swine and a small ass. In this context Aristotle refers to Illyrians as a non-Greek nation with its own climate and cultural conditions. Herodotus and Thucydides expected their readers to know of the Illyrians (Hdt. 1.196, 9.43.2; Thuc. 1.24.1). They were conceived to have spoken a language which was no dialect of Greek, the verb *illurizein* implying this (Steph. Byz. *s.v. Illuria*). For further details, see Crossland 1982, pp. 839–40.

more nationalistic, conceiving of the Trojans as barbarians and praising Homer as a 'philhellenic' poet who did not depict the Greeks in any negative way.[37] Certain historical perspectives are nevertheless visible. We have already seen that Callimachus accepted Aristotle's solution to the problem of Achilles' cruelty.

Aristarchus, on the other hand, chose a somewhat different approach. He athetized the motif of Achilles' deep sorrow over the death of his best friend, Patroclus, and thus omitted the emotional impetus of his revenge. At the same time, however, Aristarchus admits that the torture of Hector's corpse was revenge (ἐπ' ἐδικίᾳ) and as such 'pardonable' (συγγνωστός). He also explains that 'to start an injustice is more cruel [than taking revenge]', implying that Hector had behaved worse than Achilles.[38] The foremost Alexandrian scholar thus emerges as a defender of Achilles on internal textual grounds rather than on the basis of an overall historical perspective. He admits the cruelty of the hero's behaviour (ἡ αἰκία), but he no longer identifies it as a remnant of alien or even barbaric customs. Indeed, Aristarchus shared to some extent the 'philhellenic' interpretation of Homer and generally assumed that Achilles was depicted by the poet as a respectable and noble hero. Once he even athetized two lines 'because the words are contrary to Achilles' dignity'.[39] Moreover, Aristarchus clearly distinguished between Greeks and barbarians, identifying the latter with the Trojans, even though he did not inveigh as strongly against them as became common among Byzantine scholars.[40]

Aristarchus nevertheless also applied historical considerations in contexts which were in his view ethically and nationally less sensitive. Regarding the famous question whether the archaic heroes were versed in reading and writing, he insists that they were analphabetic:

One gets the impression of the use of letters of words. But it is not necessary to accept this, but the writing [mentioned here] is carving. It is possible that he engraved images, through which the father-in-law of Proetus would necessarily know. (Schol. *Il.* 6.169A)

---

[37] Schmidt 2002 and references there.   [38] Schol. *Il.* 24.6–9A, 17.126; see also Schmidt 2002, p. 173.

[39] ὅτι παρὰ τὴν ἀξίαν Ἀχιλλέως οἱ λόγοι (Schol. *Il.* 22.393–4A); see also Schol. *Il.* 2.673–5A, 20.125–8A, discussed by Schenkeveld 1970, pp. 165–6; see also van der Valk 1963–4, vol. II, pp. 397–401.

[40] Schol. *Il.* 2.130–3. The philhellenic tendency of the Byzantine scholiasts in the bT traditions can be seen in the famous statement in Schol. *Il.* 16.814–15, see also Schol. *Il.* 13.807, 17.220–32; Schmidt 2002, p. 173. As an example of the increasingly philhellenic tendencies of the scholars, consider Schol. *Il.* 5.70A, 1.454A, where Aristarchus identifies the motif of Achilles' joy over the defeat of the Greeks as οὐκ ὀρθῶς. This is later explained thus: 'it is improbable that Achilles would rejoice over the defeat of the Greeks, while Chryseis is a barbarian and hater of the Greeks [and would thus rejoice over their defeat]' (Schol. *Il.* 1.454T).

The cultural significance of Aristarchus' position emerges by comparison with subsequent interpreters, who emphatically state that 'it is impossible that those who invented all the arts did not know the letters' (Schol. *Il.* 6.168T). In this case, Aristarchus, like Aristotle, does not expect all epic lines to be exemplary for contemporary readers but instead views them in their proper historical context as a more primitive layer of the tradition. Aristarchus similarly acknowledges that 'the ancients (οἱ παλαιοί) used barter exchange and not coins' and agrees with the Alexandrian scientist Eratosthenes that Homer relied on outdated geographical notions.[41]

In the Alexandrian context it is furthermore interesting that Neoteles, the author of a treatise on archaic archery quoted by Aristarchus, adopted an Aristotelian approach when arguing that a particular Homeric line reflects the customs of 'Scythian archery'.[42] Given these echoes of Aristotle's historical approach in Alexandrian scholarship, we now have to investigate how Philo's colleagues fit into the overall picture. To what extent was their interpretation of the Binding of Isaac typical of their time and environment? Did they go further than others in their historical inquiries into their foundational text?

PHILO'S COLLEAGUES IN THE CONTEXT OF HOMERIC SCHOLARSHIP

Philo's colleagues who interpreted the Binding of Isaac clearly belong to the milieu of Alexandrian scholarship. Their historical approach to the foundational text is similar to that of Aristarchus, Callimachus and Neoteles. It is even closer than theirs to the Aristotelian tradition. Like Aristotle himself, Philo's colleagues distinguish a primitive layer of their tradition and associate it with barbarian practices. They also accept the literal sense of the problematic scene without dismissing or athetizing it or offering apologetic explanations. The level of their critical awareness as well as their willingness to compare Scripture with the literature of other nations allows us to situate them at the extreme end of the Aristotelian tradition in Alexandria. Although their approach was similar to that of Aristarchus, they were more consistent in their historical analysis. Philo's colleagues thus emerge not just as mere followers of the fashion of their

---

[41] Schol. *Il.* 7.473A; Schol. *Il.* 3.184A ('according to Homer, Phrygia is distinct from Troy, while more recent writers merge them') and Schol. *Il.* 3.306–10A.

[42] Schol. *Il.* 8.325; Porphyry fully embraced Neoteles' interpretation, stressing that Teucer 'initially drew the cord upon his shoulder as the Scythians' (Porph. 1.123, quoted by Erbse 1969–9, vol. II, p. 359); regarding Aristarchus' familiarity with Neoteles, see Schol. *Il.* 8.325.

time, but as true pioneers, who ventured further into academic inquiry than many of their contemporary Alexandrians.

The Aristotelian orientation of Philo's colleagues is visible in their reference to contemporary customs. Whereas Aristotle had referred to the Thessalians and the Illyrians as examples of nations who still implemented archaic practices, Philo's colleagues point to a similarity between Abraham's binding of Isaac and contemporary Indian customs. Lacking evidence of child sacrifice in their own time, they invoke the Indian gymnosophists, who had caught the attention of many Alexandrians in the wake of Alexander's conquests.[43] As Philo puts it:

[they furthermore say] that the gymnosophists among the Indians, on the other hand, until now (ἄχρι νῦν), whenever the great and incurable disease of old age begins to take hold of them, before they are firmly held sway, heap up a funeral pyre and burn themselves on it, even though they are perhaps able to hold out for many years. And the womenfolk, when their husbands have died before them, hasten joyfully to the same pyre, taking upon themselves to be burnt alive together with the bodies of those. (*Abr.* 182)[44]

Relying on a typically Aristotelian argument from ethnography, Philo's colleagues recall the famous Indian custom of self-sacrifice, which Josephus also uses later on in his description of Eleazar's speech to the martyrs on Massada (*BJ* 7.351–7). The Indians occupied a similarly ambiguous position to the Illyrians, having come under the influence of Greek culture but not altogether submitting to it. According to Aristotelian standards, they were a most appropriate choice to demonstrate the continuation of primitive customs which are recorded in the biblical story of the Binding of Isaac but had been discontinued by Moses.

Philo's colleagues moreover stress in a distinctly Aristotelian manner that Abraham had acted out of habit:

What is the benefit (τί προσῆκεν) of praising him [Abraham] as if he was the undertaker of a new action (ὡς ἐγχειρητὴν κεκαινουργημένης πράξεως), which in fact commoners and kings as well as whole nations have practised at certain times? (*Abr.* 183)

---

[43] The famous story of Alexander's encounter with the Indian gymnosophists is preserved also by Philo (*Prob.* 93–5), who chose the version reflecting more critically on Alexander, thus following the account of Aristobulus, one of Alexander's court historians, rather than that of Onesicritus; for details, see Niehoff 2001, pp. 152–6. For more general background information, see Wilcken 1923, pp. 174–7; Pearson 1983, pp. 86–7, 97–9, 150–87; Stoneman 1997, p. 66.

[44] The following line 'undoubtedly, one should admire them for their courage, since they hold death in contempt, out of great superiority, and rush to it as if it was immortality, running breathlessly' (*Abr.* 183) most probably derives from Philo's pen. The enthusiastic approval of (self-)sacrifice as well as the nominative case of the subject, rather than accusative + infinitive, indicate this.

Philo's colleagues react here to a more positive interpretation of Abraham and reject the idea of his original contribution. They instead argue for the common nature of Abraham's willingness to sacrifice his son. Was this argument meant as a mere calumny, as Philo had implied, or did it serve other purposes? Unfortunately, the fragment ends here and we lack further direct evidence of the views of Philo's colleagues. Philo's response to their interpretation, however, provides some important clues. It is striking how concerned he is to show that none of the Greek or barbarian customs apply to Abraham. The patriarch, he insists, was under no public pressure to perform a sacrifice in order to save his people (*Abr.* 190). More importantly, he did not follow any previous custom:

In Babylonia and Mesopotamia as well as among the people of the Chaldeans, where he [Abraham] was raised and spent most of his life, there certainly was no received custom of child sacrifice (ἔθος μὲν οὖν τὸ ἐπὶ παιδοκτονία... οὐ παραδέχεται), so as to suggest that through the continuity of the practice (τῇ συνεχείᾳ τῶν δρωμένων) his realization of the dreadful may have become more feeble. (*Abr.* 188)[45]

As if this statement was not yet enough, Philo subsequently repeats that:

there was no custom of human sacrifice in that country, as perhaps there is in some [others] – custom, which through its continuity (τῇ συνεχείᾳ) regularly weakens the perception of the terrible. (*Abr.* 193)[46]

Philo's protest in these two passages suggests that his colleagues had interpreted Abraham precisely as conforming to the prevailing custom. Philo makes considerable efforts to uproot this image, arguing that the practice of child sacrifice was not known in any of the places where Abraham had dwelt. Moreover, a significant connection is drawn between the regularity of a custom and the mental awareness it evokes in the practitioner. Philo admits that if such a custom of child sacrifice had existed, it would have weakened Abraham's 'perception of the terrible'. Can this response, too, tell us something about the position of Philo's colleagues? Did they suggest that Abraham's willingness to sacrifice his son must be seen more leniently, as it was prompted by custom rather than personal cruelty? If they had indeed made this point, they offered an interpretation highly congenial to Aristotle's solution to the problem of Achilles' cruelty.

[45] I accept Mangey's conjecture for the last part of the sentence, reading κεχρῆσθαι instead of κεκρατῆσθαι, the former being supported by the Armenian translation (Cohn and Wendland 1896–1915, vol. IV, p. 42). I have adopted Colson's felicitous translation (Colson and Whitaker 1929–62, vol. VI, p. 93).
[46] οὐκ ὄντος ἔθους ἐν τῇ χώρᾳ καθάπερ ἴσως παρ' ἐνίοις ἐστὶν ἀνθρωποθυτεῖν.

In conclusion, I would like to stress the importance of the fragment on the Binding of Isaac, which testifies to a rigorous historical approach among some Alexandrian Bible scholars. In contrast to Philo himself, who preferred the notion of a close correlation between Scripture and unchanging Nature, his colleagues adopted Aristotelian methods and contextualized the figure of Abraham. In their view, Mosaic Law was the result of a prolonged development rather than the expression of an unchanging religion. Their critical awareness and cultural tolerance are remarkable in the context of contemporary Alexandria, where Aristotle's approach was not applied with such consistency. Furthermore, the historicism of Philo's colleagues overshadows the methods of Josephus, who reverted to more monolithic conceptions of Scripture. In the introduction to his *Jewish Antiquities* he stressed the message of the Jewish Scriptures, namely that 'men who conform to the will of God and do not venture to transgress laws that have been excellently laid down, prosper in all things' (*AJ* 1.14).

The pioneering work of Philo's colleagues must be appreciated in light of the fact that historical perspectives on Judaism played a significant role in subsequent Jewish–Christian polemics. The figure of Abraham was crucial in this context. Justin Martyr in the mid second century CE developed some of Paul's ideas on Abraham's faith and circumcision into an overall historical interpretation of Judaism.[47] He stressed that Abraham's faith had preceded his circumcision and thus marked in his view the original stage of the religion. According to Justin, it was highly significant that none of the biblical heroes before Abraham had been circumcised. If God had indeed considered this ritual 'necessary' (ἀναγκαία), He 'would not have created Adam with a foreskin' (*Dialogue* 19.3). Abraham's circumcision must consequently be interpreted as a new stage, when a specific nation emerged and separated from other nations. Justin regarded this development in highly negative terms, identifying it as a move against God's will. In his view, circumcision was a sign of Divine punishment, which allocated suffering to the Jews alone (*Dial.* 15.2). The model of historical progress which we have seen in the work of Philo's colleagues was thus replaced by the notion of decline into national parochialism. Justin's own Christian identity was naturally inscribed into the early stage of Jewish history, namely before Abraham's circumcision and 'deviation' from the true faith.

Julian the Apostate, on the other hand, who was eager to enrol Jews and Judaism in his fight against Christianity, insisted on the unchanging role

---

[47] On Paul's views of Abraham there is, of course, an almost infinite literature; see esp. Watson 2007; Barclay 1998; Siker 1991, pp. 28–76, 87–102, 163–84.

of Abraham. He presented a very positive image of the patriarch as someone who had been circumcised and regularly offered sacrifices, resembling
traditional Greeks in many important respects.[48] Julian made considerable
efforts to insist on the unchanging relevance of these ancient Jewish customs. Even the dramatic historical changes following the destruction of
the Second Temple were down-played. Julian suggested that contemporary
Jews still behaved like Abraham and offered sacrifices in their private homes
(*Against the Galileans* 306A).

It is interesting too that in modernity Leopold Zunz responded to biased
Christian reconstructions of biblical history with a new concept of Jewish
spirituality. He suggested that the original prophetic spirit of Judaism,
which many contemporary Christians claimed to have preserved in the
New Testament in their own tradition, was revived in rabbinic literature.[49]
Zunz thus introduced a kind of Hegelian dynamics, where different types
of religiosity encounter each other and resurface in a new synthesis at a later
stage in history. It is, however, Abraham Geiger, with his systematic analysis
of the evolvement of Jewish history and *Halacha*, who most resembles
Philo's colleagues in ancient Alexandria. He, too, believed in real historical
progress and took pride in the various reforms of Judaism, which in his
view seriously took into account social needs and true religiosity.

---

[48] Jul. *Against the Galileans* 351A–356E, 305B–306B.   [49] For details, see Niehoff 1998b.

CHAPTER 7

Traces of text criticism among Alexandrian Jews

In this last chapter on Philo's anonymous colleagues we shall focus on diverse snippets of evidence rather than on one extended fragment. Throughout his different writings Philo refers to interpretations of Scripture which touch upon issues of text-critical work. The question thus arises whether some of the Alexandrian Bible exegetes not only were familiar with text-critical methods of Homeric scholarship but also applied them to the Jewish Scriptures. If this is indeed the case, as I shall argue, some Alexandrian Jews took the last step of integrating their foundational text into the contemporary, scholarly discourse on foundational literature.

There can be no doubt about the actual familiarity of some Alexandrian Jews with text-critical methods. Aristobulus in the second century BCE had already employed them with regard to a pagan text. Quoting a passage from Aratos, he said 'we have marked [this], removing the divine names Δίς and Ζεύς throughout the verses'.[1] Aristobulus has thus identified an interpolation in a pagan text, which, he was convinced, originally referred to the God of the Jews. He marked the problematic words (σεσημάγκαμεν) and removed (περιαιροῦντες) the names of the pagan deities, writing *theos* in their place.

Both the method of text emendation and the specific Greek terms employed by Aristobulus belong to the world of Homeric scholarship in Alexandria. Beginning with Zenodotus, the first librarian, and reaching a climax with Aristarchus in the mid second century BCE, Alexandrian scholars regularly identified corruptions in the epic text and marked them in the margins of their manuscript. Alternative readings, which were thought to reflect the original text, were also suggested. The noun σημεῖον is the standard term for such critical signs, the obelus marking a spurious line which was no longer considered to be an authentic part of the epic. The A

---

[1] Aristob. *ap.* Euseb. *Praep. evang.* 13.12 (fr. 4, ed. Holladay 1983–96, vol. III, p. 172); for details, see Chapters 2 and 4.

112

scholia to the *Iliad* contain many references to the critical signs, the σημεῖα, used by Aristarchus.[2] Seleucus wrote at least three books entitled *Concerning Aristarchus' Critical Signs* (σημείων).[3] Similarly, the notion of deletion or ἀφαίρεσις echoes Homeric scholarship. Aristarchus, for example, criticized a deletion made by his predecessor Zenodotus (Schol. *Il.* 1.400).

We can thus be sure that a central method of text criticism which was developed by Homeric scholars in Alexandria was known to such a learned exegete as Aristobulus. In the mid second century, when both Homeric scholarship reached a climax and Jewish literature flourished in the city, contacts between the two textual communities must have existed. At the same time, however, the extant fragments of Aristobulus' work suggest that he did not yet apply text-critical methods to the Jewish Scriptures, instead insisting on their general plausibility and textual integrity. The central question is whether other Jewish exegetes continued in the footsteps of Aristobulus. If so, did they, too, limit their text-critical studies to pagan texts? I shall argue, on the contrary, that there is evidence of Jewish Bible scholars submitting also their own canonical text to rigorous academic inquiry.

We have already seen in a previous chapter that the *Letter of Aristeas* provides some preliminary clues. The author reacted to fellow Jews who engaged in a marking of the biblical text as well as in what he considered 'text manipulation' (διασκευή).[4] Aristeas' perspective, I suggested, was a conservative reaction to the practice of text-critical studies among at least some Alexandrian Jews. This phenomenon must have been prominent enough to provoke such a fervent response on the part of Aristeas.

In this chapter I hope to show that some of Philo's colleagues continued this early tradition of biblical scholarship. Whereas Aristeas provided only a negative mirror image of such inquiries, Philo offers much more detailed insights. He enables us to study specific examples and even to reconstruct the overall approach of some Jewish Bible scholars in Alexandria.

FLAWS IN SCRIPTURE

Given the fact that Alexandrian Jews read only the Greek translation of the Jewish Scriptures and no longer had access to the original Hebrew text, it is not surprising that they noted flaws in the Greek style, for which they

---

[2] Lehrs 1882, p. 2, suggests that the expression refers to Aristonicus' report of a work by Aristarchus entitled περὶ σημείων.
[3] Quoted by M. L. West 2001, p. 48.   [4] *Letter*, 310–11, 30; for details, see Chapter 2 above.

held Moses responsible.⁵ Central issues which were discussed pertain to diction and redundant expressions. Many of these problems could easily have been solved by reference to the Hebrew original. None of the debating parties, however, even those who wished to preserve the biblical text, were apparently able to draw on this resource.

In his discussion of the Flood Philo makes a highly revealing statement, which gives us a first impression of the kind of text-critical environment in which he lived. He expected that his colleagues would offer the following scholarly treatment of a textual flaw in Scripture:

ἦν δὲ, φησί, κατεφθαρμένη ὅτι κατέφθειρε πᾶσα σὰρξ τὴν ὁδὸν αὐτοῦ ἐπὶ τῆς γῆς [Gen. 6:12]. Δόξει μέν τισιν ἡ λέξις ἡμαρτῆσθαι καὶ τὸ ἀκόλουθον τοῦ λόγου καὶ τὸ ἄπταιστον οὕτως ἔχειν: ὅτι κατέφθειε πᾶσα σὰρξ τὴν ὁδὸν αὐτῆς. ἀνοίκειον γάρ ἐστι θηλυκῷ ὀνόματι, τῇ σαρκί ἀρρενικὴν ἐπιφέρεσθαι πτῶσιν, τὴν αὐτοῦ. (*Deus* 140–1)

'[The earth]', [Moses] says, 'was destroyed, because all flesh destroyed "his" way upon the earth' [LXX Gen. 6:12]. The diction, however, will seem to some to be flawed, the correct sequence of the expression being the following: 'because all flesh destroyed "its" way'. For it is unsuitable to add a masculine inflection [of the personal pronoun], namely αὐτοῦ, to the feminine noun σάρξ.

Philo was expecting that some Bible exegetes in Alexandria would identify in the biblical verse a 'flaw with respect to diction'.⁶ Such colleagues assumed that the masculine personal pronoun αὐτοῦ was dependent on the immediately preceding σάρξ and thus defied the rules of grammar. In the Hebrew text, on the other hand, the masculine suffix of דרכו naturally follows the masculine noun בשר. The Greek translator must have been aware of the grammatical gender of σάρξ and probably interpreted the pronoun as a reference to God, who is mentioned at the beginning of the verse. It is thus suggested that all flesh destroyed not its own way, but God's.⁷ This is how Philo understood the LXX expression (*Deus* 142). Some of Philo's colleagues, however, unaware of the changes introduced by the Greek translator, were likely to emend the text. Philo says that they could be expected to suggest a correction of the personal pronoun, adapting its gender to the feminine noun σάρξ.

Although Philo does not say that he has actually seen such an emendation, he naturally assumes the possibility of its occurrence and thus indicates the text-critical environment of first-century Alexandria. The likelihood that such an emendation had been made is increased by the

---

⁵ For details on the question whether Alexandrian Jews knew Hebrew, see Chapter 1 as well as passing references throughout the other chapters.
⁶ ἡμαρτῆσθαι τὰ περὶ τὴν λέξιν (*Deus* 142).   ⁷ See also Harl 1986, p. 130; Wevers 1993, p. 82.

fact that John Chrysostomus was subsequently familiar with a version of the LXX where the pronoun of σάρξ appears in its adjusted feminine form.[8] Philo's formulations moreover suggest that such text-critical work was rooted in the Aristotelian tradition of Homeric scholarship. Aristotle had addressed literary flaws in the epics as ἁμαρτία and had devoted a special section of the twenty-fifth chapter of his *Poetics* to problems of diction.[9] Following him, Aristarchus continued to pay attention to problems of diction in the mid second century BCE.[10] The gender of nouns and their congruence with adjectival forms was a subject which he and Didymus carefully studied.[11]

Another issue which provoked lively scholarly discussions among Alexandrian Bible exegetes was the redundancy of expressions. While it is good Hebrew style to add emphasis by using a double expression, the conventions of the Greek language do not admit such a feature. The LXX nevertheless imitated the characteristics of the original Hebrew style and regularly rendered the Hebrew double expressions by precise Greek equivalents. The translators thus opted for a literal style, oriented towards the source rather than the receptor language, and ignored the aesthetic tastes of their anticipated readership.[12] Unaware of the underlying Hebrew text, scholarly readers of the LXX indeed struggled to understand Moses' apparently flawed and highly irritating style.

The verdict of some of Philo's colleagues often seems to have been rather harsh. Philo once reports the following reaction to a redundancy in Gen. 15:5:

The expression 'He led him out outside' [Gen. 15:5][13] points to a teaching regarding character formation. But some, out of crudeness of character, are in the habit of laughing about it (τινες εἰώθασιν ὑπ' ἀμουσίας ἤθους γελᾶν), saying: is someone [ever] led out inside or, contrariwise, led in outside?

Yes indeed, I would say, oh you mockers and very reckless! You have never learnt to trace the ways of the soul, but only of the bodies, the cursory movements of which you have investigated. Therefore it seems to you a paradox (παράδοξον), if someone is led out inside or led in outside. (*Her.* 81–2)[14]

---

[8] See John Chrysostom in Migne, *PG* 14, 280; 53, 226; *Epist. Ephesians* 62, 174.

[9] Arist. *Poet.* 1460b15, 1461a9–b9; Bywater 1909, pp. 333–46; Dupont-Roc and Lallot 1980, pp. 393–9.

[10] Schironi 2009, pp. 300–3; for a more general discussion of style in the scholia, see Nünlist 2009a, pp. 194–224.

[11] See esp. Schol. *Il.* 15.56A, 17.134–6A, 4.46A, 4.164A, 5.210A, 5.648A, 6.96A, 7.413A, 7.429A, 9.584A, 9.686A, 11.196A, 12.115A, 12.287A, 13.773A, 19.332Ab.

[12] See also Brock 1979.

[13] ἐξήγαγεν αὐτὸν ἔξω, reflecting the Hebrew expression ויוצא אתו החוצה.

[14] See also *All.* 3.241, where Philo discusses possible reactions of his colleagues to the redundant expression ἐξῆλθεν ἔξω in Gen. 39:12.

Philo's comments throw important new light on his colleagues' work. It emerges that they engaged in regular exegetical activity, 'being in the habit' of criticizing certain expressions. Indeed, they identified a redundancy which reflects the underlying Hebrew style of the LXX. They, like Philo, no longer had access to the Hebrew layer of the Bible, instead being puzzled by the highly unidiomatic style of the Greek translation. Philo's strong disapproval of them is at first sight surprising, because on other occasions he himself also points to problems of redundancy. He wonders, for example, why Moses used the expression κακίᾳ κακώσητε (Exod. 22:22):

What does it mean? Is it possible that one is evil-treated by something else than evil? For if evil-treatments are the work only of evil, it is superfluous to write what is a matter of agreement (περιττὸν τὸ ὁμολογούμενον γράφειν) and will be admitted without further words. (*Congr.* 178)[15]

If Philo himself explores problems of redundant expressions, why does he reject so fervently the work of his colleagues, who engage in precisely the same kind of inquiries? The difference between him and them must pertain to their conclusions. Philo works on the assumption that the redundancy is only apparent, not real, and offers allegorical explanations in defence of the LXX style. His colleagues, by contrast, are said to 'laugh' about the biblical expression. Did they follow in the footsteps of Zoilos, who had already in pre-Aristotelian times accused Homer of 'very ridiculous' presentations and on this account dismissed his epics as mediocre literature?[16] Or did Philo's colleagues rather adopt Aristarchus' method, taking 'laughable' features of style as a criterion for text emendation?[17] In other words, did Philo's colleagues deny Moses the epithet of an excellent author or did they assume his poetic excellence, while denying the authenticity of certain expressions? The highly fragmentary nature of our evidence does not allow us to reach a firm conclusion on this matter. It is at least likely, however, that Philo's colleagues suggested an emendation in the style of Aristarchus. In Philo's view, they had in any case gone too far in their critical research.

In another context Philo provides some further insights into the fundamental dispute between literal and allegorical readers of Scripture in

[15] See also *Fuga* 54, *Det.* 15, *Migr.* 48; for further details on Philo's scholarly inquiries, see Chapter 8 below.
[16] λίαν γελοίως πεποίηκει (fr. 8, *FGH* 2.111); see also fr. 7.
[17] See Schol. *Il.* 9.212bA, where Aristarchus justifies an athetesis by reference to 'ridiculous' (γελοῖον) style; see also Schol. *Il.* 7.195–9A, 13.423. The criterion of 'laughable' things was apparently already employed by Zenodotus (Schol. *Il.* 2.231–4).

Alexandria. His report is highly tendentious and shows how deep the difference between him and his colleagues had become:

Why does it say 'Jacob cooked a cooking'? [LXX Gen. 25:29][18]

I know that such things [redundant expressions] provoke laughter and mocking derision in uncultivated men (անէրամշունաց = ἀμούσων) and those lacking propriety of manners (անյարմարից = ἀναρμόστων)[19] as well as those who do not see any form or manifestation of virtue and who attribute their own incorrigibility and stupidity as well as perversity and impudence to the Holy Scriptures, which are verified more than anything ... the uneducated and the unskilled and those lacking study, their eyes of the soul having been blinded and become capricious, themselves dwell only on that which has been narrated in the story [i.e. the literal meaning], and come into contact and make connections only with names and words of the narration, while being unable to penetrate and look into the visions of meaning. (*Q.G.* 4.168, ed. Aucher 1826)

Philo is so annoyed by his colleagues that he does not provide any details about their interpretation.[20] His polemic indicates that he was not willing to make any compromises with Bible exegetes, who had in his opinion gone too far in their criticism of the text. If they did not offer positive solutions to problems of redundant style, Philo fervently dismissed them and their work.

Redundancies were examined by Alexandrian Bible scholars not only with regard to style, but also with a view to the repetition of information and motifs. Philo reports the following discussion:

This is the reason we give for its being said that 'God went down to see the city and the tower' [Gen. 11:5]. Not trifling is the additional expression (οὐ παρέργως δὲ πρόσκειται): 'which the sons of men built' [Gen. 11:5]. For perhaps someone of the insensitive mockers may at once say (ἴσως γὰρ ἄν τις εἴποι τῶν οὐκ εὐαγῶν ἐπιχλευάζων ἅμα): 'the lawgiver is indeed teaching us a novel piece of information, namely that the sons of men, and no others, are building towers and cities! Is not even a most insane person aware of these obvious and conspicuous facts?' (*Conf.* 142)

This passage echoes a lively dispute among Alexandrian Jews: Philo insists that the apparently superfluous explanation in the biblical verse has

[18] ἤψησεν δὲ Ιακωβ ἕψεμα, reflecting the underlying Hebrew expression ויזד יעקב נזיד. I have translated here the LXX, because this clearly was Philo's *Vorlage*, while the Armenian translation renders 'Jacob prepared a preparation' (պատրաստեաց յակոր պատրաստութիւն).

[19] The translations from Armenian to Greek are based on the *Nor Bargirk Armenian–Armenian Dictionary*, which provides typical Greek equivalents in the Ancient Armenian translation literature. Characteristically, the Greek fragment of this section preserves only Philo's answer rather than his report about his colleagues.

[20] This is rather typical of Philo's style in the *Q&A*, which addresses a less scholarly audience than the *Allegorical Commentary*, on both of which see Chapters 8 and 9.

a hidden meaning (*Conf.* 143); others refuse to take recourse to an allegorical solution. Philo expects them to reject the redundant style of the verse. Did their sarcastic remark about the novelty contained in the expression lead them to emend the text? In this case, too, the evidence is too fragmentary to know for certain, but such a prospect seems at least possible. Philo does not hide his aversion to such scholarship, speaking about his colleagues as 'insensitive mockers'. His negative judgement, however, must not prevent us from further investigating their true intentions and the nature of their hermeneutic methods.

CONTRADICTIONS BEWEEN VERSES

Another subject which especially intrigued Philo's colleagues was the question of contradictions between verses. We have seen in a previous chapter that this issue had already been examined in second-century BCE Alexandria. Demetrius and his anonymous colleagues had raised questions concerning contradictions and solved them by recourse to literary devices, such as the assumption of a significant gap created by the reticence or 'silence' of the author. For Philo's colleagues, too, contradictions in Scripture were a central concern. Thus they continued the work of earlier Jewish exegetes, but their answers to the problems no longer seem to have been as committed as the earlier exegetes' on the integrity of Scripture.

Philo is generally aware of colleagues, who 'are accustomed and like to' inquire whether things 'are consistent in the literal and plain sense of the legislation'.[21] He also knows of particular examples that were discussed. Some of his colleagues had identified a problem of contradiction in Gen. 39:1, where Potiphar is said to have a wife even though he is a eunuch (*All.* 3.236). Philo acknowledges that for literal readers there 'consequently appears to be a problem' (ἀκολουθήσει τὸ δοκοῦν ἀπορεῖσθαι). Unfortunately, he does not indicate how they dealt with the difficulty.

More information is provided in the context of Gen. 15:8, which was also considered problematic because it involved a contradiction:

> Therefore he [Abraham] inquires, saying: 'Master, by what token shall
> I know that I inherit it [the land]?' [Gen. 15:8].
> Perhaps someone may say that this contradicts [the image of him as] trusting (ἴσως ἄν τις εἴποι μάχεσθαι τοῦτο τῷ πεπιστευκέναι). For raising a question belongs to the doubter, while not asking is the behaviour of the trustful. (*Her.* 101)

This fragment provides a precious glimpse into the world of Philo's text-critical colleagues. He expects that someone will identify a

---

[21] Ταῦτα μὲν εἰ συνᾴδει τῇ ῥητῇ καὶ προχείρῳ διατάξει σκέψονται οἷς ἔθος καὶ φίλον (*Deus* 133).

contradiction between Gen. 15:8, where Abraham expresses doubt, and Gen. 15:6, where he is said to 'trust in God'. Such an exegete will furthermore examine the problem by using a Classical term of Alexandrian scholarship, namely μάχεσθαι.[22] Aristarchus paid special attention to the inner consistency of the Homeric text and studied contradictions between lines with particular care.[23] Athetesis, the marking of a line as inauthentic, was one accepted solution to such problems. Aristarchus athetizes *Il.* 8.185, for example, because the enumeration of four horses there 'contradicts' (μάχεται) the dual form of the verb in the following line.[24] Vice versa, he also argues for the authenticity of a line if it is possible to overcome the apparent contradiction and show the consistency of the different lines.[25]

This aspect of Aristarchus' work provides a meaningful background for understanding the above interpretation of Philo's colleagues. As far as the fragment shows, some Bible scholars could not recognize a deeper consistency between the respective verses, pointing instead to a glaring contrast between them. Philo unfortunately does not mention the conclusion of his colleagues. Did they adopt Aristarchus' method of athetesis and mark one of the biblical verses as inauthentic? If so, they probably dismissed Gen. 15:6, the shorter of the two conflicting verses, which is not necessary for the rest of the story.

Similar questions arose in the context of the biblical story about Abraham's servant, who is sent to find a wife for Isaac. Philo's reports are highly fragmentary but show nevertheless that the different formulations of the servant's mission were carefully compared with each other. In the course of such an analysis certain Bible exegetes pointed to glaring contradictions. Some of Philo's colleagues identified Gen. 24:7 as problematic, because it conflicts both with Abraham's original instructions as well as with the immediately following verse. The first contradiction is examined thus:

Why does it say: 'the Lord, God of heaven, and God of the earth, will send His angel before your face and you will take a wife for my son Isaac from there'? [LXX Gen. 24:7][26]

... But perhaps someone may say: does the lad still need an angel coming along, whom he bore, having already been permitted by command to complete the marriage to a familiar virgin (Gen. 24:4)? (*Q.G.* 4.90)

---

[22] See glossaries in Dickey 2007, p. 245, and Nünlist 2009a, p. 377.
[23] For details on this aspect of Aristarchus' work, see above, Chapter 3.
[24] Schol. *Il.* 8.185A; see also Schol. *Il.* 20.269–72A, 19.407, where the expression ἐναντίον ἔχων is used.
[25] See, e.g., Schol. *Il.* 9.571A, 9.619A, 11.559A, 13.365A, 22.251A, 22.318A.
[26] I have translated the LXX, Philo's *Vorlage*, rather than the Armenian translation, which omits the expression ἐκεῖθεν or מִשָּׁם.

Philo anticipates that 'someone' will interpret Gen. 24:7 in light of Gen 24:4, where Abraham commands his servant to 'go to the country where I was born, and to my kindred and take a wife for my son Isaac from there'.[27] Such a colleague would undoubtedly have noted that both verses contain the same expression καὶ λήμψῃ γυναῖκα τῷ υἱῷ μου Ισαακ ἐκεῖθεν. The Greek translator has already noted the similarity and added ἐκεῖθεν to Gen. 24:4, thus adding emphasis to the repetition of the expression. Philo moreover expects his colleague to wonder why the motif of the angel was necessary at all. Abraham, he recalls, had already given his servant specific instructions, which did not involve a Divine entourage. The argumentation of Philo's colleague thus rests both on a philological observation and consideration of contents.

Philo points to another problem related to Gen. 24:7, which he expects to be discussed by his colleagues in light of a further contradiction between verses:

What is the meaning [of the verse] 'If the woman does not wish to come with you, you shall be clear of this oath, only do not return my son there'? [Gen. 24:8]

Someone may inquire[28] why, after [Abraham] has assured [his servant] with regard to all things that the woman will come, the angel of God becoming his fellow traveller [Gen. 24:7], he now says, wavering, 'if the woman does not wish to come with you, you will be clear of this oath'. (*Q.G.* 4.91)

While Philo solves this textual problem by recourse to allegory, he expects some of his colleagues to dwell only on the literal text, in which there is a contradiction between the different accounts of the servant's mission. The reader has to decide whether or not, according to Moses, an angel was involved in bringing Isaac's wife and guaranteeing her assent.

This and the previous comments on the biblical story about the mission of Abraham's servant are highly academic and must be appreciated in the context of Homeric scholarship in Alexandria. Aristarchus had studied strikingly similar contradictions in the epic text. He investigated, for example, who prompted the horse Xantes to speak in a human voice. In *Il.* 19.407 Hera is presented as initiating its speech, while *Il.* 19.404 suggests that the horse was already speaking before the goddess appeared. Moreover,

---

[27] Note that the Greek translator explains the apparently redundant Hebrew expression ארצי ומולדתי as referring respectively to the motherland and the kindred.

[28] I have rendered the two verbs of the Armenian translation (վարանէցի եւ տարակուսէցի) with one expression, as the Armenian is undoubtedly one of the typical double translations, probably reflecting the different nuances of the Greek verb ἀπορέω. Regarding the phenomenon of double translations, see Terian 1980; regarding the more general background of Armenian translation literature, see Terian 1982.

according to *Il.* 19.418 the human speech of the horse was discontinued by the Erinyes. This verse was understood to imply that they also had a part in initiating the horse's unusual linguistic performance. Not surprisingly, Aristarchus solved the problem by athetizing one of the lines:

> 'the goddess, white-armed Hera, provided him [the horse Xantes] with human speech' [*Il.* 19.407].
> [This line] is athetized as superfluous and containing something contrary (ἀθετεῖ-ται ὡς περιττὸς καὶ ἐναντίον ἔχων). It is in discord with [the line] 'After he had thus spoken, the Erinyes held back his [Xantes'] voice' [*Il.* 19.418] – thus they clearly also granted [him speech] . . . (Schol. *Il.* 19.407A)

The epic line which is marked as spurious caused the contradiction and emerged as superfluous as far as the content is concerned. Employing the method of athetesis, Aristarchus is thus able to render the epic text more consistent. His text-critical work was highly influential among Alexandrian scholars and is likely to have had an impact also on Philo's colleagues, who shared his critical approach and were like-minded textual scholars. They, too, combined philological observations with an examination of possibly superfluous content. It is thus very likely that they solved the above problem of a contradiction by recourse to athetesis even though Philo does not refer at all to their conclusion. If this was the case, Philo's colleagues are likely to have marked Gen. 24:7 as inauthentic. The reference to the angel in that verse contradicted, as they had pointed out, two other verses. Moreover, in terms of content it emerged as superfluous. If it was dismissed as an addition by a later editor, the biblical story could re-emerge in its supposedly original consistency.

An athetesis of the verse involving the angel would have restored the image of Abraham as a hesitant figure. This motif conforms to his earlier wavering reaction to the Divine promise of an inheritance (Gen. 15:8). As we have seen above, some of Philo's colleagues pointed to a contradiction in that context, too. They stressed the contrast between Gen. 15:8 and Gen. 15:6, which portrays Abraham as trusting in God. If that problem was solved by athetesis, as I suggested, a highly consistent image of Abraham emerged from the skilful hands of Philo's colleagues.

The above investigation has thus far relied on extremely fragmentary evidence and has often had to assume that Philo's reference to an expected interpretation reflects its actual occurrence among Alexandrian Bible exegetes. Such a reconstruction of exegetical approaches which are no longer preserved in independent sources can be justified in view of the fact that Philo generally distinguishes between problems he expects to be raised by someone else and those he himself addresses.[29] Relying on his references to others, even if mentioned only as a potential interpretation, I have been able to draw a general picture of text-critical scholarship among Jewish Bible exegetes in Alexandria. Although the nature of the textual problems which had been examined emerged very clearly from Philo's polemics, the precise conclusion of his colleagues has remained rather more clouded in uncertainty. Philo's extremely negative reaction to his colleagues, however, has led to the conclusion that they must have gone much further in their text-critical work on the Jewish Scriptures than he considered legitimate. On several occasions we have proceeded by comparing the approach of Philo's colleagues to the work of Aristarchus, assuming that if they dealt with precisely the same textual problem, they may also have adopted the solution proposed by the foremost Homeric scholar in Alexandria. In this way I have argued for the plausibility of assuming that some of Philo's colleagues used athetesis in their study of the biblical text.

A CASE OF ATHETESIS IN SCRIPTURE

In this last section we turn to a longer and more explicit fragment, where Philo discusses real colleagues and provides significant evidence of their scholarly approach. This fragment allows us to gain a firmer insight into text-critical scholarship among ancient Bible exegetes and to support the conclusion that athetesis was indeed used by Alexandrian Jews.

The fragment on which we shall focus here reflects a heated dispute between Philo and his colleagues regarding the new names Abraham and Sarah are said to have received from God (Gen. 17:5–15). In the Hebrew text their change of names is rather clear. It involves the addition of the letter 'he', which effects a phonetic change and, in the case of Abraham, is said to reflect the expression המון in God's promise that he will become 'the father of many nations' (אב המון גוים). In the LXX, by contrast, the change of names hardly effects any phonetic change, the additional letters simply repeating already existing ones. Αβραμ thus becomes Αβρααμ, while Σαρα turns into Σαρρα. Also, the explanation of Abraham's change of name is no longer meaningful, as there is no similarity between the additional *alpha* and the expression πατέρα πολλῶν ἐθνῶν. Given the exclusive familiarity of Alexandrian Bible scholars with the Greek text of Scripture, it is not surprising that these verses provoked discussion and controversy.

---

[29] See *Deus* 70, *Fuga* 54, *Post.* 1, *Mut.* 83, *Spec.* 1.32, 1.213; for details on Philo's scholarship, see below, Chapter 8.

Philo's description of an individual scholar whom he particularly disliked has initially to be analysed, because it suggests the real historical existence of such a colleague. Philo provides the following tendentious report:

καὶ πρώην ἤκουσα χλευάζοντος καὶ κατακερτομοῦντος ἀνδρὸς ἀθέου καὶ ἀσεβοῦς, ὃς ἐτόλμα λέγειν· μεγάλαι δὴ καὶ ὑπερβάλλουσαι δωρεαί, ἅς φησι Μωυσῆς τὸν ἡγεμόνα τῶν ὅλων ὀρέγειν· στοιχείου <γὰρ> προσθήκῃ, τοῦ ἑνὸς ἄλφα, στοιχίεου περιττοῦ³⁰ καὶ πάλιν ἑτέρᾳ προσθέσει τοῦ ῥῶ θαυμαστὴν ἡλίκην ἔδοξεν εὐεργεσίαν³¹ παρεσχῆσθαι τὴν Ἀβρὰμ γυναῖκα Σάραν Σάρραν ὠνόμασε δὶς τὸ ῥῶ παραλαβών· καὶ ὅσα ὁμοιότροπα συνείρων ἀπνευστὶ καὶ ἐπισαρκάζων ἅμα διεξῄει· τῆς μὲν οὖν φρενοβλαβείας οὐκ εἰς μακρὰν ἔδωκε τὴν ἁρμόζουσαν δίκην· ἀπὸ γὰρ μικρᾶς καὶ τῆς τυχούσης προφάσεως ἐπ᾽ ἀγχόνην ᾖξεν, ἵν᾽ ὁ μιαρὸς καὶ δυσκάθαρτος μηδὲ καθαρῷ θανάτῳ τελευτήσῃ. (*Mut.* 61–2)

I have just now read [in a treatise by]³² a godless and impious fellow, who was jesting and railing violently, having the effrontery to say:
   'great and surpassing indeed are the gifts which Moses says the Leader of the universe provided. For by the addition of a letter, one single *alpha*, a superfluous letter, and again by the addition of another letter, a *rho*, He seems to have given from Himself an extraordinarily great gift naming Sara the wife of Abraham Sarra by doubling the *rho*.'
And at the same time he continued to go in detail through all similar cases speaking breathlessly and sneering [at them]. Not before long he paid the suitable penalty for his insanity. For a minor and trivial allegation He led him to the hanging buttress so that the stained and impure fellow came not even to a clean death.

Philo provides in this passage precious information about the profile of a colleague who was a Bible exegete and prematurely died under severe circumstances. Some scholars have taken this report to refer to a case of suicide, but Philo clearly speaks about an execution.³³ He mentions an allegation which must have been presented at a trial and seems to have been known to his readers. Moreover, the term ἀγχόνη refers to a hanging buttress and implies the death penalty. In another context Philo identifies

---

³⁰ Cohn and Wendland 1896–1915, ad loc, altogether omit the expression στοιχείῳ περιττεύει. I follow Colson and Whitaker 1929–62 and Arnaldez 1964, who accept the form restored by Markland, namely στοιχείου περιττοῦ.

³¹ Cohn and Wendland 1896–1915, ad loc, suggest a lacuna, assuming that Philo must initially have pointed to the explanation of Abraham's name. This conjecture is possible, but not necessary, as it relies on content rather than the solution of a textual problem.

³² I have translated ἀκούω here as 'reading', parallel to Philo's usage of that verb in *Post.* 1, *Congr.* 180; see also the analysis of many similar cases in Hellenistic prose by Schenkeveld 1992. Consider also the practice of reading out aloud a text, such as the reading of Alexander's treatise described by Philo in *Alex.* 9.

³³ See Shroyer 1936, p. 279; Hay 1991b, p. 92; both relying on *Spec.* 3.161 as a significant background to the above mentioned passage.

such a death by execution as 'unclean', coming to man 'from outside' (*Aet.* 20). It is interesting that Philo does not specify the allegation but suggests instead a direct connection between the nature of his colleagues' hermeneutics and his execution. In his view, the latter is a well-deserved punishment for his impious hermeneutics and reflects Divine providence. Philo's biased report resembles his presentation of Flaccus, the Roman prefect in Alexandria under Tiberius. In this case, too, he provides no information about the trial, which historically took place, but uses it to teach a lesson in Divine providence.[34] Aristeas had used the same strategy to dismiss Theopompus and Theodectus, because they had integrated biblical material in their more secular pursuits of historiography and theatre plays (*Letter*, 314–16).

Philo quotes his colleague's comments on the change of Abraham's and Sarah's names. The addition of the *alpha* is rejected by him, because it looks utterly superfluous (στοιχείου περιττοῦ), if only considered on the basis of the LXX. Furthermore, this Bible exegete has identified a theological problem, pointing to the ridiculous nature of the assumption that the ruler of the universe would honour anybody with such a trifling present. The evaluation of the biblical passage thus relies both on a philological observation and on a theological concept. Philo's colleague is said to have 'continued to go in detail through all similar cases'. This implies that he was a systematic scholar, investigating particular literary phenomena throughout Scripture.

Philo's description of this Bible exegete suggests that his work closely corresponded to Alexandrian Homer scholarship. As we have already noted, Aristarchus was especially committed to an investigation of the epic as a whole, explaining the recurrence of particular phenomena by comparison with each other.[35] Assuming with Aristotle that Homer's style was clear and concise, Aristarchus paid attention to superfluous literary features:[36] he was mostly concerned with redundant verses, unaware that they reflect the oral background of the epic, but occasionally also pointed to superfluous words.[37] In our context it is especially interesting that Aristarchus often combined philological considerations with a judgement of the content. He marked, for example, two lines as superfluous, because 'they are not

---

[34] See esp. *Flacc.* 147–52, discussed by van der Horst 2003, pp. 219–29; Niehoff 2001, pp. 40–1, 133–6.
[35] For details, see Chapter 3.
[36] On Aristarchus' commitment to the Aristotelian notion of clear and concise style in Homer's epics, see Schironi 2009, pp. 300–12; on his study of redundancies, see Lührs 1992, pp. 18–148.
[37] Regarding superfluous lines, see esp. Schol. *Il.* 6.311A, 19.407A, 21.471A; regarding superfluous words, see esp. Schol. *Il.* 1.137A, 1.194A, 1.523A, 2.123A, 3.138A.

necessary and ridiculous and contain some contradiction' (Schol. *Il.* 5.838–9A). He athetized some other lines, because he found the image conveyed in them of Athena throwing her head back 'ludicrous'.[38] On his view, the motif of horses drinking wine was 'most ridiculous'.[39] The image of 'Achilles gnashing with his teeth' was equally dismissed as 'ridiculous' (γελοῖον), while a reading of Zenodotus was rejected, because it created the 'ridiculous' impression of Zeus 'shouting from mount Ida'.[40]

Did Philo's colleague have similar text-critical objectives in mind, when sarcastically dismissing the biblical image of God in the context of Abraham and Sarah? Did he, like Aristarchus, suggest an athetesis of the respective verses? This conclusion is not only plausible but emerges quite clearly from the larger context of Philo's fragment. The individual scholar whom he had singled out for special criticism is part of a larger group or school of Bible exegetes, described by Philo in the following terms:

λέγεται γὰρ ὅτι 'οὐ κληθήσεται τὸ ὄνομά σου Ἀβράμ, ἀλλ' ἔσται τὸ ὄνομά σου Ἀβραάμ'. ἔνιοι μὲν οὖν τῶν φιλαπεχθημόνων καὶ μώμους ἀεὶ τοῖς ἀμώμοις προσάπτειν ἐθελόντων οὐ σώμασι μᾶλλον ἢ πράγμασι καὶ πόλεμον ἀκήρυκτον πολεμούντων τοῖς ἱεροῖς πάνθ' ὅσα μὴ τὸ εὐπρεπὲς ἐν λόγῳ διασῴζειν δοκεῖ σύμβολα φύσεως τῆς ἀεὶ κρύπτεσθαι φιλούσης ὑπάρχοντα μετὰ ἀκριβοῦς ἐρεύνης[41] φαυλίσαντες ἐπὶ διαβολῇ προφέρουσι, διαφερόντως δὲ τὰς τῶν ὀνομάτων μεταθέσεις. (*Mut.* 60)

> For it is said that 'your name shall no longer be called Abram, but your name will be Abraam' [LXX Gen. 17:5].

Some, however, of those who love to quarrel and always wish to attach blame to blameless things, not so much regarding external matters but the very meaning,[42] and some of those who wage an undeclared war against holy things reproach by

---

[38] γελοία δὲ καὶ ἡ ἀνανεύουσα Ἀθηνᾶ· (Schol. *Il.* 6.311A).

[39] γελοιότατος (Schol. *Il.* 8.189A).

[40] Schol. *Il.* 19.365–8A, 16.666A; see also Schol. *Il.* 24.25–30; see also van der Valk 1963–4, vol. II, pp. 391–415, who stresses the ideological considerations of Aristarchus' atheteses.

[41] Cohn and Wendland 1896–1915, ad loc, suggest a substantial emendation of the text adding οὐκ (μετὰ ἀκριβοῦς) or replacing μετά with δίχα. The manuscript text, however, is grammatically correct, thus not warranting any change, and its content becomes perfectly clear when we consider the continuation of Philo's criticism: he accuses the 'quarrelsome' Bible critics of having studied all the cases of name changes, thus grounding their attack on a broad and detailed analysis (*Mut.* 61). While Cohn and Wendland's conjecture was unfortunately accepted by the English translators Colson and Whitaker 1929–62, it has rightly been rejected by the French translator Arnaldez 1964.

[42] The expression οὐ σώμασι μᾶλλον ἢ πράγμασι is highly unusual. Colson and Whitaker 1929–62, ad loc, translated 'not so much to material things as to actions and ideas'. My own translation instead reflects the Stoic distinction between φωνή, the actual word spoken, σημαινόμενον πρᾶγμα, the meaning understood by the hearer and τυγχάνον, the actual object spoken of (*SVF* 2.166). Throughout his discussion of the changes of name Philo stresses the underlying meaning conveyed by them, see especially his reference to τὰ δὲ τυγχάνοντα implied in the change from Σάρα to Σάρρα (*Mut.* 77).

calumny, especially the changes of names, after having deprecated by means of a detailed inquiry all the things which seem to them not appropriate to preserve in the literal sense, although these are in reality symbols of nature which ever likes to hide.

Philo obviously disliked these colleagues and used highly polemical terms to warn his readers of their interpretations. His specific formulations suggest that they were sinful Jews causing internal strife within the Jewish community, because they had adopted an outsider's perspective on Scripture. Initially, the term φιλαπεχθήμων refers in Philo's writings predominantly to Jews who fail to show sufficient loyalty to their fellow Jews either by rejoicing over their misfortunes or generally behaving as complete strangers.[43] Philo stresses that joining the Jewish community involves, among other things, becoming friendly with men, while those who 'rebel from the holy laws' become 'quarrelsome' (*Virt.* 182). Significantly, he levelled the same charge against the interpreters of the Binding of Isaac, whose rigorous historical analysis we encountered in Chapter 6. In Philo's view, they, too, were 'lovers of quarrel' (*Abr.* 178).

Philo also describes his colleagues as 'attaching blame to blameless things'. The terms μῶμος and ἄμωμος regularly occur in Philo's writings in the context of sacrifice, identifying priests and animals as either ritually fit or unfit.[44] In the *Allegorical Commentary*, in particular, Philo extends his discussion to the metaphorical realm, speaking of spiritual blamelessness. Besides some general statements, he repeats one specific theme: blameless is the soul that acknowledges God as the cause of everything, preserving His gifts undamaged and perfect.[45] The arts and sciences, Philo insists, must also be recognized as having their cause and ultimate purpose in God (*Her.* 116). They are Divine gifts which must not be put to irreverent use. Philo implies that his colleagues relied on methods which had been given by God and were meant to enhance man's reverence of Him, but they employed the methods for irreverent purposes.

Philo's charge of calumny (διαβολή) is especially significant, because in half of its nineteen occurrences in Philo's writings it refers to slanders attached to Jews by Gentiles, especially the Egyptians.[46] The topical context

---

[43] See esp. *Mos.* 1.248, *Spec.* 1.241, *Jos.* 226, *Fuga* 5. Two of the ten occurrences refer to hostility shown by non-Jews to Jews (*Virt.* 34, *Flacc.* 52).

[44] *Spec.* 1.117, 166, 242, 259, 268, *Mut.* 233, *Somn.* 2.185.

[45] For Philo's general statements, see *All.* 3.141, *Cher.* 85, *Sobr.* 11; while Philo's remarks about the soul are to be found in *All.* 1.50, *Her.* 114–23.

[46] *Jos.* 66, *Mos.* 1.46, *Flacc.* 33, 89, *Legat.* 160, 170–1, 199, 241. On Philo's image of the Egyptians as ultimate Other, see Pearce 2007; Niehoff 2001, pp. 45–74.

is the ethnic conflict in Alexandria, which led to the pogrom of the Jews between 38 and 41 CE. Applying the term διαβολή to a particular kind of literal exegesis, Philo may have hinted at their adoption of a vicious external perspective. Did Philo consider these fellow Jews to be too close to Apion, who was a leading Homer scholar in Alexandria and later presided over the hostile Egyptian embassy to Gaius? Did these Jewish scholars in fact belong to Apion's circle? It is possible that such a direct connection was not yet anticipated by Philo in the *Allegorical Commentary*, which was probably written before the violent events in Alexandria.[47] It remains clear, however, that calumny was a grave sin in his eyes. Some Israelites were in his view guilty of it, when accusing Moses of having made up oracles in order to justify his choice of Ahron, which was in their understanding nothing but nepotism (*Mos.* 2.176). Philo thus suggests that the literal exegetes, whose interpretation of Scripture he identifies as calumny, were similarly rebelling against their own tradition.

While introducing his colleagues in the most polemical fashion, Philo nevertheless admits that they engaged in 'detailed inquiry'.[48] They must have been scholars committed to the literal sense only, as Philo complains that they are 'unwilling' to accept the allegorical meaning.[49] Moreover, like the individual scholar mentioned before, they also studied 'especially the change of names', thus engaging in a systematic scholarly inquiry.

A crucial glimpse into their work is provided by Philo's statement that they 'deprecated . . . all the things which seem to them not appropriate to preserve in the literal sense' (πάνθ' ὅσα μὴ τὸ εὐπρεπὲς ἐν λόγῳ διασῴζειν δοκεῖ). Philo uses the verb διασῴζω only here in the framework of Bible exegesis.[50] It is not a technical term of Homeric scholarship, but Philo seems to have used it in the sense of preserving the text rather than athetizing it. Aristobulus referred in a similar context to 'whoever wishes to retain (συντηρεῖν) the phrase about God'.[51] Philo used a paraphrastic expression to indicate that his colleagues were unable to preserve a particular verse as authentic.

---

[47] Note that it is only in the last treatise of the *Allegorical Commentary*, namely in *On Dreams*, that Philo mentions serious political tensions between the Jews and 'one of the ruling class' (*Somn.* 2.123), thus foreshadowing the violent events described in the *Embassy* and *Against Flaccus*.

[48] This term is rare, but has a clearly positive connotation in Philo's writings (see also *Agr.* 18).

[49] *Q.G.* 3.53, treating the same interpreters, who study the change of Abraham's and Sarah's names.

[50] The verb occurs thirty-three times throughout Philo's work, otherwise referring to salvation in a historical or an ethical sense (see e.g. *Abr.* 98, 177, *Legat.* 328).

[51] Aristob. *ap.* Euseb. *Praep. evang.* 8.10.12 (= fr. 2, ed. Holladay 1983–96, vol. III, p. 142); for details, see above, Chapter 4.

Moreover, the expression μὴ τὸ εὐπρεπές refers to standards of literary propriety which had been established by Homeric scholarship
in Alexandria.[52] Aristarchus frequently referred to this criterion when
analysing difficult lines in the epic. He rejected, for example, a line, because
'it is inappropriate (ἀπρεπές) that Agamemnon should say such things'
(Schol. *Il.* 1.29–31A). Similarly, *Il.* 24.130–2 was athetized, because it was
'inappropriate (ἀπρεπές) for a mother to say to her son: it is good to sleep
with a woman' (Schol. *Il.* 24.130–2A). On another occasion, Aristarchus
athetized a line as 'worthless (εὐτέλη) according to [considerations of]
both context and authorial intention', while later scholars insisted that the
poet had 'appropriately (εὐπρεπῶς)' created a relief of emotions (Schol.
Il. 15.212AB).

Philo's 'quarrelsome' colleagues must be appreciated in this context
of Homeric scholarship. Their judgement that the biblical story about
the change of Abraham's and Sarah's names cannot be maintained as
εὐπρεπές corresponds to prevalent text-critical practices among Greek
scholars. Unable either to offer a proper literal explanation or to have
recourse to allegory, they rejected certain biblical verses. Gen. 17:5 and
17:15 were thus athetized. These verses would not have been deleted from
the manuscript but, following the conventions of Homeric scholarship,
marked instead as spurious in the margins of the text. The literal Bible
exegetes can be expected to have used an obelus, as Aristarchus did, while
discussing the reasons for their criticism in a separate treatise. It is possible
that Philo quoted their views from such a treatise, which was probably
a running commentary on the Book of Genesis. Anticipating modern
Bible criticism by almost two thousand years, these Alexandrian scholars
inevitably aroused animosity in certain circles of the Jewish community.

Philo's more extended fragment of his colleagues' work has thus enabled
us to form a more precise picture of text-critical studies of the Bible in
Alexandria. Reading his polemics against the grain, we were able to glean
precious evidence of their textual considerations, which involved rigorous philology and theological concepts. Athetesis seems to have been an
accepted device among such Bible scholars. All of these characteristics
identify them as interpreters close to Aristarchus. The additional, more
fragmentary evidence which has been considered in this chapter points
in the same direction. Other textual difficulties, such as contradictions
between verses, flawed diction and repetitions, have been studied by methods which had been developed by Aristarchus. While all of these colleagues

---

[52] See glossary in Nünlist 2009a, p. 370; Schol. *Il.* 8.362, 139–40, 9.316, 334–6; 20.94–5.

belonged to the same Aristarchan milieu, they were not necessarily identical. It is quite possible that Philo was familiar with different groups of literal Bible exegetes, who investigated various aspects of Scripture in light of prevalent Homeric methods.

These findings complement our overall picture of Philo's colleagues. We have seen in earlier chapters of this part of the book that some of them approached the Bible from the point of view of comparative mythology, while others submitted the story of Isaac's Binding to rigorous historical analysis. These colleagues emerged as Aristotelian scholars, who were committed to an open comparison between the Jewish Scriptures and other literature. They held liberal views with regard to the distinction between Greeks and barbarians, advocating a community of languages and cultures. Moreover, they made a highly original contribution to Alexandrian scholarship, because they applied Aristotelian notions even more consistently to their foundational text than their Greek colleagues had done in the context of the Homeric epics. Besides these Bible scholars we have been able to distinguish others of a philological, Aristarchan orientation. They did not shrink from textual emendations of the Jewish Scriptures, hoping to restore their original consistency and beauty.

PART III

The inversion of Homeric scholarship by Philo

CHAPTER 8

Literal methods of Homeric scholarship in Philo's Allegorical Commentary

In this section of the book Philo's own work will be investigated in light of Homeric scholarship. Thus far, it has become clear that he was very critical of colleagues who adopted rigorous scholarly methods, either reading Scripture as literature in a general Aristotelian sense or engaging in text-critical studies in the style of Aristarchus. It now remains to be seen whether Philo's intimate familiarity with such scholarly methods is echoed in his own Bible exegesis. I shall argue that he did not ignore them, as may be expected, but rather used them in a sophisticated and highly innovative fashion to construct a separate discourse of Jewish hermeneutics. This is especially the case in his *Allegorical Commentary*, which will be the focus of the present chapter. Addressing an audience used to critical scholarship on the literal level, Philo seriously studied textual problems in this series of commentaries in order to justify his own allegorical interpretations. He thus created a new synthesis of approaches and conveyed a hitherto overlooked theory of allegory.

Although little attention has thus far been paid to the dimension of literal scholarship in Philo's *Allegorical Commentary*, Yehoshua Amir and Adam Kamesar have made significant progress on the question whether Philo regarded Scripture as a piece of literature.[1] Amir has stressed the ambiguity of Philo, who sometimes speaks of Scripture as a divinely inspired text, while on other occasions addressing Moses as the author of a literary work.[2] Amir has explained these contrary aspects by suggesting that Philo assumed the Platonic notion of literary inspiration, according to which the human

---

[1] Attention has been paid to the literal dimension of Philo's *Allegorical Commentary* by Kamesar 2002, who called for an investigation into the 'grammatical' dimension of Philo's work; and by Cazeaux 1984, pp. 160–70, and Pépin 1987, pp. 34–40, who both pointed to Philo's investigations into the literal text but examined its connections neither to Philo's allegory nor to Homeric scholarship; cf. also Siegfried 1875, who compared Philo's inquiries into the literal level, especially his study of redundancies, to rabbinic exegesis, assuming anachronistically that the latter served Philo as a model.

[2] Amir 1984, 1988.

author is inspired by an external, divine impetus. Kamesar, in response to Amir, has argued for Philo's more definite theoretical commitment to a literary approach, while, in his view, not making much use of literary notions in his Bible exegesis.[3]

Important new insights into the nature of Philo's exegesis can be gained by interpreting the *Allegorical Commentary* in the context of Alexandrian scholarship, both Homeric and biblical. Whereas Philo generally rejected the rigorous approach of his scholarly colleagues, he did not altogether disconnect himself from the realm of critical work, as Aristeas had previously done. In the *Allegorical Commentary* Philo engages in a hitherto unnoticed discussion with literalist Bible scholars, who had a significant presence among Jewish intellectuals in Alexandria. In this series of commentaries Philo does not yet present allegorization as a self-evident method of interpretation, but instead makes considerable scholarly efforts to trace it back to the biblical text itself.[4] At stake is the intention of Moses as the author of the Torah. Philo insists for the first time that extended allegorical interpretations are not a whimsical idea in the reader's mind, but rather something Moses himself wished to convey.

THE IMPLIED AUDIENCE OF THE *ALLEGORICAL COMMENTARY* AND ITS LITERARY ASSUMPTIONS

The implied audience of the *Allegorical Commentary* has to be established in order to appreciate Philo's intellectual context of writing. Throughout the different treatises of this series Philo is aware of the fact that his readers are hesitant to accept an allegorical interpretation or even actively resist such an approach. He occasionally urges them 'not to be astonished (μὴ θαυμάσῃς) by the rules of allegory' or wonders 'what sense this [verse] makes to those interpreting the literal sense'.[5] Philo frequently addresses such readers with personal appeals, once explaining that Moses has used a certain formulation 'urging [you] to avoid the literal interpretation (ὁρᾶς ὅτι... προτρέπτων ἀφίστασθαι τοῦ ῥητοῦ)' and once mocking the implications of the literal interpretation (τί λέγετε, ὦ γενναῖοι;).[6]

Philo's overall orientation towards an audience committed to the literal text is especially visible in his treatise *On the Confusion of Tongues*. We have already seen that he opens this with an extensive quotation of his

---

[3] Kamesar 1995.
[4] Both the *Q&A* and the *Exposition* introduce allegorical interpretations without much justification, often using highly casual formulations or relying on the 'laws of allegory'; for details see Chapters 9 and 10.
[5] *Somn.* 1.73, *Det.* 167.   [6] *Det.* 15, *Somn.* 1.93.

colleagues' literary analysis, which he rejects in no uncertain terms.[7] In the present context it must be stressed that Philo reports the interpretation of his colleagues at such length, giving them a greater platform and a fairer hearing than in the *Q&A*. This relative openness to the views of literal Bible exegetes indicates the interest Philo expected the readers of the *Allegorical Commentary* to have in them. He moreover mentions other literal exegetes whom he trusts to 'refute on their own account those writing such things and falsifying [Scripture]' (*Conf.* 14). Such a refutation, he explains, will rely on 'ready explanations from the outward sense of Scripture for the questions as they arise'. Philo thus distinguishes between literal readers, who are in his view too critical, and those sharing his basic desire to defend the biblical text. He indeed respects some of them to the extent that he presents their interpretation in a positive manner:

> Those attending only to the outward and ready things believe now that the origin of the Greek and barbarian languages has been sketched out [in the biblical story]. (*Conf.* 190)

Philo stresses that he will not censure these colleagues, 'for perhaps they, too, speak the truth', yet urges them 'not to stop here, but to attend to allegorical explanations'.[8] Literal exegetes thus emerge as his implied audience, whom he hopes to convince of the usefulness of his allegorical approach. He indeed wishes to show that Moses himself 'has provided starting points' for allegory.[9]

Responding to critical interpreters of the story of the Tower of Babel, Philo says that his allegorizations are offered:[10]

> neither in a contentious spirit nor in order somehow to meet sophistry with sophistry, but rather following the chain of logical sequence, which does not allow stumbling (προσπταίειν οὐκ ἐῶντι) but easily removes any stumbling-block which may arise, in order that the course of the narratives may be smooth (ὅπως αἱ τῶν λόγων διέξοδοι γίνωνται ἄπταιστοι). (*Conf.* 14)

---

[7] For details, see above Chapter 4.

[8] μὴ ἐπὶ τούτων στῆναι μετελθεῖν δὲ ἐπὶ τάς τροπικὰς ἀποδόσεις (*Conf.* 190).

[9] δίδωσι μέντοι πρὸς τοῦτ' ἀφορμάς (*Conf.* 191); see also *Det.* 167, where Philo highlights the problems of a verse, rejecting its literal meaning and insisting that 'necessarily' (ἀνάγκη) all this is allegorical. The allegorical interpretation is then introduced as the meaning which Moses 'wishes to convey' (ὁ βούλεται παριστάνειν).

[10] I accept the interpretation of the lacuna by Colson (n. 1, ad loc), who rejects Wendland's minimal text emendation (ad loc) and suggest instead that a reference to Philo's own allegorization must have dropped out of the text. This is corroborated by the fact that in *Conf.* 15 Philo introduces an allegorical reading of Gen. 11:1 with the expression φαμὲν τοίνυν, which indicates that a previous argument is continued rather than superseded. Moreover, Philo's discussion in *Conf.* 190 closely resembles the structure of the text as emended by Colson and Kahn: Philo briefly praises congenial literalists and then offers his own allegorization.

In this passage allegory is conceptualized as a solution to 'stumbling-blocks' in the literal text. While some of Philo's colleagues studied textual problems as indications of different compositional layers or as signs of text manipulations, Philo insists that such problems can be solved and the integrity of Scripture preserved. Recovering the smoothness of the biblical narratives with an allegorical interpretation, he aims at restoring their original logic and intention.

Engaging readers committed to literal scholarship, Philo assumes more scholarly and literary concepts in the *Allegorical Commentary* than in any other series of his writings. The treatises in this series echo Alexandrian scholarship rather closely. Above all, Philo has adopted the standard scholarly form of a running commentary (ὑπόμνημα). The *Allegorical Commentary* provides a systematic inquiry into the first chapters of the Book of Genesis, moving from one verse to another and from one problem or question to the next.[11] Eusebius correctly grasped the nature of Philo's work when presenting it as a type of aporetic literature.[12]

The numerous treatises of the *Allegorical Commentary* moreover abound with scholarly expressions reflecting systematic commentary activity on the literal level. Typical formulations are: 'let us now examine the following [expression]',[13] 'the question next in sequence'[14] as well as 'why' [was it written] and 'one must investigate'.[15] In contrast to the *Exposition* and the *Q&A*, the *Allegorical Commentary* offers numerous cross-references to other biblical verses.[16] Such additional verses are usually drawn into the discussion on the basis of an association of words. They serve to throw further light on the verse commented upon and allow a more comprehensive study of a particular phenomenon throughout Scripture. As we have already seen,

---

[11] While the *Q&A* share the general framework of a verse-to-verse commentary, we shall see in the next chapter that the questions raised there do not address textual problems but rather serve as an organizational principle.

[12] Euseb. *Hist. eccl.* 2.18.1; in modern scholarship this aspect has been recognized by some scholars but not yet fully explored, see Nikiprowetzky 1977, pp. 170–80; 1983; Borgen 1997, pp. 80–102, who stresses the ubiquity of the question and answer method throughout Philo's work and its phenomenological proximity to Greek question and answer literature.

[13] τὸ ἑπόμενον... συνεπισκεψώμεθα (*Post.* 32); διαπορητέον δὲ ἑξῆς (*Det.* 32); see also *All.* 1.101, *Det.* 57, *Gig.* 67, *Sobr.* 1.

[14] ἑξῆς κἀκεῖνο διαπορητέον (*All.* 1.101); see also *Post.* 32, 49, *Deus* 51, *Det.* 57.

[15] Διὰ τί; (e.g. *All.* 1.2, 1.33, 1.48, 1.85, *Gig.* 1, *Fuga* 60); σκεπτέον (e.g. *All.* 2.80, 3.252, *Post.* 40, *Sobr.* 31, 62, *Fuga* 157); see also the similar expressions ἄξιον δὲ σκέψασθαι (*All.* 2.42, *Post.* 22, *Conf.* 169), σκεψώμεθα (*All.* 3.28), ζητητέον (*All.* 1.91), ἴδωμεν δὲ ἑξῆς (*All.* 3.4), ἄξιον οἶμαι διαπορῆσαι διὰ τί (*Gig.* 1), νυνὶ διαπορῶμεν (*Post.* 1), ἐρευνήσωμεν (*Post.* 40), ἐρευνητέον (*Conf.* 183). In the same spirit Philo sometimes lists several questions on one verse before dealing with each of them individually (e.g. *All.* 1.33, *Fuga* 87).

[16] See also Runia 1984, pp. 227–41.

this exegetical method, together with the technical terms of inquiry, is typical of Alexandrian scholarship, both Homeric and biblical.[17]

In the *Allegorical Commentary* Philo's study of the biblical text is guided by the assumption that it was written by one author with a distinct style.[18] Philo is the first extant Bible scholar to have adopted certain technical terms of stylistic analysis which are associated in Alexandria especially with Aristarchus. In line with his Homeric predecessor, Philo pays special attention to the author's habitual and typical usage. Whereas Aristarchus explored the ways in which 'Homer customarily speaks' (εἴωθε λέγειν), Philo explains the stylistic habits of Moses (εἴωθε καλεῖν).[19] He also points out that Moses, like the ancient Greek poets, but in contrast to contemporary conventions, used the term 'intoxicant' as a synonym for 'wine' (*Plant.* 154). On another occasion it is stressed that Moses did better than Greek writers, who attributed the assignment of names to 'wise men' rather than to the first created human (*All.* 2.15).

Paying attention to Moses' particular style, Philo was sensitive to inconsistencies in the biblical text; he shared this interest with Aristarchus, but he never contemplated text emendation.[20] Aristarchus athetized lines on grounds of uncharacteristic usage of language, arguing, for example, that Homer 'would not say' such a thing or that an expression is 'not Homeric' or 'against his usage'.[21] Philo characteristically dwells on similar inconsistencies of style but uses them for his own allegorical purposes. He thus investigates, for example, why Moses simply states the fact of Cain's birth instead of gradually introducing the birth of a child, then specifying its sex and, finally, recording its name (*Cher.* 53–5). Philo admits that Moses 'changes the customary usage' (τὸ σύνηθες ἐξαλλάττων), but

---

[17] Regarding Aristarchus, see, e.g., Schol. *Il.* 1.13–16A, 7.334–5A, 8.43A, 8.328A, 11.659A; for further details, see above, Chapter 3. The background of his approach was Aristotelian, see Arist. *Apor. Hom.* fr. 142, 145–8, 150–3, 155–9; Arist. *Poet.* 1461a5.

[18] Philo, of course, investigates Moses' particular style as if he had originally written in Greek. Kamesar 1995, p. 60, has pointed out that Philo does not consider the book of Psalms to be authored by Moses himself, but rather by one of his company (*Plant.* 39, *Conf.* 39, *Somn.* 2.245).

[19] Regarding Aristarchus, see esp. Schol. *Il.* 10.10A, 14.37A, 10.515A, 5.269A, 9.338A, 2.435A, 3.152A, 6.160A, 6.400A, 7.149A, 8.107A, 14.58A, 16.123A, 22.322A; note also that Aristarchus accused Zenodotus of ignoring certain Doric forms in Homer's Greek and instead Hellenizing his language (Schol. *Il.* 1.56A, 1.68A, 3.99A, 3.206A). Regarding Philo, see esp. *Sobr.* 16, *Det.* 39, *Gig.* 6, *Her.* 22.

[20] See esp. *Her.* 22, where Philo stresses that 'while he [Moses] is in the habit of using (εἰωθὼς δὲ χρῆσθαι) two foremost designations for the Cause, namely God and Lord, here he has used neither of them, but instead the designation "master", very cautiously and exceedingly valid'; as well as *All.* 1.33, where Philo wonders why Moses uses the term 'breeze' in Gen. 2:7 and not 'wind' as in Gen. 1:2.

[21] Schol. *Il.* 24.304A, 4.140A, 7.353A, 3.334–5A. Aristarchus was so influential that even those disagreeing with him related to his arguments. Similarly, Didymus adopts a reading of Aristarchus' edition, dismissing other versions as 'contrary to Homer's custom' (Schol. *Il.* 3.10A).

he insists that Moses did not do so out of ignorance or incompetence. Moses is instead shown to be 'familiar with the proper giving of names', as proven by Gen. 4:25, where the birth of Seth is presented in the regular fashion (*Cher.* 54–5). The irregularity of Moses' style in Gen. 4:1 is consequently interpreted as a hint of the implied allegorical meaning of the verse (*Cher.* 55).

Philo, like Aristarchus and other biblical scholars, was sensitive to stylistic redundancies. Whereas Aristarchus noted especially redundant lines, unaware that they reflected the oral origins of the epic, Philo discusses mostly redundant words, which reflected – unknown to him – the underlying Hebrew. The notion of the 'superfluous' (περισσός) became central for both. Aristarchus often used it as a criterion for athetesis, while Philo assumes that Scripture does not contain anything really superfluous.[22] Philo once describes in strikingly personal terms, how he coped with a biblical redundancy:

Well knowing that he [Moses] never puts in a superfluous word (ὅτι περιττὸν ὄνομα οὐδὲν τίθησιν) . . . I began asking myself (ἠπόρουν κατ᾽ ἐμαυτόν) why he did not simply say that the intentional slayer is put to death, but rather 'by death put to death' [Exod. 21:12].

In which other way does a dying man come to his end save by death? After resorting then to a wise woman, investigation (σκέψις) by name, I was released from inquiries (τοῦ ζητεῖν ἀπηλλάγην). For she taught me that some are dead while living, whereas some are alive while dead. (*Fuga* 54)

This passage abounds with scholarly expressions stressing the dimension of inquiry and examination. Philo's personal involvement is conspicuous. He is profoundly concerned with problems which emerge from a reading of Scripture as literature. Ironically, it is Skepsis who releases Philo from further investigation. A problem of redundancy in the literal text is thus solved on the metaphorical level. In another context Philo similarly insists that Moses wrote 'in a superfluous manner (περιττῶς)' only for the purpose of 'urging [you] to depart from the literal sense'.[23]

---

[22] Regarding Aristarchus, see esp. Schol. *Il.* 1.96A, 21.471A, 6.311A and Lührs 1992, pp. 18–148, whose analysis is somewhat compromised by two facts: he focused too narrowly on cases of redundant verbs at the beginning of verses and, furthermore, examined many verses where an expression other than περισσός is used. A systematic study of the references in Erbse's index, however, confirms Lührs's important conclusion that περισσός refers to a particular category of athetesis. Note that Aristarchus also identified superfluous expressions (e.g. Schol. *Il.* 1.137A, 1.194A, 1.523A, 2.123A, 3.138A). Regarding Philo, see especially his programmatic statement in *All.* 3.147, where he insists that 'you will not find a single pointless expression' (οὐδὲν γὰρ λεχθὲν παρέργως εὑρήσεις).

[23] *Det.* 15; for similar examples, see *Gig.* 34, *Migr.* 48, *Congr.* 73, *Somn.* 2.25.

Finally, Philo is the first extant Bible scholar to have discussed a problem of punctuation, thus sharing another important concern of Homeric scholarship. He offers the following comments on Lev. 19:23, which can be read in two different ways depending on where the comma is put:

> But the language is ambiguous (ἡ δὲ λέξις ἐστὶν ἀμφίβολος), for it makes manifest one [meaning] like this: 'its fruit shall remain for three years' and then separately the expression 'and uncleansed it shall not be eaten' [Lev. 19:23], while the other [meaning] is: 'its fruit shall for three years remain uncleansed' and then separately the expression 'and shall not be not eaten'. (*Plant.* 113)

Philo's comments echo a long tradition of Homeric scholarship, ranging from Aristotle to Aristarchus. The former had already mentioned different forms of punctuation as one method of solving problems in the epic text.[24] Aristarchus similarly investigated ambiguities of punctuation, exploring the various literal meanings deriving from them.[25] It emerges that Philo was familiar with this aspect of the standardization of the Homeric text. This is not surprising, because he also knew the Alexandrian division of the epics into twenty-four songs (*Cont.* 17).

Having appreciated the distinctly literary and scholarly assumptions of the *Allegorical Commentary*, which were shared by its implied audience, we are now able to investigate Philo's exegetical achievement in a broader historical context. The most conspicuous mark of Philo's approach is the link between the literal-scholarly and the allegorical dimension. In first-century Alexandria he was the first scholar to anchor a consistently allegorical approach in serious literal scholarship, thus offering a new theory of allegory, which is rooted in Aristotelian notions of authorial intention. At the same time Philo transcends previous Aristotelian scholarship in significant and innovative ways. The novelty of his approach can best be appreciated by looking at his treatment of two Classical subjects, namely contradictions and problems of verisimilitude, which continued to attract scholarly attention until Porphyry.

CONTRADICTIONS BETWEEN VERSES

A conspicuous concern of Philo in the *Allegorical Commentary* is the question of contradictions between verses. Such inquiries are attested already among Jewish Bible exegetes of the mid second century BCE. Demetrius

---

[24] Arist. *Poet.* 1461a23; see also Bywater 1909, pp. 338–40; Dupont-Roc and Lallot 1980, p. 396.
[25] See esp. Schol. *Il.* 11.409A; and also Schol. *Il.* 1.388 (Nicanor), 14.75–6 (Nicanor), 15.128a (Nicanor and Herodianus).

referred to 'someone [who] inquired how the Israelites had weapons, since they departed from Egypt unarmed'.[26] He himself wondered whether there was no contradiction between Exod. 2:21, where Moses and Zipporah are said to marry, and LXX Gen. 25:3, where Raguel is mentioned. If the latter was Zipporah's grandfather, she lived a generation before Moses and thus could not marry him.[27] We saw in a previous chapter that these early inquiries into contradictions between biblical verses were embedded in the Aristotelian tradition, which was influential in Alexandria, especially in the work of Aristarchus. The latter paid serious attention to contradictions, studying the Homeric text from within itself.[28]

Philo is primarily an allegorical reader of Scripture, but he continues this tradition of literal exegesis. Like his Aristotelian predecessors he is committed to the authorial meaning of Scripture and investigates contradictions in the text as a challenge to the notion of one consistent author. In contrast to them, however, he no longer solves such problems on the literal level but uses contradictions as an instrument to move from the literal to the non-literal level. Philo is able to make this transition precisely because he firmly believes in the underlying consistency of the Torah (*Det.* 81).

Some examples will illustrate Philo's innovative strategy. The first one pertains to a metaphorical interpretation, which echoes his background in Aristotelian scholarship while also showing his particular contribution to the contemporary discourse. Studying the story of Paradise, Philo points to the following contradiction:

And further [God] says: 'in the day you will eat thereof, you shall die the death' [Gen. 2:17]. Yet having eaten [from the Tree of Knowledge], they not only do not die but even beget children and become the cause of life to others [Gen. 4:1]. (*All.* 1.105)

This problem of a contradiction could easily have been raised by Demetrius, his anonymous colleagues or Aristobulus, but Philo provides an answer which significantly differs from theirs. Having raised the problem, he initially pauses, asking 'what then should be said?'[29] This question is formulated in order to prepare the reader more gradually for a rather dramatic transition from the literal to the metaphorical level. Although Aristobulus had also offered metaphorical interpretations of biblical problems, he limited his exegesis to brief explanations, which solved specific

---

[26] *Ap.* Euseb. *Praep. evang.* 9.29.16.   [27] *Ap.* Euseb. *Praep. evang.* 9.29.1–3.
[28] For details, see Chapter 3.
[29] Τί οὖν λεκτέον; (*All.* 1.105); Philo uses this or a similar expression on other occasions, too (e.g. *All.* 1.91, *Post.* 34).

anthropomorphic motifs by pointing with Aristotle to the common usage of language.³⁰

Philo, by contrast, offers a more extended answer to the problem of contradiction. For this purpose he leaves the Aristotelian tradition and relies on a Classical Platonic motif, namely the notion that the pursuit of philosophy leads to an ethereal state, where the body and its earthly desires are practically non-existent.³¹ Applying this notion to Gen. 2:17, Philo suggests that 'death is of two kinds, one pertaining to man, the other in particular to the soul' (*All.* 1.105). The death of the soul is presented as a state of merely physical existence, which results from a wicked and overly material life style.³² While Adam and Eve lived in a physical sense after eating from the Tree of Knowledge, they were, in Philo's view, dead as far as their soul was concerned, because they had disobeyed God and become wicked. The contradiction between the verses is thus solved, Philo combining the scholarly technique of question and answer with a Platonic motif. At the same time he has suggested that the allegorical reading 'smoothes' the biblical narrative. Since the biblical text is not satisfactory on the literal level, containing a contradiction of verses, the allegorical meaning emerges as the unblemished message originally intended by Moses. This Philonic interpretation is clearly far more removed from the literal level and the reader's common sense than Aristobulus' previous metaphorical solutions to problems of anthropomorphism.

Philo identifies further contradictions of verses in the story of Paradise.³³ One of them pertains to God's exchange with Eve, who is punished for her sin. In this context Philo offers an emphatically allegorical solution:

'And God said to the woman: what have you done? And she said: the serpent has beguiled me and I have eaten' [Gen. 3:13]. Whereas God inquires of sense-perception concerning one thing (Gen. 3:12), she answers concerning another. For

---

³⁰ For details on Aristobulus' metaphorical interpretations, see Chapter 4. Occasionally, Philo similarly refers to the commonly accepted meanings of biblical expressions (e.g. *All.* 2.16), without using them as a basis for his overall non-literal approach.

³¹ Plato, *Phaedo* 80–81a; see also Wis. 7:13, 8:17, 15:3, where the author stresses that immortality will be achieved by the devoted student of wisdom, thus testifying to the popularity of Plato's notions in Alexandria.

³² This expression is explicitly mentioned here for the first time in the extant Greek literature, remaining rare in Philo's work (the only other occurrence being *Q.G.* 1.51).

³³ For another example see *All.* 1.101–2, where Philo inquires into the precise wording of the Divine commandments concerning the trees, noting that they are formulated either in the plural or the singular (*All.* 1.101). Given the overall context of God addressing both Adam and Eve, Philo insists that one must read the respective verses allegorically, namely as a reference to different ways of acquiring wisdom. The singular is thus said to be used with regard to few individuals, while the plural is used in view of the multitude of people who sin and fail to become wise (*All.* 1.102).

He inquires concerning [her guilt towards] man, while she does not speak about him but says something about herself, namely 'I have eaten', and not 'I have given'. Perhaps then allegorizing we shall solve the problem (μήποτ᾽ οὖν ἀλληγοροῦντες λύσομεν τὸ ἀπορηθέν) and show that the woman directly answers the question, for it is a matter of necessity that when she eats, man also eats. (*All.* 3.59–60)

In this passage Philo explicitly presents the allegorization of Eve as the solution to the textual problem on the literal level. He thus proceeds precisely in the way outlined in *On the Confusion of Tongues*, where he programmatically states that his allegorizations are meant to remove 'stumbling-blocks' (*Conf.* 14). In the case of Eve it is remarkable that Philo highlights the discrepancy between the verses even though he assumes the allegory of woman as sense-perception right from the very beginning. This equation is so natural for him that he formulates his initial question as a problem concerning God's inquiry of 'sense-perception'. Whereas the answer is thus axiomatically assumed, the textual problem is nevertheless expounded. Philo does this because he is concerned about Moses' authorial intention. He suspects that his colleagues in Alexandria may accuse him of offering a whimsical interpretation which, in their view, has nothing to do with the original meaning of the biblical text. Addressing the contradiction of verses, Philo suggests to fellow exegetes that the literal text is problematic and therefore requires a new perspective. The latter is offered in a surprisingly hesitant mode, Philo stressing that 'perhaps then' allegory will solve the problem. He evidently assumes an audience used to considering textual problems, but unfamiliar with allegory.

Our final example illustrates the extent to which Philo makes efforts to identify problems of contradiction, which will help him to anchor his non-literal interpretations in Scripture.[34] Focusing on Abraham's epithet 'elder', Philo raises the following questions:

Does not everyone reading in the most holy books know that the wise man Abraham is introduced (εἰσάγεται) as more short-lived than almost all his own forefathers? But none of those, I think (οἶμαι), even though they lived long lives, were described as elders, but only Abraham. At all events the Oracles say that 'Abraham was an elder advanced in years and the Lord blessed Abraham in everything' [Gen. 24:1]. (*Sobr.* 17)

Philo appeals here in a surprisingly general way to readers versed in Scripture, who will appreciate the contradiction of passages. He must have meant the list of forefathers recorded in Gen. 5:4–31, where the average age is close to 800, while Abraham reached only the age of 175 (Gen. 25:7). The

---

[34] For a similar example, see *All.* 3.236.

biblical praise of Abraham's longevity thus appeared to him odd given the significantly longer lives of earlier generations. At the same time, however, Philo could have appreciated Abraham's longevity in comparison with that of his descendants. From this perspective he could have acknowledged the feasibility of the epithet, because Ishmael and Joseph, for example, reached only the ages of 137 and 110 respectively.[35] It is thus only in view of previous generations that Abraham's epithet appears problematic. Philo clearly prefers to focus on the predecessors and even adds some rather uncertain evidence, namely his vague reminiscence that none of Abraham's forefathers was called 'elder'. He mentions this point in order to stress the contradiction between the biblical passages. Philo is evidently delighted to identify a textual problem on the literal level, regarding such a procedure as an excellent scholarly preparation for his own interpretation. He thus hopes that his readers will more easily recognize that Moses 'customarily called' (εἴωθε καλεῖν) biblical heroes either old or young as a reference to their respective maturity or foolishness (*Sobr.* 16).

Philo's combination of extended allegorical interpretations with scholarly inquiries into contradictions of verses is highly exceptional. Living in first-century Alexandria, he made a very significant and hitherto overlooked contribution to the development of allegorical theory. Using textual problems in order to question the hegemony of literal readings, Philo suggests that an allegorical meaning was intended by the author. The roots of his approach cannot be traced to the Stoics, who ignored authorial intention in the context of allegory, as we saw in connection with Aristobulus.[36] Indeed, Zeno's famous discussion of a contradiction between epic lines leads to a clear preference of one of them rather than to allegory.[37]

Aristotle, on the other hand, is a significant precedent for Philo. Luc Brisson has stressed that Aristotle accepted allegory as one way of saving myths.[38] In the extant fragments of his *Aporemata Homerica* there is an example of an allegorical solution to a contradiction between Homeric

---

[35] Gen. 25:17, 50:22. Isaac lived roughly the same number of years as his father (Gen. 35:28).

[36] For details, see Chapter 4.

[37] '[Homer] has written some things in accordance with opinion, while others in accordance with truth (τὰ μέν κατὰ δόξαν, τὰ δὲ κατὰ ἀλήθειαν) so that he may not appear to contradict himself in those passages in which contradictory things seem to have been said' (*SVF* 1.274); see also Buffière 1956, pp. 146–8, who suggests that this fragment belongs to Zeno's early stage of thought, when he was still connected to Antisthenes and before he embarked on his own allegorical project; Steinmetz 1986, pp. 19–21, who proposes to distinguish between Zeno's text-critical work on Homer's epics and his allegorical interpretation of Hesiod; Pontani 2005b, pp. 29–31.

[38] Brisson 2004, pp. 38–40; see also Montanari 1993, p. 260.

lines.[39] Treating the conflicting descriptions of the sun, once as omniscient and once as relying on a messenger, Aristotle proposes three solutions. One of them suggests that 'Lampetia was a messenger to Helios as vision is to man'.[40] Significantly, Aristotle neither uses the term 'allegory' nor claims exclusive authority for this solution.

Philo, approaching the Jewish Scriptures in the first century CE, is a striking mirror image of Aristotle. Specifically Platonic motifs abound in his work and yet he is still committed to studying textual problems on the literal level, elaborating upon them in the spirit of Aristotle's questions and answers. At the same time, however, Philo clearly transcends Aristotle as well as his Alexandrian follower Aristobulus. He no longer limits his exegesis to brief explanations of the literal text, having recourse where necessary to non-literal interpretations, but focuses on the allegorical meaning, which he takes to realms far distant from the literal text. Philo's approach thus relies on a delicate balance between the literal and the allegorical meanings of Scripture. On the one hand, he stresses problems in the literal text in order to make room for allegory, and, on the other hand, he assumes authorial intention and anchors allegory within the literal text. The literal dimension of Scripture is thus not dismissed but shown to be problematic to a degree that renders the allegorical meaning plausible, if not necessary. This twofold position creates the characteristic complexity and ambiguity of Philo's work.

Philo's position in Alexandria is special because he combined two worlds which had hitherto remained apart. While Aristobulus and Aristarchus continued Aristotle's approach, allegorists such as Apollodorus and some anonymous allegorists mentioned in Philo's work relied on Stoic models. Aristarchus, for example, generally did not resort to allegory but occasionally solved a contradiction between epic lines by arguing that 'these expressions are not meant literally'.[41] Apollodorus as well as Philo's allegoristic colleagues in first-century Alexandria pointed to the supposed etymologies of words as an indication of their allegorical meaning.[42]

---

[39] Note also that Aristotle offered a 'physical' interpretation of Helios' cattle, taking it as a reference to the number of days in the lunar year (Arist. *Apor. Hom.*, fr. 175; ed. Rose 1886). It is no longer clear precisely what prompted Aristotle's allegorical reading, perhaps the unusual calculation of the herds or the emphasis on their immortality; see also the comments by Hintenlang 1961, pp. 131–7, who stresses the unusual occurrence of allegory in Aristotle's exegetical work.

[40] Arist. *Apor. Hom.*, fr. 149 (ed. Rose 1886). See Chapter 3 above.

[41] τὰ τοιαῦτα δὲ κυρίως οὐ λέγεται (Schol. *Il.* 2.45A). Note that Aristarchus offered metaphorical interpretations of concrete verbs also in contexts disconnected from contradictions between verses (Schol. *Il.* 1.37A, 2.670A, 5.21A, 5.299A, 8.408A, 11.390A, 13.420A, 22.356A).

[42] For details on Apollodorus' allegories, see Chapter 4 above; regarding Philo's anonymous colleagues, see esp. Hay 1979–80; 1994; Goulet 1987, who provides the most detailed study of Philo's allegorical

Heraclitus the Allegorist, probably writing at the beginning of the second century CE, followed Philo's approach most closely, offering similar, albeit far less scholarly and less Platonic interpretations of the Homeric epics.[43] As Filippo Pontani and Donald Russell have recently stressed, Heraclitus insisted that Homer himself had intended the allegorical interpretation of his epics.[44] If Homer, he says in his famous prologue, 'meant nothing allegorically (εἰ μηδὲν ἠλληγόρησεν), he would be impious through and through'.[45] While Heraclitus hardly uses scholarly expressions and does not dwell on literal problems in the way Philo does, he nevertheless discusses questions which had been treated in Homeric scholarship.[46] Once he refers to a contradiction between verses as an argument for assuming Homer's allegorical intentions. Homer, he explains, 'has given us a very lucid account of this [allegorical] mode of expression' in *Il.* 9.222–4, where Odysseus' talk about the harvest contradicts its immediate context of war.[47] Heraclitus draws the same conclusion as Philo would have done, namely that 'we understand the true significance from the pair of contrasting opposites'.[48]

PROBLEMS OF VERISIMILITUDE

Problems of verisimilitude are another important concern in Philo's *Allegorical Commentary*. In this area, too, he continues a tradition of literal Jewish Bible exegesis, which is attested approximately two centuries earlier. Demetrius had referred to a discussion of the question why did 'Joseph at the meal give a fivefold portion to Benjamin even though he was incapable of taking in such quantities of meat?'[49] Similarly, Aristobulus inquired into the perplexity of the burning bush, which 'burns irresistibly, [but] does not consume anything entirely'.[50] We have already seen in previous chapters that Demetrius' anonymous colleagues as well as Aristobulus were firmly rooted in the Aristotelian tradition of Homeric scholarship. Philo

---

colleagues, but synthesizes the evidence too much. Philo himself also offered some allegories in Stoic style, which have attracted much scholarly attention, see esp. Buffière 1956; Pépin 1987; Amir 1971; Kamesar 2004; Stein 1939, pp. 162–85.

[43] Concerning the date of Heraclitus' *Homeric Problems*, which still lack mystical, Neoplatonic motifs, see Buffière 1962, pp. ix–x; Pontani 2005a, pp. 9–13, stressing stylistic indications; Russell and Konstan 2005, pp. xi–xiii.

[44] Pontani 2005a, pp. 26–30; Russell 2003, esp. pp. 228–9; see also Lamberton 2002, pp. 191–2.

[45] Her. *Hom. Probl.* 1.1 (text and trans. by Russell and Konstan 2005).

[46] See esp. Her. *Hom. Probl.* 6.5 (ἀκριβῶς διαθρήσας) and 9.2 (οὐκ ἄπιστον).

[47] Her. *Hom. Probl.* 5.14; see also Pontani 2005a, pp. 185–6, providing the background of Homeric scholarship on the Homeric line.

[48] Δι' ἐναντίων ἀλλήλοις πραγμάτων τὸ δηλούμενον ἐπιγιγνώσκομεν (Her. *Hom. Probl.* 5.16).

[49] *Ap.* Euseb. *Praep. evang.* 9.21.14.   [50] *Ap.* Euseb. *Praep. evang.* 8.10.16.

continues to address problems of verisimilitude but no longer solves them with short literal explanations, instead using them as a springboard for allegorical interpretations in a spiritual, Platonic mode. This synthesis is highly innovative and ushers in a new approach, which subsequently resurfaces in Porphyry's *Cave of the Nymphs*.

Philo opens his treatise *On the Posterity of Cain* with a programmatic statement, asking:

> whether we should understand the statements in the books in which Moses acts as an interpreter more figuratively (τροπικώτερον), as the impression at hand made by the words is greatly at variance with truth (τῆς ἐν τοῖς ὀνόμασι προχείρου φαντασίας πολὺ τἀληθοῦς ἀπᾳδούσης). (*Post.* 1)

Judging the biblical account of Cain going out from God's face (Gen. 4:16) to be utterly implausible, Philo investigates why Moses nevertheless presented him thus.[51] He initially stresses that God is omnipresent, any literal flight from Him being 'impossible' (ἀδύνατον). Philo then insists that 'the only thing left' (λοιπὸν ἂν εἴη) is to grasp that 'nothing of the propositions is meant literally' (τῶν προταθέντων οὐδὲν κυριολογεῖται).[52] Instead, the reader is invited to choose 'the way of allegory dear to philosophical men' (*Post.* 7). Philo then develops an extended allegory of the soul, describing in Platonic terms how it longs to leave behind the material realm in order to perceive of God, while men such as Cain turn their heart from God and remain blind.[53]

Philo subsequently anchors another allegory in a problem of verisimilitude, inquiring 'why [Cain], even though alone, is introduced as founding and building a city.'[54] In this context Philo exaggerates the problem beyond the necessities of the literal text. He not only stresses that Cain was utterly alone, because his parents would have refused to cooperate with him, but also suggests that Cain would have had to build a city with all the architectural equipment of a metropolis like Alexandria (*Post.* 49–50). Seeing the unlikelihood of such a construction by one individual, Philo concludes that the verse 'is not only a paradox, but contrary to reason'.[55] His solution is an invitation to resort to allegory:

---

[51] Note that the notion of verisimilitude borders here on the notion of impiety, Philo assuming on theological grounds that the verse in its literal sense departs from the truth. See also *Conf.* 134, where the literal reading of a similar anthropomorphic verse is dismissed as 'impiety' (ἀσέβεια).

[52] This and the previous quotation can be found in *Post.* 7; for a similar discussion of a problem of verisimilitude, see *Somn.* 1.65.

[53] See esp. *Post.* 13–21. The Platonic background of Philo's notion of the soul has been established by Runia 1986, pp. 467–75; 2001, pp. 222–59.

[54] *Post.* 49, referring to Gen. 4:17.

[55] τὸ μὲν γὰρ οὐ παράδοξον μόνον ἀλλὰ καὶ παράλογον, *Post.* 50.

Perhaps then, as these things diverge from the truth, it is better to say allegorically (μήποτ᾽ οὖν ἐπειδὴ ταῦτα τῆς ἀληθείας ἀπᾴδει βέλτιον ἀλληγοροῦντας λέγειν ἐστίν) that Cain intended to set up his own creed as one builds a city. (*Post.* 49–50)

In this passage Philo hesitantly introduces his allegorization of the biblical passage, suggesting that 'perhaps then' it is better to have recourse to the underlying meaning. His argument for an allegorical reading of Cain as the founder of a wicked creed, which relies on sophistic arguments, rests on the suggestion that the literal text 'diverges from the truth'. Philo makes special efforts to elaborate on the unrealistic nature of the verse, using Aristotelian notions of paradox and contrariness to reason, which had also been employed by Aristobulus.[56] Unlike these predecessors, however, Philo prepares his readers for a rather dramatic move to an extended allegory. His detailed study of the problem of verisimilitude indicates how important it was for him to anchor allegory in the literal text, thus hoping to convince his literalist readers of its plausibility.

Many other examples could be adduced. We will focus here on three which reflect Philo's Alexandrian environment particularly well.[57] The first example pertains to the issue of cleansing fruit trees, which Philo discusses in light of agricultural experience:

While now the statement that a tree is cleansed is reasonable and supported by truth, the statement that a fruit [is cleansed] is not at all confirmed by manifest fact (οὐ πάνυ τῷ ἐνεργεῖ πεπίστωται), for no gardener cleanses figs or grapes or any fruit at all. And yet he [Moses] says: 'its fruit shall for three years remain uncleansed and shall not be eaten' [LXX Lev. 19:23], as if it were customary [for the fruit] always to be cleansed.

It must be said now that these [statements] are one of those delivered in the underlying meanings, the literal meaning being very much out of accord (Λεκτέον οὖν ὅτι καὶ τοῦθ᾽ ἕν ἐστι τῶν ἐν ὑπονοίαις ἀποδιδομένων τοῦ ῥητοῦ μὴ σφόδρα συνᾴδοντος). (*Plant.* 112–13)

Philo shares here with his readers an agricultural experience which he expects to be widely known. He thus appeals to their concrete sense of reality in order to expose a problem of verisimilitude in the biblical text. Significantly, Philo does not assume the whole of Scripture should be taken

---

[56] Arist. *Poet.* 1460b33, *Apor. Hom.*, fr. 147, 167; for details on Aristobulus, see Chapter 4.

[57] For additional examples, see esp. *Somn.* 1.166–70, where Philo discusses a divergence from the truth in order to show that the description of the patriarchs is meant as an allegory about virtue; *Det.* 13–16, where Philo dismisses the verisimilitude of Gen. 37:14, stressing that it is utterly implausible to assume that Jacob sent Joseph to his brothers, going for him on an errand, since he was a rich man and thus not in need of a servant.

allegorically, but rather only those passages which are not 'smooth'. In the case of the present difficulty Philo argues that Moses intended to show how the fruits of education are to be properly treated.

Another problem of verisimilitude pertains to the biblical reference to Cain's wife, who had never been mentioned before (Gen. 4:17). Philo clearly formulates the question, which had apparently been raised already before him, namely:

Which wife did Cain know? For until now no creation of a woman other than that of Eve, created from Adam's ribs, is mentioned. (*Post.* 33)

Philo then offers his own allegorical solution, after dismissing another literal interpretation:

If someone will say (εἰ δὲ φήσει) that Cain married his sister, he will make a false statement in addition to saying something unholy, for he [Moses] introduces Adam's daughters as having been born much later (Gen. 5:4). What then must we say? (τί οὖν χρὴ λέγειν;)
He [Moses], as I believe (ὥς γε οἴομαι), calls 'woman' the opinion of impious reasoning . . . (*Post.* 34)

Philo appears to refer here to an existing discussion in Alexandria. He rejects the literal solution according to which Cain married his sister on two grounds. It is in his view 'unholy' to suggest that a sibling marriage would have been implied by Moses, who generally rejected the famous sibling marriages in Egypt.[58] Moreover, Philo considers the reference to Adam's daughters in Gen. 5:4 to be irrelevant in this context, because it appears in the biblical text after Cain's marriage. This argument is rather weak, because Gen. 5:4 provides a summary of all of Adam's children at the end of his life, mentioning the daughters only now, because in a patriarchal system they are evidently of little importance in the previous story. Philo's argumentation is nevertheless understandable in the context of his overall exegetical project. Insisting on the problem of verisimilitude on the literal level, he can offer allegory as a solution to the problem.

Philo also identifies problems of verisimilitude which echo a lively Alexandrian discussion on geographical issues. In the wake of Alexander's conquests, geography became a focus of Homeric scholarship (Strabo 1.3.3), thus complementing Classical Aristotelian concerns for verisimilitude. The Alexandrian scholar Eratosthenes led the critical camp in the second century BCE, altogether denying the value of Homer as a geographer. In his view, the epics were written only for the purpose of entertainment

---

[58] See *Spec.* 3.22–5; Niehoff 2001, pp. 94–9.

and appeal to the soul.[59] Homer was often found to say foolish things with no connection to geographical facts.[60] Apollodorus, a student of both Eratosthenes and Aristarchus, devoted a special commentary to the Homeric *Catalogue* where he treated questions of verisimilitude regarding geographical matters. The extant fragments indicate that he addressed critical issues raised by Eratosthenes but showed that Homeric passages contain an essential truth beneath the fictitious story (Strabo 10.2.10–16).

Following the Roman conquest of the East, geographical questions once more engaged scholarly interest. Well aware of the new knowledge gained under Rome's rule and familiar with Homeric scholars, such as Aristarchus, Aristonicus and Aristodemus, Strabo took a special interest in the epics.[61] In response to Eratosthenes' influential views, Strabo developed a complex notion of myth and argued that Homer's main purpose was to educate rather than to amuse.[62] If his geographical descriptions were found to ignore or even contradict known facts, such as the seven mouths of the Nile or the precise position of the island of Pharos, one must initially inquire whether they may reflect the state of knowledge or the linguistic conventions of Homer's time.[63] Overall, Strabo argued, Homer did not wholly invent stories but sometimes employed myths, which always preserve at least traces of real persons and events (1.2.14). This is so, because Homer made detailed inquiries and knew geographical facts but often chose to add fictional elements so as to arouse the interest of his audience (1.2.30). In Strabo's view, Homer thus created some 'impossible' scenes 'to gratify the taste for the marvellous and entertaining'.[64] The story of the wanderings of Odysseus, for example, which had been exposed to sharp criticism, was said to have been transmitted by Homer 'for our instruction, using allegory'.[65]

A late contemporary of Strabo, Philo shows a remarkably similar interest in the geographical problems of the Jewish Scriptures. Reflecting these distinctly Alexandrian pursuits, he inquires, for example, into the precise location of the four rivers of Paradise:

It is worth inquiring why (ἄξιον δὲ διαπορῆσαι διὰ τί) the two rivers Pheison and Geon encompass countries, the one Evilat, the other Ethiopia, while none of the others [does so]. Yet the Tigris is said to be facing the Assyrians, while the

---

[59] ψυχαγωγία (Strabo 1.2.3).   [60] Strabo 1.2.7, 1.2.12, 1.2.14–15, 1.2.19.
[61] See Strabo 1.2.1 for his awareness of Rome's contribution to geographical studies; see also Biraschi 2005, pp. 82–3; Dueck 2000, pp. 31–40, who stresses Strabo's deep interest in Homer and points to his personal background as one of the reasons for this.
[62] Strabo 1.2.8, 1.2.7; see also Schenkeveld 1976, pp. 52–64; Dueck 2000, p. 34; Biraschi 2005, p. 83.
[63] Strabo 1.2.10, 1.2.24.   [64] τερατείας καὶ τέρψεως χάριν (Strabo 1.2.35).
[65] ἀλληγορῶν (Strabo 1.2.7).

Euphrates is not said to be facing anything [Gen. 2:11–14]. And yet in reality (πρὸς τὸ ἀληθές) the Euphrates flows round several countries and has many facing it.

But the biblical story is not about a river, but about the improvement of character. (*All.* 1.85)

Following contemporary interests in geography, Philo notes in this passage that the biblical description of the Euphrates differs from that of the other rivers and inquires whether it corresponds to reality. Philo emphatically concludes that Scripture diverges from the truth and an allegorical solution is called for. Unlike Strabo, however, he is not satisfied with a brief solution to the problem but takes it as a starting point for an extended allegory on the improvement of character. He instructs his readers how to develop prudence and courage, which will protect them from folly and cowardice. Justice, by contrast, symbolized by the river Euphrates, which is 'not facing anything', does not provide this kind of protection and cannot serve as a palisade against vice.[66]

The novelty and importance of Philo's approach can be appreciated in comparison with Porphyry. He is the first exegete after Philo who offers a similar combination of Aristotelian scholarship and sustained allegory. Whether or not he knew Philo's writings, his *Cave of the Nymphs* strongly resembles the *Allegorical Commentary*. Porphyry introduces his discussion of the cave by stressing that 'the poet does not narrate these particulars from historical information (οὐ καθ᾿ ἱστορίαν)'.[67] This emerges from the fact that those who have reported on the island have not mentioned the cave at all. Like Philo, Porphyry uses this problem of verisimilitude to anchor allegory in the literal text:

Since this narration is full of obscurities (τοιούτων ἀσαφειῶν πλήρους ὄντος τοῦ διηγήματος), it can be neither a fiction casually devised for the purpose of [the reader's] delight (εἰς ψυχαγωγίαν) nor an exposition of a topical history, but something allegorical must be indicated in it by the poet, who mystically places an olive near the cave.[68]

Porphyry explicitly dismisses Eratosthenes' approach, which was based on the notion of Homer's epics as offering only literary delights. Acknowledging that the epic is not a scientifically accurate book, Porphyry stresses that the textual difficulty provides a key for unlocking its deeper allegorical meaning. In line with Philo's readings of Scripture, Porphyry discovers in the passage from the *Odyssey* a story about the soul and its ascent from the

[66] *All.* 1.86–7; for a similar example, see *Somn.* 2.246.
[67] Porph. *Cave of the Nymphs* 2, lines 14–17; ed. Nauck 1886, p. 55.
[68] Porph. *Cave of the Nymphs* 4, ll. 17–21; ed. Nauck 1886; trans. Th. Taylor 1991 with changes.

material to the spiritual realm. Strikingly, Porphyry concludes his treatise by insisting that 'interpretations of this kind' must not be considered 'forced (βεβαισμένας)' or 'nothing more than conjectures of ingenious men (εὑρεσιλογούντων πιθανότητας)'.[69] These apologies sound as if Porphyry in the third century CE still faced the same kind of critical colleagues as Philo had addressed in his *Allegorical Commentary*.

In conclusion, the *Allegorical Commentary* shows that Philo was deeply immersed in the literal methods of Homeric scholarship with its Aristotelian background in Alexandria. At the same time, Philo offered sustained allegorical readings of Scripture, frequently resorting to Platonic motifs. Whereas the Platonic tradition had thus far been reticent about literary scholarship on the epics, Philo broke new ground as a Platonist by adopting the methods of Aristotelian scholarship. Moreover, he established allegory as a serious form of interpretation which was grounded in the authorial intention of the biblical text. His approach can be identified as a significant extension of the Aristotelian tradition, thus offering an important alternative to Stoic allegory, which derived from etymology and ignored the author's own thoughts.

Combining earlier hermeneutic traditions in a novel way, Philo created a separate discourse of Jewish exegesis. Whereas his predecessors had engaged Aristotelian scholarship in order to compare the Jewish Scriptures with the literature of other nations, he wished to show that in the field of biblical hermeneutics the literary problems which had also been discussed in the context of Homer could be solved. In other words, Philo was well aware of the fact that the questions of Homeric and biblical scholarship were strikingly similar, but he insisted that the answers necessarily differed radically. Stressing the uniqueness of the Jewish Scriptures, Philo assumed that they ultimately transcend literary analysis. Philo thus departed from Aristotelian scholarship, even inverting it, and initiated a new path of religiously committed exegesis, which became very attractive among his later readers.

[69] Porph. *Cave of the Nymphs* 18; ed. Nauck 1886.

CHAPTER 9

Philo's Questions and Answers *as a manual of instruction*

In this chapter we continue to investigate Philo's own work in the light of Homeric scholarship. Taking into account the variety of his exegetical series, I focus in the present chapter on the *Questions and Answers on Genesis and Exodus* (*Q&A*). This series has from the inception of modern scholarship been recognized as similar to the *Allegorical Commentary*, because both are running commentaries covering largely the same biblical material.[1] Moreover, the *Q&A* involves a similar kind of literal and allegorical interpretation, beginning with a close reading of each verse and then leading the reader to its spiritual meaning.

Recently, the discussion of Philo's *Questions and Answers* has been enriched by investigating the implied audience of each series. Following a collection of articles, assembled by Hay (1991a), a rather broad consensus has emerged regarding the fact that Philo's different series address different audiences. Whereas the *Commentary* is acknowledged as a work appealing to specialists, the *Q&A* is generally taken to imply a far more general audience.[2]

The precise role of the *Q&A* within Philo's overall work still remains to be examined. Important new light can be thrown on this issue by investigating the nature of the questions raised in this series. Known to Eusebius as τὰ ἐν Γενέσει καὶ τὰ ἐν Ἐξαγωγῇ ζητήματα καὶ λύσεις (*Hist. eccl.* 2.8.1), the *Q&A* self-evidently belongs to the genre of the question and answer literature.[3] Beyond this general identification, however, no easy definitions

---

[1] Massebieau 1888, pp. 10–33, 59–65; Cohn 1899.

[2] Birnbaum 1996; van den Hoek 1997; Sterling 1999; Royse 2009. The question of chronology has also been discussed in Hay's collection of articles (1991a). While Abraham Terian and Greg Sterling argued for the priority of the *Questions and Answers*, interpreting them as preliminary notes to the *Allegorical Commentary*, Méasson and Cazeaux stressed the independence of the two series as well as their different genres. On the latter view, the *Q&A* is a catechetic work appealing to a broad audience, whereas the *Commentary* addresses far more specialized readers. For a more detailed discussion of the chronology of Philo's works in the context of his overall intellectual development, see Neihoff in press, c.

[3] This was noted by Cohn 1899, p. 403; it has been emphasized by Royse 2009, pp. 34–5.

apply. Sze-kar Wan has already shown that in comparison with Aristotle's *Aporemata Homerica* Philo's *Q&A* addresses a less sophisticated audience, raises only rarely problems of the Classical kind and provides considerably lengthier answers.[4]

Given this gap between Aristotle's scholarship and Philo's *Q&A*, it is necessary to examine how this series fits into the larger context of zetetic literature in the Hellenistic period. This task is rendered considerably more difficult by the fact that no comparable collection of questions and answers has survived from contemporary Alexandria. The most important point of reference is thus the *Allegorical Commentary*, where Philo uses critical questions of Aristotelian scholarship in order to address academic colleagues and develop his own allegorical approach in Platonic style.[5] The very straightforward approach of the *Q&A*, which offers direct instructions to the readers without probing into the intricacies of the biblical text, indicates an altogether different purpose. I shall suggest that the *Q&A* provides a unique glimpse into the world of Jewish education in Alexandria at a time when Philo may already have become an authoritative figure in the community.

THE IMPLIED AUDIENCE OF THE *QUESTIONS AND ANSWERS*

The first indication of Philo's implied audience in the *Q&A* is a new balance of references to other interpreters.[6] While the *Allegorical Commentary* was written mainly with a view to critical colleagues, frequently referring to their interpretations and even the details of their work, the *Q&A* primarily addressed readers for whom allegory was an accepted method of interpretation, which required no apologetics. In this series Philo limits his reports about critical colleagues, providing instead more details about other allegorical readers.[7]

---

[4] Wan 1993. Stressing the particular audience of the *Q&A*, Wan also argues that it must be seen as an independent treatise, which did not necessarily precede the *Allegorical Commentary*.

[5] For details, see Chapter 8.

[6] For an excellent overview of Philo's references, see Hay 1991b.

[7] Note that Philo occasionally provides some details of literal interpretation, which did not challenge his own; see, e.g., *Q.G.* 4.196, where he says the following: 'What is the meaning (of the expression) "after Isaac became old, his eyes grew weak in sight" (Gen. 27:1)? Those giving a literal explanation (որ զճառեալ պատմութիւնս գործեն) say that on account of a dispensation (յապագս մատակարարութեան) the prophet failed in sight, but later on he became once more fortified and keen-sighted. But the dispensation is a blessing so that not the wicked, but the one worthy of blessings may obtain it. For to me it seems that the answer is easily satisfying (հաւանարար հատուցանել զպատասխանին). But not in this place lies the beauty of the text, but rather in the natural opinions, which it is customary to affirm among those who allegorize.'

Critical scholarship is no longer presented in a way which allows the reader to form his or her own opinion, but rather as an abbreviated symbol of the negative Other. The *Q&A* significantly lacks extended fragments of critical Bible scholarship, such as the interpretation of the Tower of Babel, which was analysed in Chapter 5. Even on those rare occasions when Philo refers in both series to the same critical colleagues, he uses more polemical language in the *Q&A* and provides less information about their academic methods. In the *Allegorical Commentary*, for example, he explains that some of his colleagues engage in 'a detailed inquiry' into the changes of Abraham's and Sarah's names (*Mut.* 60). He goes on to report that they identify certain biblical motifs as 'not appropriate to preserve in the literal sense'. Philo even refers in this context to one particular scholar, who sarcastically says: 'great and surpassing indeed are the gifts which Moses says the Leader of all provided . . .' (*Mut.* 61). In the *Q&A*, by contrast, Philo does not refer to his colleagues' scholarly concerns, but mocks them in such a general way that the reader can only be astonished by the foolishness of such exegetes. In the context of Sarah's change of name Philo thus says:

Again some of the senseless[8] may make fun (ծաղր արաացէն) of the addition of one letter, the *rho*. And they are laughing about it and making fun so that they are not willing to expose the inward usefulness of the things themselves and to follow the traces of truth. (*Q.G.* 3.53, ed. Aucher 1826)

Philo makes similar statements regarding Abraham's change of name:

Some of those lacking culture and refinement,[9] rather more precisely out of foolishness and exclusion from the company of God, ridicule and reproach (ծաղր նախատանաց) the One pure by nature, and say in a blameworthy and reprehensible manner: oh, what a great gift! The Creator and Lord of All gave one letter by means of which He magnified the name of the patriarch, increasing it, so that it has three syllables instead of two. (*Q.G.* 3.43)

While Philo refers in both series to the same critical exegetes, in the *Q&A* he ascribes the sarcastic comments of the individual scholar to the group as a whole. To be sure, in the *Allegorical Commentary*, too, Philo vehemently criticizes his colleagues. At the same time, however, he also acknowledges their scholarly inquiries and provides sufficient evidence of their academic

---

[8] յանզգամաց = ἀφρόνων, πονηρῶν. The translations from Armenian to Greek are based on the *Nor Bargirk Armenian–Armenian Dictionary*, which provides typical Greek renditions of Armenian vocabulary in the ancient translation literature.

[9] ոմանք յանէրածշըուաց է յանսպարուց = ἔνιοι δὲ ἀμουσῶν καὶ ἀχορευτῶν.

methods to allow us to reconstruct their approach as a serious form of text criticism.[10] In the *Q&A*, by contrast, he focuses exclusively on polemics and subsequently even recommends in a highly condescending manner that his colleagues should engage in some study in order to appreciate Scripture properly (*Q.G.* 3.43).

More importantly, Philo now locates his critical colleagues outside 'the company of God', thus stressing the illegitimacy of their position. He assumes a strikingly orthodox position, in Walter Bauer's sense of an attempt to impose uniform structures on an earlier variety of views.[11] In Judaism the emergence of orthodox structures is usually associated with the rabbinic movement, but Philo clearly anticipates the sages of the Land of Israel.[12] The fact that the rabbis were increasingly able to define 'correct' ideas, because they had assumed sufficient political authority to do so, throws important light on Philo. His decision to 'excommunicate' and silence his colleagues indicates a growing self-confidence on his part and probably also an increase of real power within the Jewish community of Alexandria. Whereas in the *Allegorical Commentary* he seeks dialogue with Jews holding the opposite views, in the *Q&A* he is in a position to dismiss them altogether. He no longer expects text-critical scholars to read his work. Rather than engaging them in a discussion, Philo now constructs his own community, which strictly conforms to his convictions.

Philo's move from a more dialogical to a more orthodox position is conspicuous in his references to literal interpretations. It is striking that views, which are presented in a polite fashion in the *Allegorical Commentary*, are vehemently dismissed in the *Q&A*, their authors being personally ridiculed. Philo speaks here, for example, about a wrong opinion offered by 'unrestrained and gluttonous people with a belly' (*Q.G.* 1.18), while in the *Allegorical Commentary* he discusses the same interpretation as a plausible, yet ultimately unsatisfactory explanation (*All.* 2.9–10). Philo similarly reacts to those offering a literal interpretation of Cain's statement 'am I my brother's keeper?!' (Gen. 4:9). He altogether rejects such a reading in the *Q&A*, because it leads to anthropomorphic notions of God and thus to 'atheistic opinion' (*Q.G.* 1.69). In the *Allegorical Commentary*, by contrast, he argues gradually and by comparison with Abraham that Cain's words

---

[10] For details, see Chapter 7.

[11] Bauer 1971; for a useful survey of the history of Bauer's reception in modern scholarship, see Harrington 1980; see also the more recent account by Ehrman 2003, pp. 163–80.

[12] On the emergence of orthodox structures in rabbinic literature, see esp. Boyarin 2000; Niehoff 2006; cf. Schremer 2010, who is sympathetic to Bauer's approach but wishes to minimize the role of Christianity in the emergence of rabbinic orthodoxy.

should not be taken literally (*Det.* 57–60). Furthermore, in the *Q&A* Philo briefly dismisses those who 'wrongly assume' Gen. 6:6 to be a reference to God's actual repentance.[13] In the parallel passage in the *Allegorical Commentary*, on the other hand, he initially provides a rather more detailed picture of their interpretation and then criticizes it as a sinful thought (*Deus* 20–2).

Not surprisingly, the *Q&A* generally lacks direct positive appeals to literal readers. Philo no longer addresses them, as he does in the *Allegorical Commentary*, bidding them, for example, 'not to stop here, but to attend to allegorical explanations' (*Conf.* 190). Philo instead distances himself more explicitly from colleagues committed only to the literal sense and constructs firm boundaries between Us and Them. He does so by referring, for example, to an interpreter 'who errs against right thinking' or to literal exegetes, who 'pretend to believe'.[14] Right and wrong opinions are clearly delineated and associated respectively either with Our authentic group of Jewish allegorical readers or with the Other camp of literal exegetes.

Like-minded allegorical readers, by contrast, receive renewed attention in the *Q&A*. There is no parallel, for example, in any of Philo's other writings to the extended list of allegorical interpretations of the tree of life in the Garden of Eden. In the *Allegorical Commentary* Philo focuses on only one allegory, barely mentioning another (*All.* 1.56–9), but in the *Q&A* he provides the following detailed account:

Some say that the tree of life is the earth, because it causes everything to sprout for the life of both man and all other things . . . And some say that the tree of life is a name for the seven circles which are in heaven.

And some [identify the tree as] the sun, because it is really and truly in the middle of the planets and the cause of the seasons, through which everything comes into being. And some say that the tree of life is the government of the soul, because it invigorates and fortifies the faculty of the senses . . .

But distinguished and excellent men say that the tree of life is the best of virtues in man, piety, through which exclusively the mind becomes immortalized. (*Q.G.* 1.10)

Philo addresses here an audience used to allegorical interpretations, which no longer need to be justified. Moreover, he expects his readers to take a keen interest in a variety of allegorical readings, providing many different options which may appear rather similar to the outsider. Philo also grades his allegorical colleagues and identifies the last interpreters in the above list as 'distinguished and excellent men'. Those who had taken

---

[13] οὐκ εὖ δὲ ὑπονοοῦσιν (*Q.G.* 1.93, ed. Petit 1978); for further examples, see *Q.G.* 4.2 (referring to those 'gone astray in their beliefs'), *Q.E.* 2.45, *Q.G.* 4.60–1, 4.233.

[14] *Q.G.* 1.58, 2.79; see also *Q.G.* 2.64, 3.3, 4.233.

the biblical tree as a symbol of the earth are not especially praised. It thus emerges that Philo listed the different allegorizations available to him in a hierarchical order, presenting the less attractive ones at the beginning and guiding the reader to the desired climax at the end.

Another difference between the *Q&A* and the *Allegorical Commentary* is visible in the attribution of allegorical interpretations to other exegetes. Some of the interpretations, which are introduced as deriving from others in the *Q&A*, are presented as Philo's own in the *Allegorical Commentary*. In *Q.G.* 1.8, for example, Philo mentions 'some, believing Paradise to be a garden, have said that since the moulded man is sense-perception, he rightly goes to a sense-perceptible place'. In the parallel passage in the *Allegorical Commentary* Philo presents virtually the same interpretation yet speaks of it as his own idea (*Cher.* 44–5).[15] Even if other allegorists are mentioned in both series, they are 'many' in the *Q&A*, but only 'some' in the *Allegorical Commentary*.[16] In the latter Philo assumes the role of *the* representative allegorical reader, who offers a controversial interpretation accepted only by few. In the *Q&A*, on the other hand, he speaks from the point of view of a comfortable majority and mentions other similar interpretations which may already have been known to his audience.

Philo's considerably greater self-confidence in the *Q&A* is also reflected in the fact that he now presents allegorical interpretations as 'natural' (*Q.G.* 4.243). Instead of introducing them hesitantly and with a view to convincing critical scholars, he can simply appeal to his readers as 'us, who naturally allegorize'.[17] On another occasion Philo goes even further, speaking of us 'the students of Moses,[18] manifestly knowing the intention of our teacher . . . , [who] allegorically indicates . . . ' (*Q.G.* 3.8). In this skilful rhetorical move Philo associates allegorical exegesis with a natural understanding of Moses' original message. He and his allegorical followers emerge as authentic 'students of Moses'.

The *Q&A* thus reflects an author who self-confidently addresses an audience which he expects to be congenial and attentive. Philo speaks here to the convinced, stressing 'our' group identity vis-à-vis 'Other' critical and literal readers. It is likely that such an audience emerged at a more advanced stage of Philo's career, namely after he succeeded in drawing attention among Alexandrian Jews. While Jewish Bible scholars had traditionally been inclined towards a literary Aristotelian approach, a considerable number of the community may have been attracted by Philo's

---

[15] See also *Q.G.* 1.10 in comparison with *Migr.* 37; Hay 1991b, pp. 89–93.
[16] See *Q.G.* 3.11 (բազմաց բան), cf. *Her.* 280–1 (ἔνιοι, τινές).
[17] Մեզ որ այլաբանութեամբ բնութիւնն է (*Q.G.* 4.243).
[18] մեք մովսեսի ձանոթքս = ἡμεῖς γνώριμοι Μωυσέως (*Q.G.* 3.8).

allegorical exegesis at the time when he composed the *Q&A*. Leopold Cohn's conclusion that the *Q&A* follows the *Allegorical Commentary* is thus attractive.[19] It is indeed likely that this series may address a different audience at a later stage of Philo's career.

LITERAL AND ALLEGORICAL INTERPRETATIONS
IN THE SERVICE OF EDUCATION

Having appreciated the implied audience of the *Q&A* as well as Philo's increasingly self-confident position within the Jewish community of Alexandria, we now have to examine the characteristic features of his exegesis in this series. The brevity and simplicity of the *Q&A* are immediately conspicuous. Short questions and clear answers are presented in a user-friendly fashion. David Runia has drawn attention to the fact that Philo adduces here far fewer comparative verses than in the *Allegorical Commentary*, thus further clarifying the picture.[20] At the same time, however, the lucidity of the *Q&A* also implies a limitation of scholarship on the literal level. In particular, Philo has abandoned the prevalent method of Homeric and earlier biblical scholarship to study in depth any line or verse by comparing it with its parallels throughout the whole literary corpus.[21]

Another important feature of the *Q&A* is Philo's general insistence on the veracity and clarity of Scripture. He does not stress textual problems, as he did in the *Allegorical Commentary*, where he sometimes even dwelt on difficulties beyond the necessities of the literal text in order to prepare his readers for his move to allegory. In the *Q&A*, by contrast, textual 'stumbling blocks' are played down. Philo often comments on the literal text with a brief statement on its clarity. Such comments have a rather apologetic connotation, since in the *Allegorical Commentary* he had recognized a significant problem in the same verse. In the *Q&A* Philo stresses, for example, that the story of Eve's creation from Adam's rib 'is clear (յայնի)' in the literal sense (*Q.G.* 1.25).[22] In the *Allegorical Commentary*, on the other hand, he exclaimed:

The literal sense of these words is mythological, for how could anyone accept the idea that a woman or any human being is created from man's rib? (*All.* 2.19)

---

[19] Cohn 1899, pp. 403–4; Cohn's view has been accepted by Royse 2009, pp. 60–1; contra Massebieau 1888, p. 10.

[20] Runia 1991.

[21] Regarding the technique of comparing verses within the same work, see Chapters 3 and 8.

[22] For additional examples, see *Q.G.* 3.1 in comparison with *Her.* 96; and *Q.G.* 1.74, 2.37, 3.15, 3.25, 3.28, 3.30, 3.32, 3.45; see also Wan 1993, p. 35, who counted fifty-five examples where Philo presents the literal text as 'clear'.

Philo similarly treats the serpent in Paradise. Although he admitted in the *Allegorical Commentary* that, taken literally, this image is mythical (*Agr.* 96–7), in the *Q&A* he makes considerable efforts to show the plausibility of the biblical text (*Q.G.* 1.32). Having recourse to the notion of a miracle and to historical conjecture, Philo no longer introduces his own allegorical interpretation as a solution to a problem of verisimilitude, but rather as an additional meaning next to the acceptable literal sense. Furthermore, Philo acknowledged in the *Allegorical Commentary* that there is a problem of verisimilitude in the story of Sarah's barrenness, because a woman said to be sterile cannot suddenly bear children (*Mut.* 143). This problem is no longer addressed in the *Q&A*, where Philo simply says that the biblical note about Sarah's barrenness points to Divine providence (*Q.G.* 3.18).[23] In this case, too, the *Q&A* emerges as having been written in a more pious spirit. Rather than highlighting problems of verisimilitude in the style of the *Allegorical Commentary*, Philo insists on the truth value of the biblical text.

Another striking example of this exegetical tendency can be found in Philo's discussion of the rivers of Paradise. Following geographical inquiries into Homer's epics, Philo had in the *Allegorical Commentary* questioned the veracity of the literal text.[24] He admitted that there was a gap between Scripture and geography, stressing that the Euphrates 'in reality flows round several countries and has many facing it' (*All.* 1.85). In the *Q&A*, by contrast, he writes the following:

The sources of the Tigris and the Euphrates are said to flow from the Armenian mountains. But there is no Paradise (դրախտ) nor are there the two other sources of the river.

Unless perhaps Paradise is somewhere remote from our inhabited world[25] and has a river flowing under the earth, which waters many and great veins . . . And these are the supposed sources, or rather the out-flowings of the river, but properly the supposed sources, because in every respect the Holy Writings are true.[26] (*Q.G.* 1.12)

In this passage Philo still shows an awareness of the textual problem he had previously discussed. Instead of using it, however, as a justification of allegory, he now insists programmatically on the absolute truth value of 'the

---

[23] For further examples, see esp. *Q.G.* 1.6 in comparison with *All.* 1.43 and *Plant.* 33–5; *Q.G.* 1.3 in comparison with *Fuga* 179–80.

[24] For details, see Chapter 8.

[25] հեռի ի մերմէ բնակութենէ աշխարհիս = ἔξω τῆς καθ᾿ ἡμᾶς οἰκουμένης.

[26] վասն յամենայնին անսուտ զոլ ածային զրոց = καὶ γὰρ πανταχοῦ ἀληθής ἐστιν ἡ ἱερὰ γράφη.

Holy Writings' and offers a solution also on the literal level. He suggests that Paradise may be situated outside the inhabited world and thus lies beyond human measurements and maps. In other words, Scripture is true, even if we cannot assert its veracity by means of empirical proof. This solution significantly differs from Philo's earlier acknowledgement that the literal text is not true to reality. Philo has in the meantime joined the camp of more conservative Homeric scholars, who had similarly interpreted a problem of verisimilitude regarding Menelaus' wanderings. While some interpreters rejected this story as untrue, others suggested that these wanderings must have taken place 'outside Oceanus' (Strabo 1.2.35).

Assuming the veracity of Scripture in *Q&A*, Philo offers a surprisingly uniform version of questions and answers, which considerably differs from his style in the *Allegorical Commentary*. We may recall that the latter showed a high degree of ambiguity and polyphony, because Philo constantly wavered between problematizing the literal text and using it as an anchor for allegory. In the *Q&A*, by contrast, the literal and the allegorical meaning are conceived as straightforward and complementary messages, leading the reader to a proper religious attitude. Paradoxically, the literal text is considered to be of much higher truth value, while receiving far less attention than in the *Allegorical Commentary*.

Philo is no longer apologetic about his allegorical interpretations, presenting them instead with new self-confidence. Generally neither relying on his earlier Aristotelian approach nor on the Stoic method of etymology, Philo places the allegorical interpretation naturally and without further ado next to the literal meaning.[27] Characteristic introductions are 'symbolically this means', 'as for the deeper meaning' or this biblical detail 'should be thought as a symbol' or simply 'to me it seems'.[28] Stressing that the biblical text is clear on the literal level, Philo offers his allegorical interpretations with surprising freedom. He hardly has recourse to textual problems, and even contradictions between verses, which are occasionally discussed in the *Q&A*, are no longer used to justify his move to allegory.[29]

The importance of the *Q&A* consists in Philo's new use of the question and answer format. It serves for the first time as a framework for organizing and transmitting a corpus of coherent teaching. Yannis Papadoyannakis identified such a use in early Christian collections and stressed its didactic

---

[27] Note the few exceptions where Philo problematizes the literal text in order to prepare his readers for the allegorical interpretation. *Q.G.* 1.39, 3.33, 4.88, 4.168, 4.175.

[28] See, e.g., *Q.G.* 1.6, 3.25, 3.28, 1.8, 3.27, 1.31, 1.10, 1.11, 1.13.

[29] Regarding the lack of references to textual problems, see esp. *Q.G.* 1.6, 3.45, 3.30, 3.32, 4.152; regarding contradictions, see esp. *Q.G.* 1.15, 1.19, 2.49; *Q.G.* 2.74 in comparison with *Sobr.* 31–48; *Q.G.* 1.59 in comparison with *Sacr.* 11.

orientation. The writer or compiler thus imitates the teacher's authoritative position in the classroom and provides guidance regarding the field of inquiry as well as its limitations.[30] Characteristically, such collections are often written with a view to Other positions, thus outlining what is perceived to be the correct path. Philo's *Q&A*, written in the first century CE, is thus an important precedent for this kind of Christian literature.

Philo's didactic use of the question and answer format is immediately visible in the very general nature of his questions. He often simply asks 'why it is written'?[31] These διὰ τί or τί ἐστιν questions create a framework for discussing major portions of the Torah in a verse-by-verse fashion.[32] They are intended to raise the reader's curiosity and focus his attention on a particular verse. Philo thus creates a platform to expound his own views. The didactic orientation of the *Q&A* is furthermore prominent in passages where Philo praises the biblical verse as 'most exemplary' (δογματικώτατον) or of 'most universal application' (καθολικώτατον).[33] In the *Q&A* he similarly testifies to having been prompted by the biblical verse to 'see' (տեսանեմ) a religious truth, while in the parallel passage in the *Allegorical Commentary* he addressed a textual problem.[34]

Philo often formulates his questions in such a way as to imply the answer, thus firmly guiding the reader towards the correct solution. A good example of this type of question can be found in Philo's discussion of anthropomorphic images. In this context he regularly raises questions with an emphasis on the fact that God has no share whatsoever in human feelings. He can thus ask:

Why does [Moses] say 'He led the animals to man to see what he would call them', since God does not doubt (οὐ γὰρ ἐνδοιάζει θεός)? (*Q.G.* 1.21, ed. Petit 1978)

In this and other similar cases the question precludes an answer which would assume God's anthropomorphic features.[35] Philo's 'solution' is

---

[30] Papadoyannakis 2006, esp. pp. 94–9.

[31] See also Wan 1993, pp. 33–5, who identifies this type of question as 'rhetorical' in contrast to the Classical Aristotelian type, which raises real critical questions on the literal text; contra Borgen and Skarsten 1976–7, who stressed that the *Q&A* and the *Allegorical Commentary* address similar kinds of question.

[32] The question of the original scope of Philo's work is still debated. A more limited scope with roots in the reading cycle of the synagogue has been assumed by Marcus 1953, vol. I, pp. x–xv; Royse 1976–7; Royse 2009, pp. 37–8. By contrast, Cohn 1899, pp. 403–4, argued that the *Q&A* originally extended beyond the books of Genesis and Exodus, since John of Damascus refers to Φίλωνος ἐκ τῶν ἐν τῷ Λευιτικῷ ζητημάτων.

[33] *Q.G.* 1.70, cf. on the same verse *Det.* 48 (τὸ παραδοξότατον); *Q.G.* 1.72, cf. on the same verse *Det.* 91 (ἀκόλουθον).

[34] *Q.G.* 4.90, cf. *All.* 3.42 (οὐ δυνατόν).

[35] For further examples in the context of anthropomorphism, see *Q.G.* 1.55 (ed. Petit 1978) οὔτε ἐνδοιασμὸς οὔτε φθόνος περὶ θεόν, *Q.G.* 1.42, 1.47; for other examples of Philo inserting his own

indeed nothing but an emphatic restatement of the message implied already in the question. He stresses that 'doubting is truly foreign to the Divine power' and 'truly, the deity has neither doubt nor envy'.[36] The question and answer format is no longer an instrument for probing the intricacies of the biblical text, but rather a springboard for religious teaching. The answers consequently assume a far more central place. Philo takes the opportunity to explain in detail how God's true nature can be grasped (*Q.G.* 1.21). He also instructs his readers that Moses used two ways of describing God, namely either as utterly different from man, acknowledging His true nature, or as similar to man, speaking pedagogically.[37]

In the *Q&A* Philo presents his answers, too, in a conspicuously didactic form. Several congenial answers are often listed in stenographic style, thus providing a user-friendly overview.[38] Appealing to readers who are apparently less scholarly than those of the *Allegorical Commentary*, Philo moreover writes in short sentences and often summarizes his thoughts in a single key sentence.[39] He obviously wants to make sure that the reader grasps his message. This didactic style differs remarkably from Philo's procedure in the *Allegorical Commentary*, where he expressed himself in complicated sentence structures, often addressing a perplexing variety of issues at the same time. Conforming to its general orientation, the *Q&A* is highly consistent and offers complementary rather than contrary answers. These build on each other, relying on the same allegorical code, which needs only to be briefly recalled rather than explained in detail.[40] An easily accessible and coherent teaching thus unfolds in the pages of the *Q&A*.

A few examples may illustrate the kind of straightforward instruction Philo wishes to convey. Discussing the biblical expression 'this is the book of the coming into being of heaven and earth' (Gen. 2:4), he directly explains that the Book of Genesis is meant, which reports the 'things which truly have come into being'.[41] In the *Allegorical Commentary*, on the other hand, he offered rather more complicated speculations about the

---

solution already in the question, see *Q.G.* 1.60 (ed. Petit 1978), where he says ὅπα τοίνυν φιλαύτου καὶ φιλοθέου διαφοράν; *Q.G.* 1.61, 1.65, 1.66, 1.68, 1.73.

[36] ἀλλότριον γὰρ ὄντως θείας δυνάμεως τὸ ἐνδοιάζειν (*Q.G.* 1.21; ed. Petit 1978); ἀληθῶς οὐκ ἐνδοιάζει (*Q.G.* 1.55; ed. Petit 1978).

[37] τὸ δὲ δεύτερον παιδείας καὶ εἰσαγωγῆς (*Q.G.* 1.55).

[38] See, e.g., *Q.G.* 1.27, 1.30, 1.32, 1.35, 1.41, 1.51, 1.52, 1.64, 1.76.

[39] See, e.g., *Q.G.* 1.29, where Philo says: '[Moses] says something very tangible and sense-perceptible…' (cf. *All.* 2.49–52); *Q.G.* 1.42, 1.53, 1.56, 1.57; see also Cohn 1899, p. 403, who noted Philo's tendency in the *Q&A* to abbreviate complicated explanations of the *Allegorical Commentary*.

[40] See, e.g., *Q.G.* 1.31, where Philo introduces the symbolical meaning of the serpent, which is then taken up again in *Q.G.* 1.48.

[41] τὰ ἐπ' ἀληθείας γεγονότα (*Q.G.* 1.1; ed. Petit 1978).

Divine Logos (*All.* 1.19–20). Similarly, in the *Q&A* Philo uses the biblical statement 'it is not good for man to be alone' (Gen. 2:18) as an opportunity to praise marital love and concord as a 'strengthener of character' (*Q.G.* 1.17). In the *Allegorical Commentary*, by contrast, he dramatically turned to Moses to inquire why indeed man should not be alone (*All.* 2.1–8). Finally, the biblical image of Adam naming the animals is used in the *Q&A* to provide a lucid summary of insights, which were rather more scattered in the *Allegorical Commentary*.[42]

In conclusion, the importance of the *Q&A* as a manual of instruction must be emphasized. It is the first extant compilation of questions and answers on a foundational text, which uses the zetetic form to organize the transmission of a particular religious teaching. While thus far in the Aristotelian tradition the questions tended to be of central importance, usually addressing a text-critical problem, Philo gives new priority to the answers. Assuming the veracity of Scripture on both the literal and the allegorical level, he offers a manual of correct answers to rather general questions. A monolithic and hierarchical discourse emerges, which ultimately inverts traditional Homeric scholarship. Philo indeed wishes to protect his audience from the doubts of truly critical inquiry, offering allegorical interpretations in a new and highly self-confident manner which is only rarely anchored in the literal text.

THE ALEXANDRIAN CONTEXT

It now remains to be seen how Philo's *Q&A* fits into the Alexandrian context. Can a particular group of students or perhaps even a school be identified? Whereas most scholars have located Philo's teaching activities in the context of the Alexandrian synagogues, a reconstruction which is possible but cannot be proven, Gregory Sterling has offered an important new perspective by arguing for the possibility that Philo instructed students in a private setting.[43] Following Sterling's distinction between a more

---

[42] '[Moses] clarified the great complexity of those who are involved in philosophy, explaining that these names exist through attribution, but not by nature. For [he explained] that a proper and suitable name was each suited naturally to whatever [object] through the ingeniousness of the wise man, who is also pre-eminent in knowledge. And the attribution of names was most proper to the one not only wise, but also first born of the earth. For it was necessary that the ruler of mankind and the king of all earth-born creatures should achieve this great honour, so that he, as the first indeed who saw the animals and the first who himself became worthy of ruling over all [the animals] should become also the first author and inventor of names' (*Q.G.* 1.20; ed. Aucher 1826 and Petit 1978); cf. *All.* 1.90–1, *Mut.* 63.

[43] Sterling 1999; cf. Wolfson 1947, vol. 1, p. 79; Nikiprowetzky 1977, pp. 179–80; Royse 1976–7; Perrot 1984, pp. 129–32. Some of the above scholars have even attempted to identify a division of weekly

sophisticated audience for the *Allegorical Commentary* and simpler readers of the *Q&A*, I would like to highlight the unique role of the latter. While I interpreted the *Allegorical Commentary* in a strictly academic context, I shall argue that the *Q&A* provides important information about more general Jewish education.

Initially, a negative qualifier is in order. The *Q&A* does not provide elementary instruction in the Jewish Scriptures. Philo presupposes a basic knowledge of the biblical stories and does not raise the kinds of question which were used by primary schoolteachers to familiarize their pupils with the basic plot. A famous papyrus records the following questions, which were meant to alert Greek school boys to the most salient facts of the Homeric epics:

Who were the gods on the side of Troy? Who was the king of the Trojans? [Who was] their general . . . ?[44]

Philo's questions in the *Q&A* are obviously of a much more advanced nature. While this series addresses a less sophisticated audience than the *Allegorical Commentary*, it still preserves the form of a running commentary. Philo may well have written for Jews who had already received a basic instruction in the synagogue. 'A man of the ruling class', whom Philo once quotes, portrays the Jews on the Sabbath as 'reading the holy books' and 'unfolding what may not be clear'.[45] Philo's implied readers in the *Q&A* may well have heard such clarifications and were now ready for some further instruction.

No hard evidence has survived to reconstruct the precise institutional framework of Philo's teaching activities, and yet some revealing clues are available. On two important occasions Philo draws a picture of Jewish pedagogy, namely in his *Dialogue on the Rationality of Animals* with his nephew Julius T. Alexander and in his famous description of Bible studies among the Therapeutae. These settings cannot be verified by comparative material, but they are immediately relevant because they belong to the later period of Philo's career, when he had already assumed a prolific public role and come into close contact with Rome.[46] These treatises moreover reflect

---

Torah portions in Philo's treatises. This view, however, relies on a very speculative reconstruction of the original literary units of the *Q&A* and cannot explain Philo's rather more selective approach, which does not cover all the biblical material equally.

[44] *PSI* 19, quoted by Marrou 1950, p. 233; and by Jacob 2004, p. 37.

[45] εἴ τι μὴ τρανὲς εἴη διαπτύσσοντες (*Somn.* 2.127); see also Leonhardt 2001, pp. 89–91; Philo's descriptions of Sabbath instruction in the *Exposition* notably lack references to Bible exegesis (see *Mos.* 2.216, *Spec.* 2.61–2).

[46] See also Sterling 1999, pp. 157–8, who stresses that the setting of the dialogue cannot be historically verified. Concerning the date of the dialogue with Alexander, which mentions the Jewish embassy to

Philo's educational values and thus provide a rather accurate picture of what he aimed at in the *Q&A*.

Philo's dialogue with Alexander and Lysimachus, another family member, assumes the context of private instruction. Such meetings seem to have been convened at changing intervals, depending on the circumstances. Lysimachus, for example, mentions public and family affairs which may interrupt philosophical inquiries (*Alex.* 4).[47] Another feature of private instruction is prominent: a slave enters the room, bringing a book which will be the object of the following discussion (*Alex.* 9). In this setting Philo assumes a remarkably authoritative posture. He agrees to explain his views only on condition that Lysimachus will sit quietly and not interrupt him (*Alex.* 5). This suggestion is promptly rejected as being 'contrary to philosophy', but then accepted for the benefit of the instruction which Lysimachus hopes to gain by the 'conversation' (*Alex.* 6). He thus agrees to the following relationship between student and teacher:

So I sit quietly, modestly and with restored humility as is proper for a student and here you are seated in front of me on a platform looking dignified, respectable and erudite, ready to begin to teach your teaching. (*Alex.* 6)[48]

This strictly hierarchical setting closely parallels the structure of the *Q&A*, where Philo also poses as an authoritative speaker. Here, too, the questions are not real, because the views of Alexander are dismissed from the beginning. Lysimachus does not raise difficulties but comes to Philo wishing to hear more of his views on the matter. Such a procedure is self-consciously distinguished from a free philosophical dialogue, where the conversation partners are expected to be equals challenging each other. Philo's dialogue is so monolithic or perhaps even 'orthodox' that in the end he disqualifies his nephew's view as 'opposite to the sacred doctrine' (*Alex.* 75).

An even more interesting picture emerges in the context of the Therapeutae. This group consists of devoted allegorical readers like Philo, spending most of their days reading 'the Holy Scriptures, seeking wisdom in their ancestral philosophy by way of allegorizing' (*Cont.* 28). According to Philo, they took the literal meaning as 'symbols of something whose hidden nature

---

Rome (*Alex.* 54), see Terian 1988, pp. 45–50; regarding the place of *On the Contemplative Life* within Philo's work, see Niehoff 2010c; J. E. Taylor 2003, who draws attention to significant historical circumstances reflected in this treatise.

[47] See also *Alex.* 75, where the possibility of postponing further discussion is considered.

[48] Translation by A. Terian, quoted by Sterling 1999, p. 157, from Terian 1981, which was not available to me.

is revealed in the underlying meaning'.[49] The Therapeutae share not only Philo's general allegorical approach, but also his distinctly non-apologetic position in the *Q&A*. Philo explains that this group views the whole Torah as a kind of living creature, the body corresponding to the literal meaning and the soul to the allegorical interpretation (*Cont.* 78). These two levels complement each other in precisely the same way as Philo suggests in the *Q&A*. They are conceived to be naturally parallel rather than one being subordinate to the other and requiring justification by literary criticism or etymology.

Philo reports on the centrality of the question and answer format among the Therapeutae.[50] During the symposia the president provides a festive exposition for the whole group and 'inquires into some question (ζητεῖ) in the Holy Scriptures or solves (ἐπιλύεται) one previously raised by someone else'.[51] This exegetical exposition is significantly identified as a form of leisurely 'instruction' (διδασκαλία), which involves some repetition, shunning clever rhetoric and superficial effect (*Cont.* 75–6). The questions are not discussed in a strictly academic context but serve instead as a prelude to the immediately following hymns and religious festivities.[52]

Strictly hierarchical structures characterize the Therapeutae, too. The president of the group speaks only when absolute silence prevails. His exposition is not addressed to equals, but rather to an audience 'not similarly clear-sighted' (*Cont.* 75). The members of the group are not expected to argue with him, as would be typical of a Classical Greek symposium,[53] but rather to try to follow the course of his exposition:

They listen with ears pricked up and eyes fixed on him always in exactly the same posture, signifying comprehension and acceptance by nods and glances, their praise of the speaker by cheerfulness and slightly turning their faces, their perplexity by a gentler movement of the head as well as the finger-tip of their right hand. (*Cont.* 77)

Applause and acceptance rather than open discussion are anticipated. Obviously not in a position to argue with the speaker, the members of

---

[49] ἐπειδὴ σύμβολα τὰ τῆς ῥητῆς ἑρμηνείας νομίζουσιν ἀποκεκρυμμένης φύσεως ἐν ὑπονοίαις δηλουμένης (*Cont.* 28); see also *Cont.* 78; Klinghardt 1996, p. 196, who generally pointed to the similarity between the Therapeutae allegory and Philo's own procedure in the *Q&A*; cf. J. E. Taylor 2003, pp. 126–53, who associates the allegorical approach with the 'extreme allegorists' mentioned in *Migr.* 86–93 and concludes that the former, too, were not observant. This conclusion, however, is not warranted, see my review in *SCI* 23 (2004), pp. 305–9.
[50] The centrality of Scriptural study among the Therapeutae was noted by Wendland 1896, pp. 748–50, who used it for his argument in favour of the Jewish character of the group, which emerged in his view in scholarly circles.
[51] *Cont.* 75; for a detailed analysis of the Therapeutae symposium, see Niehoff 2010c.
[52] *Cont.* 80; see also Deutsch 2006.   [53] See also König 2008.

the group may only aspire to imbibe and comprehend the speaker's words. This is true not only on special occasions, when the president addresses them, but also on regular Shabbats when a senior member expounds the Torah. Then, too, Philo indicates, the Therapeutae are exposed to a didactic discourse, which they accept silently, indicating their 'praise by looks or nods' (*Cont.* 31).

Philo undoubtedly offered an idealizing picture of the Therapeutae, filtering their practices through his own tendentious views, but it is nevertheless appropriate to ask whether he wrote his *Q&A* with them in mind. Did he perhaps even anticipate that they would use his treatises either in their daily study or in the special group sessions? His style of allegorical exposition in a question and answer format would undoubtedly have suited them very well. One can easily imagine the president of the group consulting Philo's *Q&A* and selecting each time one of the solutions conveniently listed on every verse. Furthermore, the Therapeutae seem to have been open to exegetical literature written by prominent writers. As Philo says:

They also have treatises of men of old, who were the founders of their school (οἳ τῆς αἱρέσεως ἀρχηγέται) and left behind them numerous memorials of the form used in allegorical interpretation, which they take as a kind of archetype and imitate their method of exposition (μιμοῦνται τῆς προαιρέσεως τὸν τρόπον). (*Cont.* 29)

Although Philo was not a founder of the Therapeutic school, he could easily have been considered by them as an allegorical exegete worthy of imitation. His own encomium of the group suggests cordial relations.[54] Even if Philo's *Q&A* had not become part of their curriculum, the framework of biblical instruction among the Therapeutae suited him particularly well. Indeed, Philo's description offers a vivid picture of the kind of teaching activity he himself anticipated in his *Q&A*.

Philo's *Q&A* thus provides unique insights into one aspect of Jewish instruction in first-century Alexandria. This series is the first extant work which puts the verse-by-verse commentary to didactic use for a wider audience, which had already received primary education but had no directly scholarly interests. The considerable breadth of the *Q&A* suggests a serious demand for Philo's instruction and points to regular teaching activity. This teaching probably took place in Alexandria and followed the same lines of pedagogy as suggested in the dialogue with Alexander and the description of Bible studies among the Therapeutae.

---

[54] See also F. Daumas in: Daumas and Miquel 1963, pp. 32–4, 48–9, who argued for a continuous, personal relationship between Philo and the Therapeutae; Wendland 1896, p. 740, who suspected that some of the similarities between Philo and the Therapeutae were the result of Philo's interpretation.

The *Q&A* marks an important turning point in Philo's career. While the *Allegorical Commentary* shows him in his initial controversies with critical colleagues of an Aristotelian orientation, the *Q&A* assumes a convinced audience, interested to learn more about Philo's views. The highly authoritative style of the *Q&A* also indicates the emergence of orthodox structures, used to create a committed community around Philo's more conservative approach to biblical studies. It remains to be explored whether this setting had any direct influence on the emergence of Christian Bible studies in Alexandria.[55]

---

[55] Clement of Alexandria, of course, is a key figure in this context. On his positive attitude towards Philo, see Runia 1993a, pp. 132–56. Van den Hoek 1997, pp. 79–85, suggested that the main connection between Philo and Clement was literary: Philo's works were known to Clement. At the same time, van den Hoek intriguingly wonders whether the scholarly nature of Christian exegesis in Alexandria had any connection to an earlier 'school of biblical scholarship' (p. 82).

CHAPTER 10

Philo's Exposition of the Law *at a significant distance from Alexandrian scholarship*

The last series of Philo' exegetical writings that we shall analyse in this book is the *Exposition of the Law*, which is generally recognized as belonging to a different genre from the *Allegorical Commentary* and the *Q&A*.[1] Abraham Terian and David Runia rightly stressed this difference, insisting that Philo's treatise *On the Creation* belongs together with the *Lives of the Patriarchs* and should not have appeared in the English translation of his works before the three books of *Allegorical Commentary* on the creation.[2] The structure of the *Exposition* was appreciated by the modern Hebrew translators of Philo's works, who published its different treatises in their proper order.[3] The Hebrew reader of Philo thus moves from the *Creation* directly to the *Lives of the Patriarchs* and from there to the *Decalogue* and *On the Special Laws*. In this way Philo's argument about the law of Nature, which unfolds in these different aspects of the Jewish religion, is easily recognized as a prominent theme of the series.[4]

The *Exposition* no longer follows the conventions of a running commentary, offering instead a broad paraphrase or summary of the biblical material.[5] Leopold Cohn and Louis Massebieau have explained this feature by reference to the particular audience of this series.[6] In their view, Philo addressed a wider Jewish audience in Alexandria than he had previously envisioned in the *Allegorical Commentary* and the *Q&A*, while not yet reaching out to an even broader non-Jewish audience, as he subsequently

---

[1] See Runia 2001, pp. 5–8; Royse 2009, pp. 45–50, and references there.
[2] Terian 1997; Runia 2001, pp. 1–4. The connection between the *Lives of the Patriarchs* and *On the Creation of the World* is particularly stressed by Philo in *Abr.* 1–3, on which see also Massebieau 1888, pp. 36–7; Borgen 1997, pp. 66–7.
[3] Daniel-Nataf 1986–, vols. II and III.
[4] On the development and function of this argument in the *Exposition*, see Chapter 6; the structure and coherence of the *Exposition* have been emphasized by Borgen 1996.
[5] Philo's summary is of a different kind from the Midrash known as 'rewritten Bible' from the Land of Israel, on which see Alexander 1988; contra Borgen 1997, pp. 63–79.
[6] Cohn 1899, pp. 404–15, and Massebieau 1888, pp. 33–41.

169

did in his apologetic and historical works. More recently, Ellen Birnbaum has pointed to indications that non-Jewish readers, ignorant of the basic facts of Judaism, were also implied in the *Exposition*.[7]

It is thus time to re-examine the question of Philo's audience in the *Exposition* and to ask what role his more paraphrastic exegesis played in the context of his career. In particular, what did his break with the conventions of Alexandrian commentary activity signify? I shall argue that Philo addressed a wider, non-Jewish audience at a stage in life when he had already become involved in the political affairs which led to the embassy to Rome. It is even possible that he wrote with Roman readers in mind, presenting to them an overview of Scripture with some echoes of his earlier questions and answers.

THE IMPLIED AUDIENCE OF THE *EXPOSITION*

The bird's-eye perspective on Scripture which is conspicuous in the *Exposition* provides a first indication of its implied audience. Philo opens his treatise *On the Creation of the World* with a comparison of lawgivers, which leads to praise of Moses. Philo stresses that, in contrast to others, Moses prefaced his laws with a 'most impressive exordium', thus providing a proper philosophical framework for the observance of his laws.[8] Explaining that Moses' exordium consists of an account of the creation, Philo obviously does not anticipate any prior knowledge of the Book of Genesis (*Opif.* 3). His procedure differs strikingly from both the *Allegorical Commentary* and the *Q&A*, where he addressed Alexandrian Jews, used to reading Scripture, and offered a verse-by-verse commentary without introduction or general explanations.

Furthermore, in the *Exposition* Philo begins his discussion of the creation with two general considerations, namely the unspeakable beauty of the topic and the contrary view of an uncreated, eternal world (*Opif.* 4–7). It is remarkable that Philo stresses these two topics also in the opening of his treatise *On the Eternity of the World*, which addresses an audience conspicuously ignorant of Judaism (*Aet.* 1–18). Philo explains there that Moses is the lawgiver of the Jews and that he presented the notion of a created world in the 'Holy Books' of which there are five (*Aet.* 19). Philo's style of approaching the subject of creation is thus very similar in two treatises which address a non-Jewish audience and probably belong, as I shall argue, to a later stage of his career.

---

[7] Birnbaum 1996.   [8] *Opif.* 1–2; for further details, see Runia 2001, pp. 100–2.

Among all the writings of Philo it is the *Exposition* that describes the translation of the Jewish Scriptures into Greek.[9] While the *Allegorical Commentary* and the *Q&A* simply assumed the existence of the LXX, which was the basis of all of Philo's exegesis, he now considers it necessary to explain how the Hebrew Scriptures came to be known in the Greek-speaking world.[10] Abraham and David Wasserstein have noted that Philo's version of the story is curiously focused on the positive impression the Torah made on non-Jews.[11] Philo stresses that 'the sanctity of our legislation has been admired not only among the Jews, but also among all other nations' (*Mos.* 2.25). He evidently hopes that his readers will emulate King Ptolemy, who 'conceived an ardent affection of our laws', and that they will 'overthrow their peculiar ways' in exchange for the Mosaic Laws (*Mos.* 2.31, 44).

In the *Exposition* Philo is moreover aware of the fact that his readers require some explanation about the structure of the Jewish Scriptures. Initially, he explains the following basic facts:

The first of the five books, in which the Holy Laws are written down, is called Genesis, from the creation of the world, an account of which it contains at its beginning. It has received this title in spite of its embracing numberless other matters . . . (*Abr.* 1, trans. Colson with changes)

In this passage, too, Philo assumes an audience unfamiliar with the Torah. He introduces the division into five 'books' (βίβλοι), paying particular attention to the nomenclature of the first. Philo justifies the name 'Genesis' despite the apparent gap between this designation and the overall content of the book, because the (created) world contains all the different things narrated in it (*Abr.* 2). The Greek name of the biblical book must have emerged in Alexandria. Earlier biblical scholars apparently emulated their Homeric colleagues, who standardized the epic texts by dividing them into recognizable books and giving a name to each.[12] It is striking that the names of the individual Homeric books also refer to events at the opening of each so that the reader, knowing the text by heart, can easily identify the beginning of a new book. While this nomenclature was natural for an

---

[9] *Mos.* 2.25–44; following Goodenough 1933, I take the biography of Moses to be part of the *Exposition*, whether or not it was intended as its preface, as suggested by Runia 2001, p. 1; contra Royse 2009, p. 47.

[10] On Philo's exclusive use of the LXX and his lack of access to the Hebrew original, see Chapters 1 and 8.

[11] Wasserstein and Wasserstein 2006, pp. 38–9.

[12] Regarding the division of the Homeric epics into songs, which is standardized by the Alexandrian scholars but not reflected in the early papyri, see Nünlist 2006; S. West 1967, pp. 18–25; contra Jensen 1999.

audience immersed in the foundational text, whether Homeric or biblical, it is rather more surprising for a reader making his first acquaintance with the corpus. It was the latter kind of reader to whom Philo explained why the name 'Genesis' was indeed justified.

Philo offers further comments on the division of the Torah, distinguishing different literary genres, namely the creation account as well as a historical and a legislative part.[13] In this context he resumes an earlier discussion on the literary nature of Scripture, while significantly updating it in view of a wider audience. In the *Exposition* he makes the following encompassing statement:

> It must now be explained why he [Moses] started his law book with history, while placing the commandments and prohibitions second. For he did not, like any historian, aim at leaving behind to later generations a record of ancient deeds for the useless purpose of pure entertainment (τοῦ ψυχαγωγῆσαι) but instead treated history from the beginning, starting with the creation of everything, in order to show two most essential principles: first, that the Father and Maker of the world was in truth also its lawgiver, second, that the one who observes the laws will embrace also the attendance of Nature and will live in accordance with the ordering of the universe, so that his deeds are in harmony with and attuned to his words and his words to his deeds. (*Mos.* 2.48)

Philo discusses here the structure of the Torah in light of the notion that literature provides nothing but entertainment. He insists on a clear distinction between 'useless' literature (ἀνωφελῶς), which only seeks the reader's pleasure, and the Jewish Scriptures, which convey 'essential principles' (δύο τὰ ἀναγκαιότατα) anchored in Nature herself. The Torah emerges as a special kind of historical work, treating ancient events in a truthful and pedagogic manner. The vital point of this argument is the assumption that there is an intrinsic connection between the creation and the laws, both parts of Scripture reinforcing each other.

Philo's implied audience must have been non-Jews who required an explanation about the different parts of the Torah as well as its structure. The particular orientation of the above passage emerges when we compare it with Philo's earlier treatments of amusing versus educational literature. In the *Allegorical Commentary* he approaches the subject when discussing the story of Sarah's and Hagar's competition for offspring from Abraham. A textual problem is characteristically used to lead to a discussion on the allegorical level. Philo inquires why Sarah is once more introduced in

---

[13] *Praem.* 1–3, *Mos.* 2.45–7; the latter summarizes the creation and the genealogical part under one broader category of history, on which see also Kamesar 2009, pp. 74–5.

Gen. 16:3 as Abraham's wife. Rejecting the idea that Moses 'practised the worst form of prolixity, namely tautology', Philo argues that there must be another, more hidden reason for his formulation (*Congr.* 73). Moses' style is justified by an allegorization of Sarah as philosophy, the true wife of the learner, who demands utmost devotion, while the maid, Hagar, represents the preliminary studies, including poetry, whose attractions must not be confused with those of the lady herself. Philo's readers are thus warned not to submit to the pleasures of the preliminary studies lest they 'be charmed' (ψυχαγωγούμενοι) by them. They should instead pursue their ultimate aim, namely the study of philosophy (*Congr.* 78).

In Philo's view, Scripture indicates that Abraham remained faithful to his wife, philosophy, even when wedding Hagar. Abraham's virtue is further-more highlighted by adducing Plato's innovative definition of philosophy as the wisdom of 'things divine and human'.[14] Irmgard Männlein-Robert has shown that Plato thus distinguished philosophical inquiry from poetry, insisting that only the former leads to true insight, while Homer's epics deceive the reader by presenting far-removed imitations of the truth.[15] Philo adopted the Platonic formulation and approach, contrasting the philosophy sought by Abraham to the charms of poetry (*Congr.* 77).

In the *Allegorical Commentary* Philo returned to the topic of amusing literature in the context of Isaac's name, which signifies 'laughter' (Gen. 21:5). As God provided this joy, Philo wishes to show that no ordinary, but 'serious' pleasure is involved. The Divine Scriptures, Philo explains, convey an intellectual joy which derives from recognizing the truth:

> In the poetic work of God (ἐν δὲ τῇ τοῦ θεοῦ ποιητικῇ) you will not find anything mythical or fictional, but the canons of truth all inscribed, which do not cause any harm (ἀσινεῖς). You will find no metres and rhythms and tuneful verses charming (ψυχαγωγοῦντα) the ear with their music, but the consummate works of Nature herself, which have a harmony of their own. (*Det.* 125)

Here Philo contrasts the Jewish Scriptures with metrical poetry, undoubtedly referring primarily to Homer's epics. The truth of Nature is associated with the Torah, while myth and fiction characterize other poetical works. Philo's statements echo an earlier Alexandrian discussion which we have already encountered, aiming at a separate discourse of Jewish hermeneutics. Eratosthenes led the critical camp in second-century

---

[14] *Congr.* 79; Pl. *Resp.* 485a10–b3.
[15] Männlein-Robert 2002, esp. pp. 16–17, where she also argues that the Stoics, who are often credited with the formulation of this definition of philosophy, held rather different views, seeking to re-establish the traditional value of Homer's poetry.

BCE Alexandria, altogether denying the value of the Homeric epics as a source of scientific knowledge. In his view, they were written only for the purpose of entertainment and appeal to the soul (ψυχαγωγία).[16] Homer was often found to say foolish things with no relation to the facts.[17] In response to Eratosthenes' influential position, Strabo developed a complex notion of myth and argued that Homer's main purpose was to educate rather than amuse.[18] Generally, Strabo argued, Homer did not wholly invent stories but sometimes employed myths, which always preserve at least a trace of real persons and events (1.2.14).

In both passages of the *Allegorical Commentary* Philo engages literary notions of the Alexandrian discourse in order to portray the Jewish Scriptures as truthful literature, which educates its readers in a manner vastly superior to that of merely charming poetry. In the *Exposition* Philo continues to integrate some of these earlier themes and stresses the essential teachings of the Torah. At the same time, however, his account is newly focused on the sequence of the five books of the Pentateuch. More importantly, he no longer uses Plato's definition of philosophy but places his discussion in the more general context of history writing.[19] Homer is less central in the *Exposition*. His poetry is no longer the foil against which any argument about literature is developed. Instead, the connection between the Mosaic legislation and the creation account has moved into the foreground of Philo's discussion.

These differences between the *Allegorical Commentary* and the *Exposition* indicate their different audiences. In his earlier work Philo addressed Alexandrian Jews who were intimately familiar with both the Jewish Scriptures and Homer's epics. Consequently Philo insisted on the superiority of the Torah, associating it with Plato's definition of philosophy, while rejecting the comparative literary approach of some of his Aristotelian colleagues.[20] In the *Exposition*, on the other hand, Philo addresses an audience that is unfamiliar with the Torah and requires a basic explanation of Mosaic Law in the context of the creation.

Philo's audience in the *Exposition* indeed seems to be interested in the overall values and customs of Judaism rather than in intricate literary

---

[16] *Ap.* Strabo 1.2.3.   [17] Strabo 1.2.7, 1.2.12, 1.2.14–15, 1.2.19.

[18] Strabo 1.2.8, 1.2.7; see also Schenkeveld 1976; Dueck 2000, p. 34; Biraschi 2005, p. 83.

[19] Cf. Kamesar 2009, pp. 74–7, who traces Philo's formulations back to Aristotelian notions found in the *Tractatus Coisilianus*, stressing that Philo identified the Torah with non-mimetic literature. Although I agree with the latter conclusion, I believe that Philo's views are more firmly rooted in the specific Alexandrian discussions of Homer. Moreover, Aristotle worked with a rather positive notion of myth, as we saw in Chapter 5, but Philo dismissed myth with the early Plato as a deceitful narrative.

[20] For details on the latter, see Chapter 5.

questions. Mosaic Law especially intrigued his readers, not always from a sympathetic point of view. It is striking that Philo opens his four treatises *On the Special Laws* with a discussion of circumcision, because 'it is ridiculed among many' (*Spec.* 1.1). It is equally noteworthy that Philo calls the detractors to 'desist from childish mockery' by considering that the Egyptians, too, practise circumcision (*Spec.* 1.3). In this context he is even willing to count the Egyptians, whom he generally abhors, among the 'great nations', whose example should encourage his readers to revise their prejudices.[21]

Philo's argumentation in the *Exposition* significantly differs from his approach in the *Allegorical Commentary* and the *Q&A*. In the former he briefly discussed circumcision as an issue of correct Bible interpretation. Addressing a Jewish audience in Alexandria, Philo stressed that allegorical readers must not neglect the laws in their literal sense (*Migr.* 89–93). They should not behave as though they were 'living alone by themselves in a wilderness' but acknowledge the bonds of the society they live in.[22] In the *Q&A*, where the topic of circumcision already receives more attention, Philo offers for the first time health reasons in its defence and mentions also other nations who practise it (*Q.G.* 3.46–50). Instructing his students in Alexandria, he stresses the superiority of the Mosaic legislation over Egyptian customs. In contrast to the latter, Moses ordained circumcision only for the boys, rather than for boys and girls, and demanded the operation immediately after birth rather than during adolescence (*Q.G.* 3.47–8).

While Philo continues in the *Exposition* to use some of his previous justifications of circumcision, resorting to the spiritual explanation mentioned in the *Allegorical Commentary* and the health reasons of the *Q&A*, he introduces a new perspective for his non-Jewish audience. Rather than stressing the internal coherence of Jewish society, as well as its superiority, Philo now associates the Jews with other nations foreign to his audience. He invites his readers to appreciate that the Jews are not the only ones 'mutilating the bodies of themselves and their nearest' (*Spec.* 1.3). If Philo makes such efforts in the *Exposition* to revise the image of the Jews as highly isolated and odd, we must ask who his particular audience was. Who, in other words, could be expected to strongly dislike circumcision as a peculiar marker of the Jews?

The earliest non-Jewish writers mentioning circumcision generally presented it as a widespread custom, tracing the Jewish practice back to the

---

[21] *Spec.* 1.3; on the bad reputation of the Egyptians in Philo's writings, see Niehoff 2001, pp. 45–74; Pearce 2007.

[22] *Migr.* 90; the social aspect of Philo's argument has been emphasized by Barclay 1998 contra Boyarin 1994, pp. 13–38.

Ethiopians and the Egyptians.[23] It was in Rome that circumcision became not only a well-known marker of the Jews, but also a special focus of scorn. Tacitus, Horace and Petronius did not hide their disdain.[24] The author of the *Historia Augusta* assumed that the Bar Kochba Revolt had broken out, because the Jews 'were forbidden to mutilate their genitals', while Antoninus Pius in the second century CE legislated against the circumcision of non-Jews as part of the ritual of conversion.[25] These highly negative attitudes must have been influential in Rome even earlier, because Josephus, writing in first-century Rome for a non-Jewish audience, explicitly responded to them. Strikingly, he recalls Apion's mockery of circumcision rather than that of an indigenous Roman writer.[26] Already Josephus has noted that Apion's rhetoric does not fit his Alexandrian background, because the Egyptians themselves were generally circumcised during this period.[27] In Alexandria mockery of circumcision would not have resonated very well. It thus follows that Apion, the head of the Egyptian embassy to Rome, began to scorn the practice as specifically Jewish only after arriving in the capital. Echoing local resentment of the Jews, he is the first known writer to promote this slander in Rome.

Josephus responded to the persistent criticism of circumcision which Apion had advocated in Rome by drawing attention to the fact that the Egyptians, too, practised it. Herodotus, he stressed, 'informed us that they have taught others to circumcise' (*Ap.* 2.142). Apion and his views on circumcision must also have been highly relevant to his direct contemporary Philo. The latter's justification of the ritual in the *Exposition* resembles Josephus' argumentation in one crucial respect. Both Jewish writers refer to the Egyptian practice in order to convince an unsympathetic audience that the Jews are not odd and isolated. Philo thus emerges as an important predecessor of Josephus, engaging approximately fifty years earlier in a similar kind of Roman discourse.

It now remains to be investigated when and how Philo began to orient himself towards a non-Jewish audience attuned to Roman prejudices. Moreover, did he directly address an audience in Rome? While these

---

[23] See esp. Herodotus 2.36; Strabo 16.5; discussed by M. Stern 1974–84, vol. I, pp. 1–6, 261–315; Schäfer 1997, pp. 93–5.

[24] Tac. *Hist.* 5.5, 2; Hor. *Sermones* 1.9, 70; Petron. *Sat.* 102.13–14; see also M. Stern 1974–84, vol. II, p. 41; vol. I, pp. 324–6, 443–4; Schäfer 1997, pp. 98–100; Isaac 2004, pp. 472–4.

[25] *Hist. Aug.*, *Hadrian* 14.2, the historicity of which is discussed by Isaac 2004, p. 473; Schäfer 1997, pp. 103–5; *Dig.* 48.8, 11, discussed by Isaac 2004, p. 461.

[26] This reference remains very general, Apion being presented as 'scoffing at circumcision' (χλευάζει περιτομήν), without a precise quotation from his work (*Ap.* 2.137).

[27] *Ap.* 2.141–4; see also Barclay 2007, pp. 240–2.

questions cannot be answered with certainty, there are some clues pointing in the direction of the ethnic conflict in Alexandria which called for
Philo's diplomatic services in Rome. In a famous passage in the *Exposition* he bemoans the fact that he lost his leisure time for philosophical
inquiry, instead being 'swept away' by civil turmoil.[28] We must also take
into account that Philo's embassy in Rome was kept there for a prolonged
time, as Gaius was reluctant to receive them. Considering that the embassy
is likely to have stayed in Rome also after Gaius' assassination in January
41, leading to talks with his successor Claudius, it becomes clear that Philo
probably spent at least three years in the capital (38–41 CE).[29] If Apion, the
head of the parallel Egyptian embassy, had written works which were still
influential in Rome at the end of the first century CE, it is likely that Philo
similarly used his time in the capital to present a more positive image of
the Jews and their customs.

ECHOES OF ALEXANDRIAN QUESTIONS AND ANSWERS

The *Exposition*, as we have already observed, is no longer a running commentary on the biblical text, but a free narrative of the biblical material.
Unlike the *Allegorical Commentary*, this series generally does not raise text-
critical questions in order to introduce and justify allegory. Allegory is
rather taken for granted as a legitimate method of interpretation, which is
regularly integrated in the flow of the narrative, especially in the *Lives of the
Patriarchs*.[30] Unlike the *Q&A*, the *Exposition* does not use the question and
answer format as an organizing principle either. Philo's narrative instead
focuses on the main themes and characters of the Torah, presenting the
material in chronological order and with emphasis on the coherence of the
subject matter. The treatise *On the Creation of the World* even ends with a
summary of the things to be learnt from the account (*Opif.* 170–7).

Written mainly for a non-Jewish audience, which was hardly sympathetic
to Judaism, the *Exposition* rarely exposes problems in the biblical text.
Direct questions on a particular biblical verse are rather infrequent. The
questions on Scripture, which nevertheless come up, were not originally

---

[28] *Spec.* 3.1–3; this passage has often been interpreted in the context of the ethnic conflict in Alexandria
and has been used to date the *Exposition* to the mature stage of Philo's career; for an overview of the
scholarship, see Vermes and Millar 1973–87, vol. III.2, pp. 842–4.
[29] See also Harker 2008, pp. 10–21.
[30] See, e.g., *Abr.* 54, 68, 99, 119, 147, 200, 236; *Jos.* 58, 125 and *Jos.* 28, where Philo explains that 'all
or most of the law book is an allegory', using the term in a very broad sense, including general
parenthesis; *Dec.* 1, where Philo promises to explain the underlying allegorical meanings of the laws,
where necessary, but hardly does so throughout his four treatises on Mosaic Law.

conceived in this context. They either reflect Philo's own inquiries in his earlier treatises or echo discussions of Jewish colleagues in Alexandria which he considered relevant to his present narrative.

The different treatises of the *Exposition* are not equally removed from the original commentary format of Philo's work. His treatise *On the Creation of the World* remains closest to the earlier zetetic style, whereas the *Lives of the Patriarchs* departs from it most dramatically. In the former there are still quite a lot of direct quotations of verses roughly according to their sequence in Scripture, while the few allegorical interpretations that are offered are textually justified.[31] In the *Lives*, on the other hand, Philo hardly refers to specific verses but instead dwells extensively on the allegorical meaning of certain passages without having recourse to textual problems. Philo's treatises *On the Decalogue* and *On the Special Laws* assume a midway position, quoting few explicit verses and generally limiting allegory while raising some interesting questions.

In his treatise *On the Creation* Philo occasionally recalls textual problems which he had discussed at length in the *Allegorical Commentary*. In the present context he no longer studies them for their own sake but provides brief summaries in order to strengthen his overall argument. Philo's original concern for the non-mythological nature of Scripture, which had been hotly debated among his colleagues, is still echoed, yet with considerably less fervour.[32] Having provided a summary of the story of Paradise, Philo thus stresses:

These are no mythical fictions such as poets and sophists delight in, but modes of making ideas visible, bidding us resort to allegory according to the underlying interpretations. Following a probable conjecture (εἰκότι στοχασμῷ), one would say that the aforementioned serpent is properly a symbol (σύμβολον) of pleasure. (*Opif.* 157)

The motif of a clever serpent speaking in a human voice defies, of course, scientific standards of verisimilitude. Philo admitted in the *Allegorical Commentary* that the literal story was highly unlikely and amounted to a myth (*Agr.* 96–7). He solved the problem by allegorizing the serpent as pleasure, stressing that 'in the underlying interpretations the mythical is removed out of our way' (*Agr.* 97). In the *Exposition* Philo repeats significant aspects of this argument, using the same hermeneutic key term αἱ δι' ὑπονοιῶν ἀποδόσεις. It is at the same time conspicuous that he now declares the biblical story to be non-mythical, while earlier on he admitted, with critical colleagues in the Jewish community in mind, that

---

[31] Examples of biblical quotations can mostly be found in *Opif.* 129, 131, 134, 148, 153.
[32] For details on the dispute about myth, see Chapter 5.

the biblical text was mythical on the literal level. Philo's argumentation has thus become more linear, starting with the foregone conclusion and then providing some thoughts in support of it. In the *Allegorical Commentary*, by contrast, he proceeded in a dialectical way, initially accepting the critical views of his colleagues and then offering a solution from an altogether different hermeneutic realm.

A similar echo of earlier textual inquiries resurfaces in *Opif.* 153–7. Philo says in this passage that the story about Paradise 'seems symbolical rather than literal', because 'never yet have trees of life or understanding appeared on earth'. Discussing Gen. 2:8 in the *Allegorical Commentary*, Philo dwelt in detail on the question whether the image of God planting a garden was mythological (*All.* 1.43–5). The urgency of this problem is hardly felt any longer in the *Exposition*, where Philo briefly mentions it in the context of his overall allegorical interpretation.

In *The Lives*, too, Philo occasionally refers to questions he has previously discussed. In the *Life of Joseph*, for example, he addresses again the issue of Potiphar, who was at once a eunuch and a husband. In the *Allegorical Commentary* he pointed to this problem of contradiction and solved it with an allegorical interpretation, suggesting that Potiphar signifies the mind devoid of wisdom.[33] In the *Exposition* this solution appears again. It is remarkable, however, that the problem itself is no longer discussed in the paraphrase of the literal story. Philo instead integrates the allegorization of Potiphar in the separate paragraphs which explore the underlying meaning of the biblical passage.[34] In this context the allegory is repeated and Philo explains that 'therefore also, most paradoxical, this eunuch mated with a wife' (*Jos.* 60). The expression 'most paradoxical' still echoes the original problem of contradiction that had engaged Philo's attention in the *Allegorical Commentary*. The problem itself, however, is no longer the starting point of the discussion, nor is the solution the climax of the argumentation. Philo instead mentions the answer in passing during his overall exposition of the allegorical meaning of the biblical story.

A slightly more complex picture emerges with regard to questions of colleagues, which Philo integrates in his *Exposition*. While he shows a strong preference for certain like-minded colleagues, he still refers to more critical views, hoping thus to be able to provide conclusive answers. This is especially the case in his treatise *On the Creation of the World*, where Philo sometimes dwells on the details of a particular verse even to the extent of interrupting the flow of his narrative.

---

[33] *All.* 3.236, referring to Gen. 39:1.   [34] *Jos.* 37–40, 58–60.

An inquiry which Philo reports most approvingly relates to the creation of man (Gen. 1:26–7):

Someone might inquire (ἐπιζητήσειε δ᾽ ἄν τις) into the reason why it is that man was created last with regard to the creation of the cosmos for, as the Holy Writings reveal, the Creator and Father made him last after all the others.

Indeed, those who immerse themselves further in the laws and investigate thoroughly and with all scrutiny, as much as is possible into the things concerning them,[35] say that God, after giving man a share in his kinship with regard to the logical faculty, which was the best of all gifts, did not begrudge him any of the others either but prepared everything in the cosmos for him as to the most familiar and beloved creature, wishing that upon being created he should not lack anything to live and to live well. (*Opif.* 77)

The question discussed in this passage derives from the context of the verse rather than from a crux in the text itself. It is asked whether the sequence of creation, with man placed at the end, may indicate his low value. At stake is the precise message of Scripture. The solution provided by Philo's colleagues is much to his liking, because it confirms man's centrality in God's creation, a notion he himself stresses (*Opif.* 79–88). Both the question and the solution are remarkably conservative. No difficulty is identified in the biblical text and no literary criticism is expressed. The zetetic tradition had originally been far more subversive, as we saw in previous chapters. The question in the above quoted passage rather looks as if it had been invented for the sake of providing an interesting solution. It serves as a springboard for an interpretation which may have been ready beforehand. This feature fits the milieu in Alexandria that saw an inflation of Homeric questions. Aristarchus complained about this phenomenon, accusing its practitioners of 'wanting to invent ζητήματα'.[36] Philo's literal exegetes seem to have belonged to an environment where questions were no longer put to actual text-critical use but rather served more general hermeneutic purposes. In certain circles they had become something of a stylistic device. These colleagues of Philo did not participate in the discourse of hard-core text criticism but rather belonged to a milieu that was loosely inspired by scholarly methods without rigorously applying them.

Philo's comment that his colleagues investigated Scripture 'as much as is possible' (ὡς ἔνι μάλιστα) indicates that, as far as he was concerned, they accepted certain limits of investigation. They seem to have recognized that the Bible contains things that are beyond full human comprehension. On this crucial issue Philo wholeheartedly agreed with them. He himself

---

[35] λέγουσιν οὖν οἱ τοῖς νόμοις ἐπὶ πλέον ἐμβαθύναντες καὶ τὰ κατ᾽ αὐτοὺς ὡς ἔνι μάλιστα μετὰ πάσης ἐξετάσεως ἀκριβοῦντες.

[36] Schol. *Il.* 10.372.

occasionally expressed awe vis-à-vis Scripture, stressing, for example, that 'necessarily only God knows the really true reason' for a particular crux in the biblical text (*Opif.* 72).

This impression of Philo's colleagues is corroborated by the fact that they show no intellectual affinity with the Aristotelian tradition, which was most influential in text-critical Alexandrian scholarship.[37] Instead, their reference to God as 'giving man a share in his kinship with regard to the logical faculty' and not 'begrudging him' any gift rather indicates a Platonic orientation. The *Timaeus* depicts man as a creature endowed with divine reason and inclined to 'the genre of philosophy'.[38] God's lack of envy is a central theme in Plato's creation account (*Tim.* 29e). Philo's colleagues emerge as sharing Platonic assumptions, while lacking signs of attachment to rigorous scholarship in Aristotelian style. Philo approved of their approach to Scripture, himself sharing a Platonic background. He was happy to integrate their question and answer method into his *Exposition*, thus benefiting from another opportunity to highlight the centrality of man in the creation of the world.

Another kind of scholarly inquiry into Scripture met with ambivalence on Philo's part. An illuminating example is the discussion of God's anthropomorphic words 'let us make man in our image and likeness' (Gen. 1:26). Philo himself tended to avoid the problem of the plural by adapting this verse to the more monotheistic expression κατ᾽ εἰκόνα θεοῦ in the following verse. Philo thus paraphrases Gen. 1:26 as Moses 'says that man was created after the image of God and in his likeness'.[39] While pre-emptively solving the problem by omitting the crux itself, Philo nevertheless refers to the obvious difficulty:

Should someone not without justification (οὐκ ἀπὸ σκοποῦ) raise the difficulty why he [Moses] attributed (ἀνέθηκεν) the creation of man not to one demiurge only as with all the others, but as if to many. For he [Moses] introduces (εἰσάγει) the Father of everything speaking thus: 'Let us create man according to our image and likeness' [Gen. 1:26].

I would [rather] ask whether the One to whom everything is subordinate is in need of anything whatsoever? He who had no need of any collaborator when He created the heaven and the earth and the sea – should He not have been able to make such a humble and perishable creature as man without helpers, just by Himself?! (*Opif.* 72)

---

[37] For details on Aristotle's influence on Alexandrian scholarship, see esp. Chapters 1, 4 and 6.

[38] Cf. Philo, *Opif.* 77–8 to Plato, *Tim.* 47a–b, 34a–35b; 41e–42d. Note that the expression τὸ φιλοσοφίας γένος is unique to Plato and Philo until Plutarch also mentions it (Plut. *Plat. Quaest.* 999E); see also Runia 2001, pp. 201–3, 248–51.

[39] Τὸν ἄνθρωπόν φησι γεγενῆσθαι κατ᾽ εἰκόνα θεοῦ καὶ καθ᾽ ὁμοίωσιν (*Opif.* 69).

The question raised here relates to the Torah as a literary work and dwells on its particular style. It is asked why the author 'attributed' a particular expression to one of the characters and 'introduced' him by a speech considered unusual. This approach is literary and reflects the spirit of Aristotelian scholarship which we have already identified in many examples of Bible exegesis among Philo's predecessors and colleagues. Philo was clearly ambivalent about this question on Gen. 1:26. Instead of lavishing praise on its potential expounder, as he did in the previous case, he admits that the question is raised 'not without justification'. Philo furthermore provides only a partial report, omitting the answer which may have been provided by literary critics. He instead formulates his own question in a highly pointed, if not sarcastic tone. It is thus difficult to know how some of his colleagues would have solved the problem. We may, however, gain a clue from Philo's apologetics. When sharply asking his readers whether one can really think of God, the creator of the whole cosmos, as someone in need of collaborators when it comes to the creation of man, Philo seems to give an ironic twist to an already existing argument. Some of his colleagues seem to have suggested that God is presented as requiring a helper for the creation of man.

Philo's own solution to the problem reflects a Platonic spirit. Following the *Timaeus*, he devotes considerable efforts to proving that the plural in ποιήσωμεν has ethical significance. God relied on 'others as if on collaborators' so as to shun responsibility for man's evil inclinations.[40] Only man's spiritual aspects, Philo insists, were created in the Divine image, while all his inferior qualities originated from God's assistants. Philo's theological solution based on Plato's *Timaeus* replaces another interpretation by literal exegetes, who had been inspired by Aristotle's approach. In his case, too, Philo used a question, which had already been raised or was likely to be raised, in order to elaborate his own ideas in the context of his *Exposition*.

The question and answer format resurfaces also in Philo's treatises on Mosaic Law. He even anticipates that some congenial colleagues will raise similar questions and possibly provide 'more convincing' answers, which 'will benefit both them and me' (*Spec.* 1.214).[41] At the same time, however, it is noteworthy that Philo, unlike Aristeas, does not raise questions

---

[40] *Opif.* 75; cf. Pl. *Tim.* 41b–e, where the lower deities are said to be responsible for the inferior bodily aspects of man. Being created themselves, they ensure that man will not be immortal. Philo, by contrast, does not explain the origin and nature of God's collaborators; see also Runia 2001, pp. 222–35.
[41] See also *Spec.* 2.159, 3.178.

concerning the very meaning of specific laws.[42] The *Decalogue* and its sequel in *On the Special Laws* are instead explained in a straightforward narrative, which reflects remarkable self-confidence. Regarding the second commandment of the Decalogue, for example, which prohibits the worship of other gods, Philo does not hesitate to criticize the different forms of polytheism, praising the Jewish belief in one God alone (*Dec.* 52–81). Overall, he stresses the ethical value of Mosaic Law, explaining how each of the specific injunctions leads to a morally elevated style of life. In Philo's view, Moses aimed at a perfect measure of self-restraint which acknowledges bodily needs while regulating their expression and subordinating them to higher values.[43]

The questions on the Decalogue and the special laws are thus of a surprisingly textual and literary nature, treating relatively minor details rather than fundamental issues of law observance. Given their basic orientation, it is not surprising that they resemble the questions and answers in what appear to be Philo's earlier works.[44] A typical problem of contradiction, for example, is identified in the story of the Divine revelation on Mount Sinai. Philo offers the following comment:

One may properly inquire why he [Moses] considered it right to pronounce each of the Ten Commandments not to the multitude but as if to one, while many thousands were collected in one spot. (*Dec.* 36)

Philo addresses a similar problem in the *Allegorical Commentary*, where he inquires into the precise wording of the Divine commandments concerning the trees of Paradise. Noting that they are formulated both in the plural and the singular, he identifies a contradiction between the Divine instruction to a single person and the context of Adam and Eve being addressed (*All.* 1.101). Characteristically, the problem is solved by recourse to allegory. Philo interprets the problematic verse as a reference to different ways of acquiring wisdom. In his view, the singular is used with regard to few righteous individuals, while the plural is used in view of the multitude of people, who sin and fail to become wise (*All.* 1.102). Although Philo discusses a similar problem of contradiction in the *Exposition*, he does not use it as an introduction to allegory. His answer rather conveys a straightforward lesson:

---

[42] Cf. *Letter*, 129, where certain animals are regarded as impure even though God created them, too. An exception in Philo's work is *Spec.* 2.129, where he addresses the question, raised by others, why parents are not mentioned in Scripture as inheriting their children.

[43] For details, see Niehoff 2001, pp. 94–110, and bibliography there.

[44] For other examples, see *Spec.* 4.66, *Dec.* 32.

One answer which must be given is that He wishes to teach the readers of the sacred Scriptures a most excellent lesson, namely that each single person, when he is law-abiding and obedient to God, is equal in worth to a whole nation. (*Dec.* 37)

A new type of question which appears in Philo's works on Mosaic Law is animated by general considerations rather than textual inquiries and seems to engage the views of non-Jewish onlookers. Philo shows compassion for his people, defending them against negative evaluations from outside. His enormous concern at the opening of his treatise on the Decalogue to explain why the laws were not given in the city must be interpreted in this context. Philo starts his discussion by referring to 'those raising the question why he promulgated the laws not in the city but in the depths of the desert' (*Dec.* 2). Unlike previous questions this inquiry is not based on a particular verse, but rather on general knowledge. It could easily have been raised by someone who had not read the Jewish Scriptures and assumed that legislation was intrinsically connected to the city. In the Hellenistic world famous lawgivers, such as Solon and Lycurgus, were indeed connected to particular city-states.

Lest the Jews appear to be a parochial nation, lacking urban culture and proper legislation, Philo carefully responds to the above question. He even devotes fifteen paragraphs to it, providing his own answers as well as one that he has heard. His line of defence is an appeal to the ascetic sense of his readers, who would appreciate the ethereal simplicity of the desert. The city, by contrast, is depicted as a dangerous place, where pride, corruption and impiety threaten man (*Dec.* 3–17). Philo rightly hoped that this argumentation would be attractive in the eyes of his readers, who may well have been attuned to the revival of orthodox Stoic views in Rome and to Seneca's warnings of the corruptions of a voluptuous life in the city.[45] Philo's questions and answers on the austerity of Jewish festivals point in the same direction (*Spec.* 2.193).

In conclusion, the relatively few questions which occur in the *Exposition* either summarize Philo's inquiries in what appear to be his earlier treatises or respond to more general problems, which he suspected to be on the minds of his non-Jewish audience. In this series Philo no longer works with the text and other Jewish exegetes in mind but primarily addresses the general concerns of an audience who have heard about the Jews but have not come into close contact with their writings. The *Exposition* is thus furthest removed from Philo's detailed commentary activity, which emerged at the beginning of his career in a distinctly Alexandrian environment.

[45] For details on the similarities between Philo and Seneca in this respect, see Niehoff 2010c.

Philo's three series of exegetical writings reflect both his rapid career and the changing circumstances of his time. In the *Allegorical Commentary* he makes an impressive début, showing his expertise in the literal methods of Homeric scholarship and responding to more critical colleagues in the Jewish community. The *Q&A* emerged from the hands of a rather authoritative teacher, who had already succeeded in gathering students around his more conservative approach. In both series Philo was concerned to establish a separate discourse of Jewish hermeneutics, which relies on critical methods shared by Homeric scholarship, while using them to demonstrate the uniqueness of the Jewish Scriptures. In the *Exposition*, by contrast, Philo turned to a non-Jewish audience, using exegetical motifs in an overall narrative designed to defend the Jews against current prejudices. Philo realized that this was rather urgent at a time when contemporaries such as Apion appealed to Roman readers, presenting anything but favourable images of the Jews.

Epilogue

Stressing the importance of Alexandria as *the* centre of literal Homeric scholarship in the Hellenistic world, I have analysed for the first time Jewish exegetical works in light of the Alexandrian scholia to Homer. The scholia have never been translated from Greek into any other language and are available only in the form of running comments on the Homeric text, rather than in thematic arrangement, thus rendering access to them very difficult. Their relevance to Alexandrian Bible exegesis has thus far not been recognized.

My comparison of Homeric and Biblical hermeneutics has shown that Jewish intellectuals in Alexandria were acutely aware of the academic methods developed at the Museum. While there were lively controversies among Alexandrian Jews regarding the nature and legitimacy of Homeric scholarship, the overall picture is one of impressive creativity in dialogue with the surrounding culture. Jewish Bible scholars offered the first critical studies of the canonical text, thus anticipating modern research by more than two thousand years.

Each of this book's three parts has treated a separate category of Alexandrian Bible exegesis. The first has examined the early sources from the Ptolemaic period, throwing completely new light on each of them. The *Letter of Aristeas* is shown to be conservative, defending the biblical text against critical methods. The fragments from Demetrius have been read with special emphasis on his references to already existing questions and answers, which are used to reconstruct the history of this genre from Aristotle onwards. Aristobulus, hitherto often assumed to have been a Stoic, has been identified as an Aristotelian in the context of Aristotelian Homer scholars in Alexandria.

The second part of the book has identified fragments of anonymous Jewish exegetes in Philo's works. Reading his polemics against such colleagues in the light of the scholia, I have offered a new reconstruction of anonymous Bible exegesis in Alexandria. It emerges that some Jewish scholars applied rigorous literary methods to Scripture, comparing mythical stories to their counterparts in Homer's epics, interpreting the Binding of Isaac in the context of ancient child sacrifice and offering text emendations of various kinds.

In the last section of the book I have investigated Philo in the context of his colleagues and predecessors. He emerges as a relatively conservative figure who applied literary techniques with considerable caution, insisting on the unity and authenticity of the biblical text. At the same time, however, I have been able to show that Philo created a new synthesis between literal approaches of an Aristotelian orientation and Platonic allegory. In this respect he became a pivotal figure, who laid the foundation for subsequent syntheses in Greek literature, such as the one offered by Porphyry.

In this section on Philo I have also been able to throw new light on the implied audiences of Philo's different series of works. It became clear that the *Allegorical Commentary* belongs to the Alexandrian context, when Philo engaged the views of his critical colleagues in the Jewish community. The *Questions and Answers* reflects a mature teacher, who was speaking to a convinced following. The *Exposition of the Laws* addresses a wider, largely non-Jewish audience probably at a stage when Philo was involved in the political events of his time and travelled to Rome as the head of the Jewish delegation. These new insights into the different cultural contexts of Philo's works will enable us in the future to reconstruct the chronology of Philo's writings and to write a much needed intellectual biography of this figure who was central to ancient Judaism, Hellenistic philosophy and nascent Christianity.

The results of my book considerably change our understanding of Alexandrian Judaism and, more generally, the juncture between Judaism, Hellenism and Rome at a crucial point in the history of Western civilization. Initially, the great variety of Jewish voices has become evident. From now on we should no longer speak of one prevalent type of Hellenistic exegesis or regard Philo as *the* representative of Hellenistic Judaism. It has also become clear that there were fruitful contacts between Jews and Greeks even in the field of literal exegesis, which has often been intuitively regarded as quintessentially Jewish and thus not comparable. The book furthermore throws new light on the development of the different philosophical schools in Alexandria, showing that the Aristotelian school was more influential than has often been thought, while the Stoic school only became visible with the rise of Rome. Subsequent Christian and rabbinic Bible exegesis now require a reassessment in light of the new evidence from Alexandria.

References

Acosta-Hughes, B. (2002) *Polyeideia: the Iambi of Callimachus and the Archaic Iambic Tradition* (Hellenistic Culture and Society 35). Berkeley.

Alesse, F., ed. (2008) *Philo of Alexandria and Post-Aristotelian Philosophy.* Leiden.

Alexander, P. S. (1988) 'Retelling the Old Testament', in *It Is Written: Scripture Citing Scripture. Essays in Honour of B. Lindars*, ed. D. A. Carson and H. G. M. Williamson. Cambridge: 99–121.

    (1998) '"Homer the Prophet of All" and "Moses Our Teacher": Late Antique Exegesis of the Homeric Epics and of the Torah of Moses', in *The Use of Sacred Books in the Ancient World*, ed. L. V. Rutgers, P. W. van der Horst and L. M. Teugels (Contributions to Biblical Exegesis and Theology 22). Leuven: 127–42.

Algra, K. (2003) 'Stoic Theology', in *The Cambridge Companion to the Stoics*, ed. B. Inwood. Cambridge: 153–78.

Almagor, E. (2005) 'Who Is a Barbarian? The Barbarians in the Ethnological and Cultural Taxonomies of Strabo', in *Strabo's Cultural Geography: the Making of a Kolossourgia*, ed. D. Dueck, H. Lindsay and S. Pothecary. Cambridge: 42–55.

Amir, Y. (1971) 'Philo's Allegory in Relation to Homeric Allegory', *Eshkolot* 6: 35–45. [in Hebrew]

    (1974) 'Homer und Bibel als Ausdrucksmittel im 3. Sybillenbuch', *Scripta Classica Israelica* 1: 73–89.

    (1984) 'Moses as the Author of the Torah in Philo's Writings', *Proceedings of the Israel Academy of Sciences and Humanities* 6: 83–103. [in Hebrew]

    (1988) 'Authority and Interpretation of Scripture in the Writings of Philo', in *Mikra: Text, Translation, Reading and Interpretation of the Hebrew Bible in Ancient Judaism and Early Christianity*, ed. M. J. Mulder. Assen: 421–53.

Arnaldez, R. (1964) *Philon d'Alexandrie. De mutatione nominum* (Les œuvres de Philon d'Alexandrie 18). Paris.

Assmann, J. (1992) *Das kulturelle Gedächtnis: Schrift, Erinnerung und politische Identität in frühen Hochkulturen.* Munich.

Aucher, I. B. (1826) *Philonis Judaei paralipomena Armena.* Venice.

Baldry, H. C. (1965) *The Unity of Mankind in Greek Thought.* Cambridge.

Baltes, M. (1998) *Der Platonismus in der Antike: Grundlagen, System, Entwicklung*, vol. v: *Die philosophische Lehre des Platonismus*. Stuttgart.

Barclay, J. M. G. (1996) *Jews in the Mediterranean Diaspora: From Alexander to Trajan (323 BCE – 117 CE)*. Edinburgh.

(1998) 'Paul and Philo on Circumcision: Romans 2:25–9 in the Social and Cultural Context', *New Testament Studies* 44: 536–56.

(2007) *Against Apion: Translation and Commentary* (Flavius Josephus: Translation and Commentary 10). Leiden.

Bauer, W. (1971) *Orthodoxy and Heresy in Earliest Christianity*. Philadelphia; Eng. trans., ed. and supp. by R. A. Kraft of German orig. 1934.

Bauks, M. (2007) 'The Theological Implications of Child Sacrifice in and beyond the Biblical Context in Relation to Genesis 22 and Judges 11', in *Human Sacrifice in Jewish and Christian Tradition*, ed. K. Finsterbusch, A. Lange and K. F. D. Römheld (Studies in the History of Religions 112). Leiden: 65–86.

Baumgarten, A. I. (1997) *The Flourishing of Jewish Sects in the Maccabean Era: an Interpretation* (Supplements to the Journal for the Study of Judaism 55). Leiden.

(2002) 'Bilingual Jews and the Greek Bible', in *Shem in the Tents of Japhet: Essays on the Encounter of Judaism and Hellenism*, ed. J. L. Kugel (Supplements to the Journal for the Study of Judaism 74). Leiden: 13–30.

Berthelot, K. (2010) 'Philon d'Alexandrie, lecteur d'Homère: quelques éléments de réflexion', in *Prolongements et renouvellements de la tradition classique*, ed. A. Balansard, G. Dorival and M. Loubet. Aix-en-Provence: 93–100.

Bickerman, E. J. (1975) 'The Jewish Historian Demetrius', in *Christianity, Judaism and Other Greco-Roman Cults: Studies for Morton Smith at Sixty. Part II*, ed. J. Neusner (Studies in Judaism in Late Antiquity 12). Leiden: 72–84.

(1976–86) 'Some Notes on the Transmission of the Septuagint', in *Studies in Jewish and Christian History*, ed. E. J. Bickerman (Arbeiten zur Geschichte des antiken Judentums und des Urchristentums 9). 3 vols. Leiden: vol. 1, 137–66.

(1988) *The Jews in the Greek Age*. Cambridge, Mass.

Biraschi, A. M. (2005) 'Strabo and Homer: a Chapter in Cultural History', in *Strabo's Cultural Geography: the Making of a Kolossourgia*, ed. D. Dueck, H. Lindsay and S. Pothecary. Cambridge: 73–85.

Birnbaum, E. (1996) *The Place of Judaism in Philo's Thought: Israel, Jews, and Proselytes* (Brown Judaic Studies 290, Studia Philonica Monographs 2). Atlanta, Ga.

(2001) 'Philo on the Greeks: a Jewish Perspective on Culture and Society in First-Century Alexandria', *Studia Philonica Annual* 13: 37–58.

(2004) 'A Leader with Vision in the Ancient Jewish Diaspora: Philo of Alexandria', in *Jewish Religious Leadership: Image and Reality*, ed. J. Wertheimer. 2 vols. New York: vol. 1, 57–90.

Blank, D. and Atherton, C. (2003) 'The Stoic Contribution to Traditional Grammar', in *The Cambridge Companion to the Stoics*, ed. B. Inwood. Cambridge: 310–27.

Blumell, L. (2007) 'A Jew in Celsus' "True Doctrine"?: an Examination of Jewish Anti-Christian Polemic in the Second Century CE', *Studies in Religion* 36: 297–315.

Böhm, M. (2005) *Rezeption und Funktion der Vätererzählungen bei Philo von Alexandria: Zum Zusammenhang von Kontext, Hermeneutik und Exegese im frühen Judentum* (Beihefte zur Zeitschrift für die neutestamentliche Wissenschaft und die Kunde der älteren Kirche 128). Berlin.

Borgen, P. (1996) 'Philo of Alexandria – a Systematic Philosopher or an Eclectic Editor?', *Symbolae Osloenses* 71: 115–34.

  (1997) *Philo of Alexandria: an Exegete for his Time* (Supplements to Novum Testamentum 86). Leiden.

Borgen, P. and Skarsten, R. (1976–77) '*Quaestiones et Solutiones*: Some Observations on the Form of Philo's Exegesis', *Studia Philonica* 4: 1–15.

Bousset, W. (1915) *Jüdisch-christlicher Schulbetrieb in Alexandria und Rom. Literarische Untersuchungen zu Philo und Clemens von Alexandria, Justin und Irenaeus* (Forschungen zur Religion und Literatur des Alten und Neuen Testaments, N.F. 6). Göttingen.

Boyarin, D. (1994) *A Radical Jew: Paul and the Politics of Identity* (Contraversions: Critical Studies in Jewish Literature, Culture, and Society 1). Berkeley.

  (2000) 'A Tale of Two Synods: Nicaea, Yavneh and the Making of Orthodox Judaism', *Exemplaria* 12: 21–62.

Boys-Stones, G. R. (2001) *Post-Hellenistic Philosophy: a Study of its Development from the Stoics to Origen.* Oxford.

  (2003) 'The Stoics' Two Types of Allegory', in *Metaphor, Allegory, and the Classical Tradition: Ancient Thought and Modern Revisions*, ed. G. R. Boys-Stones. Oxford: 189–216.

Bréhier, É. (1908) *Les idées philosophiques et religieuses de Philon d'Alexandrie.* Paris.

Brisson, L. (2004) *How Philosphers Saved Myths: Allegorical Interpretation and Classical Mythology.* Chicago.

Brock, S. P. (1979) 'Aspects of Translation Technique in Antiquity', *Greek, Roman, and Byzantine Studies* 20: 69–87.

Brodersen, K. (2002) *Die Wahrheit über die griechischen Mythen. Palaiphatos' 'Unglaubliche Geschichten'* (Universal-Bibliothek 18200). Stuttgart.

Buffière, F. (1956) *Les mythes d'Homère et la pensée grecque.* Paris.

  (1962) *Héraclite. Allégories d'Homère* (La Collection des Universités de France). Paris.

Burkhardt, H. (1988) *Die Inspiration heiliger Schriften bei Philo von Alexandrien.* Giessen.

Bywater, I. (1909) *Aristotle. On the Art of Poetry: a Revised Text with Critical Introduction, Translation and Commentary.* Oxford.

Calame, C. (2003) *Myth and History in Ancient Greece: the Symbolic Creation of a Colony.* Princeton, NJ.

Canfora, L. (2002) 'Aristotele "Fondatore" della Bibliotheca di Allesandria', in *Scritti in onore di Italo Gallo*, ed. L. Torraca. Napoli: 167–75.

Carlier, C. (2008) *La cité de Moise: le peuple juif chez Philon d'Alexandrie.* Turnhout.

Carroll, M. (1895) *Aristotle's Poetics, C. XXV in the Light of the Homeric Scholia.* Baltimore.

Cazeaux, J. (1984) 'Philon d'Alexandrie, exégète', *Aufstieg und Niedergang der Römischen Welt* II.21.1: 156–226.

Charles, R. (2009) 'Hybridity and the Letter of Aristeas', *Journal for the Study of Judaism* 40: 242–59.

Clauss, M. (2003) *Alexandria. Schicksale einer antiken Weltstadt.* Stuttgart.

Cohen, N. G. (1985) '"Agraphos Nomos" in Philo's Writings – a New Examination', *Daat* 15: 5–20. [in Hebrew]

(1987) 'The Jewish Dimension of Philo's Judaism – an Elucidation of *de Spec. Leg.* IV 132–150', *Journal of Jewish Studies* 38: 165–86.

(1995) *Philo Judaeus: His Universe of Discourse* (Beiträge zur Erforschung des Alten Testaments und des antiken Judentums 24). Frankfurt am Main.

Cohn, L. (1884) 'Untersuchungen über die Quellen der Plato-Scholien', *Jahrbücher für classische Philologie, Supplementband* 13: 773–864.

(1892) 'The Latest Researches on Philo of Alexandria', *Jewish Quarterly Review* 5: 24–50.

(1899) 'Einteilung und Chronologie der Schriften Philos', *Philologus, Supplementband* 7: 385–436.

Cohn, L. and Wendland, P. (1896–1915) *Philonis Alexandrini opera quae supersunt.* 6 vols. Berlin.

Collins, J. J. (2000) *Between Athens and Jerusalem.* 2nd edn. Grand Rapids.

(2010) 'Early Judaism in Modern Scholarship', in *The Dictionary of Early Judaism*, ed. J. J. Collins and D. C. Harlow. Grand Rapids: 1–23.

Collins, N. L. (2000) *The Library in Alexandria and the Bible in Greek* (Supplements to Vetus Testamentum 82). Leiden.

Colson, F. H. and Whitaker, G. H. (1929–62) *Philo, with an English Translation.* 10 vols. (Loeb Classical Library). London.

Cornford, F. M. (1937) *Plato's Cosmology: the Timaeus of Plato* (International Library of Psychology, Philosophy, and Scientific Method). London.

Cribiore, R. (2001) *Gymnastics of the Mind: Greek Education in Hellenistic and Roman Egypt.* Princeton, NJ.

Crossland, R. A. (1982) 'Linguistic Problems of the Balkan Area in Late Prehistoric and Early Classical Periods', in *The Cambridge Ancient History*, vol. III.1: *The Prehistory of the Balkans; and the Middle East and the Aegean World, Tenth to Eighth Centuries B.C.*, ed. J. Boardman, I. E. S. Edwards, N. G. L. Hammond and E. Sollberger. 2nd edn. Cambridge: 834–49.

Dähne, A. F. (1834) *Geschichtliche Darstellung der jüdisch-alexandrinischen Religions-Philosophie.* 2 vols. Halle.

Daniel-Nataf, S., ed. (1986–) *The Writings of Philo of Alexandria.* Jerusalem. [in Hebrew]

Daube, D. (1953) 'Alexandrian Methods of Interpretation and the Rabbis', in *Festschrift Hans Lewald: bei Vollendung des vierzigsten Amtsjahres als ordentlicher Professor im Oktober 1953.* Basel: 27–43.

Dauge, Y. A. (1981) *Le Barbare. Recherches sur la conception romaine de la barbarie et de la civilisation* (Collection Latomus 176). Bruxelles.

Daumas, F. and Miquel, P. (1963) *Philon d'Alexandrie. De vita contemplativa* (Les œuvres de Philon d'Alexandrie 29). Paris.

Dawson, D. (1992) *Allegorical Readers and Cultural Revision in Ancient Alexandria.* Berkeley.

Deines, R. and Niebuhr, K.-W., eds. (2004) *Philo und das Neue Testament: Wechselseitige Wahrnehmungen I. Internationales Symposium zum Corpus Judaeo-Hellenisticum Novi Testamenti (Eisenach/Jena, Mai 2003)*. Tübingen.

Deutsch, C. (2006) 'The Therapeutae, Text Work, Ritual, and Mystical Experience', in *Paradise Now: Essays on Early Jewish and Christian Mysticism*, ed. A. D. DeConick (SBL Symposium 11). Atlanta, Ga.: 287–311.

Dickey, E. (2007) *Ancient Greek Scholarship: a Guide to Finding, Reading, and Understanding Scholia, Commentaries, Lexica, and Grammatical Treatises, from their Beginnings to the Byzantine Period* (American Philological Association Classical Resources 7). Oxford.

Diehl, E. (1903–6) *Procli Diadochi In Platonis Timaeum commentaria.* 3 vols. (Bibliotheca Teubneriana). Leipzig.

Diels, H. (1903–7) *Die Fragmente der Vorsokratiker: Griechisch und Deutsch.* 2 vols. Berlin.

Dillery, J. (2003) 'Putting Him Back Together Again: Apion Historian, Apion Grammatikos', *Classical Philology* 98: 383–90.

Dillon, J. M. (1983) 'The Formal Structure of Philo's Allegorical Exegesis', in *Two Treatises of Philo of Alexandria: a Commentary on the De gigantibus and Quod Deus sit immutabilis*, ed. D. Winston and J. M. Dillon (Brown Judaic Studies 25). Chico, Calif.: 77–87.

  (2003a) *The Heirs of Plato: a Study of the Old Academy, 347–274 B.C.* Oxford.

  (2003b) 'The Timaeus in the Old Academy', in *Plato's Timaeus as Cultural Icon*, ed. G. J. Reydams-Schils. Notre Dame, Ind.: 80–94.

Dindorf, W. (1855) *Scholia Graeca in Homeri Odysseam.* 2 vols. Oxford.

Dueck, D. (2000) *Strabo of Amasia: a Greek Man of Letters in Augustan Rome.* London.

Dupont-Roc, R. and Lallot, J. (1980) *Aristote. La Poétique: le texte grec avec une traduction et des notes de lecture.* Paris.

Effe, B. (1970) *Studien zur Kosmologie und Theologie der aristotelischen Schrift 'Über die Philosophie'* (Zetemata 50). Munich.

Ehrman, B. D. (2003) *Lost Christianities: the Battles for Scripture and the Faiths We Never Knew.* New York.

Else, G. F. (1986) *Plato and Aristotle on Poetry.* Chapel Hill.

Engels, J. (1999) *Augusteische Oikumenegeographie und Universalhistorie im Werk Strabons von Amaseia* (Geographica historica 12). Stuttgart.

Erbse, H. (1969–99) *Scholia Graeca in Homeri Iliadem (Scholia Vetera).* 7 vols. Berlin.

Feldman, L. H. (2002) 'Philo's Version of the Aqedah', *Studia Philonica Annual* 14: 66–86.

Festa, N. (1902) *Palaephati Περὶ ἀπίστων* (Mythographi graeci 3.2). Leipzig.

Finkelberg, A. (1996) 'Plato's Method in *Timaeus*', *American Journal of Philology* 117: 391–409.

Finkelberg, M. (2004) '"She Turns about in the Same Spot and Watches for Orion": Ancient Criticism and Exegesis of *Od.* 5.274 = *Il.* 18.488', *Greek, Roman, and Byzantine Studies* 44: 231–44.

(2006) 'Regional Texts and the Circulation of Books: the Case of Homer', *Greek, Roman, and Byzantine Studies* 46: 231–48.

Finkelberg, M. and Stroumsa, G. G., eds. (2003) *Homer, the Bible, and Beyond: Literary and Religious Canons in the Ancient World*. Leiden.

Fornaro, S. (2007) 'Palaephatus', in *Brill's New Pauly: Encyclopaedia of the Ancient World*, ed. H. Cancik, H. Schneider and C. F. Salazar. Leiden: 376–7.

Fraade, S. D. (2006) 'Rewritten Bible and Rabbinic Midrash as Commentary', in *Current Trends in the Study of Midrash*, ed. C. Bakhos (Supplements to the Journal for the Study of Judaism 106). Leiden: 59–78.

(2007) 'Rabbinic *Midrash* and Ancient Jewish Biblical Interpretation', in *The Cambridge Companion to the Talmud and Rabbinic Literature*, ed. C. E. Fonrobert and M. S. Jaffee (Cambridge Companions to Religion). Cambridge: 99–120.

(2009) 'Qumran *Yahad* and Rabbinic Habura: a Comparison Reconsidered', *Dead Sea Discoveries* 16: 433–53.

Frankel, Z. (1854) 'Über palestinische und alexandrinische Schriftforschung', Programm zur Eröffnung des jüdisch-theologischen Seminars zu Breslau, *Jahresbericht* 1: 1–42.

Fraser, P. M. (1972) *Ptolemaic Alexandria*. 3 vols. Oxford.

Frazer, J. G. (1921) *Apollodorus. The Library*, vols. I: I–III (Loeb Classical Library). London.

Freedman, H. (1939) *Midrash Rabbah: Translated into English with Notes, Glossary and Indices*, vols. I–II: *Genesis*. London.

Freudenthal, J. (1869) 'Zur Geschichte der Anschauungen über die jüdisch-hellenistische Religionsphilosophie', *Monatsschrift für Geschichte und Wissenschaft des Judentums* 18: 399–421.

(1874) *Hellenistische Studien*, vol. I: *Alexander Polyhistor und die von ihm erhalten Reste jüdischer und samaritanischer Geschichtwerks*. Breslau.

Früchtel, L. (1950) 'Zur Äsopfabel des Kallimachos', *Gymnasium* 57: 123–4.

Gallavotti, C. (1969) 'Tracce della Poetica di Aristotele negli scolii omerici', *Maia* 21: 203–214.

Gambetti, S. (2009) *The Alexandrian Riots of 38 C.E. and the Persecution of the Jews: a Historical Reconstruction* (Supplements to the Journal for the Study of Judaism 135). Leiden.

Gera, D. L. (2003) *Ancient Greek Ideas on Speech, Language, and Civilization*. Oxford.

Geus, K. (2002) *Eratosthenes von Kyrene: Studien zur hellenistischen Kultur- und Wissenschaftsgeschichte* (Münchener Beiträge zur Papyrusforschung und antiken Rechtsgeschichte 92). Munich.

Gfrörer, A. F. (1831) *Kritische Geschichte des Urchristenthums.* 2 vols. Stuttgart.

Glucker, J. (1978) *Antiochus and the Late Academy* (Hypomnemata 56). Göttingen.

Goldhill, S., ed. (2008) *The End of Dialogue in Antiquity*, Cambridge.

Goodenough, E. R. (1933) 'Philo's *Exposition of the Law* and his *De Vita Mosis*', *Harvard Theological Review* 26: 109–25.

Goodman, M. (2000) 'Josephus and Variety in First-Century Judaism', *Proceedings of the Israel Academy of Sciences and Humanities* 7.6: 201–13.

Goulet, R. (1987) *La philosophie de Moïse. Essai de reconstitution d'un commentaire philosophique préphilonien du Pentateuque* (Histoire des doctrines de l'Antiquité classique 11). Paris.

Grabbe, L. L. (1988) *Etymology in Early Jewish Interpretation: the Hebrew Names in Philo* (Brown Judaic Studies 115). Atlanta, Ga.

Gruen, E. S. (1998) *Heritage and Hellenism: the Reinvention of Jewish Tradition* (Hellenistic Culture and Society 30). Berkeley, Calif.

(2002) *Diaspora. Jews amidst Greeks and Romans.* Berkeley, Calif.

(2008) 'The *Letter of Aristeas* and the Cultural Context of the Septuagint', in *Die Septuaginta Texte, Kontexte, Lebenswelten. Internationale Fachtagung veranstaltet von Septuaginta Deutsch (LXX.D), Wuppertal 20.-23. Juli 2006*, ed. M. Karrer and W. Kraus (Wissenschaftliche Untersuchungen zum Neuen Testament 219). Tübingen: 134–56.

Gudeman, A. (1927) 'Λύσεις', in *Paulys Real-Encyclopädie der classischen Altertumswissenschaft: Neue Bearbeitung*, ed. G. Wissowa. Stuttgart: 2511–29.

Gutman, Y. (1958–63) *The Beginnings of Jewish-Hellenistic Literature.* 2 vols. Jerusalem. [in Hebrew]

Hacham, N. (2005) 'The *Letter of Aristeas*: a New Exodus Story?', *Journal for the Study of Judaism* 36: 1–20.

Hackforth, R. (1959) 'Plato's Cosmogony (*Timaeus* 27dff)', *Classical Quarterly* NS 9: 17–22.

Hadas, M. (1951) *Aristeas to Philocrates: Letter to Aristeas.* New York.

Hadas-Lebel, M. (2003) *Philon d'Alexandrie: un penseur en diaspora.* Paris.

Halevi, E. (1973) 'The Aggadists and the Greek Grammatikoi', in *A Reader in Aggadic Literature*, ed. A. Shinan. Jerusalem: 153–61. [in Hebrew]

Harker, A. (2008) *Loyalty and Dissidence in Roman Egypt: the Case of the Acta Alexandrinorum.* Cambridge.

Harl, M. (1986) *La Genèse* (La Bible d'Alexandrie 1). Paris.

Harrington, D. J. (1980) 'The Reception of Walter Bauer's Orthodoxy and Heresy in Earliest Christianity during the Last Decade', *Harvard Theological Review* 73: 289–98.

Harris, H. A. (1976) *Greek Athletics and the Jews* (Trivium: Special Publications 3). Cardiff.

Hay, D. M. (1979–80) 'Philo's References to Other Allegorists', *Studia Philonica* 6: 41–75.

ed. (1991a) *Both Literal and Allegorical: Studies in Philo of Alexandria's Questions and Answers on Genesis and Exodus*, (Brown Judaic Studies 232). Atlanta, Ga.

(1991b) 'References to Other Exegetes', in *Both Literal and Allegorical: Studies in Philo of Alexandria's Questions and Answers on Genesis and Exodus*, ed. D. M. Hay (Brown Judaic Studies 232). Atlanta, Ga.: 81–97.

(1994) 'Defining Allegory in Philo's Exegetical World', in *Society of Biblical Literature 1994 Seminar Papers*, ed. E. H. Lovering (SBL Seminar Papers 33). Atlanta, Ga.: 55–68.

Heinze, R. (1892) *Xenokrates: Darstellung der Lehre und Sammlung der Fragmente*. Leipzig.

Hengel, M. (1974) *Judaism and Hellenism: Studies in their Encounter in Palestine during the Early Hellenistic Period*. Philadelphia.

(2001) 'Judaism and Hellenism Revisited', in *Hellenism in the Land of Israel*, ed. J. J. Collins and G. E. Sterling (Christianity and Judaism in Antiquity 13). Notre Dame, Ind.: 6–37.

Hintenlang, H. (1961) *Untersuchungen zu den Homer-Aporien des Aristoteles*. Inaugural Dissertation. Ruprecht-Karl-Universität Heidelberg.

Holladay, C. R. (1983–96) *Fragments from Hellenistic Jewish Authors*. 4 vols. (SBL Texts and Translations 20, 30, 39, 40; Pseudepigrapha 10, 12, 13, 14). Chico, Calif.

Honigman, S. (2003) *The Septuagint and Homeric Scholarship in Alexandria: a Study in the Narrative of the Letter of Aristeas*. London.

Howard, G. (1971) 'The *Letter of Aristeas* and Diaspora Judaism', *Journal of Theological Studies* NS 22: 337–48.

Hughes, D. D. (1991) *Human Sacrifice in Ancient Greece*. London.

Ierodiakonou, K., ed. (1999) *Topics in Stoic Philosophy*, Oxford.

Inowlocki, S. (2005) '"Neither Adding nor Omitting Anything": Josephus' Promise Not to Modify the Scriptures in Greek and Latin Context', *Journal of Jewish Studies* 56: 48–65.

Inwood, B. and Donini, P. (1999) 'Stoic Ethics', in *The Cambridge History of Hellenistic Philosophy*, ed. K. Algra, J. Barnes, J. Mansfeld and M. Schofield. Cambridge: 675–740.

Isaac, B. H. (2004) *The Invention of Racism in Classical Antiquity*. Princeton, NJ.

Jacob, C. (2004) 'Questions sur les questions: archéologie d'une pratique intellectuelle et d'une forme discursive', in *Erotapokriseis: Early Christian Question-and-Answer Literature in Context. Proceedings of the Utrecht Colloquium, 13–14 October 2003*, ed. A. Volgers and C. Zamagni (Contributions to Biblical Exegesis and Theology 37). Louvain: 25–54.

Jacobson, H. (1983) *The Exagoge of Ezekiel*. Cambridge.

Jaeger, W. (1948) *Aristotle: Fundamentals of the History of his Development*. Oxford.

Janko, R. (1987) *Aristotle. Poetics I, with the Tractatus Coisilianus* (Hackett Classics). Indianapolis.

Jensen, M. S. (1999) 'Dividing Homer: When and How Were the *Iliad* and the *Odyssey* Divided into Songs?' *Symbolae Osloenses* 74: 5–91.

Jost, I. M. (1821) *Geschichte der Israeliten seit der Zeit der Maccabaer bis auf unsre Tage*, vol. II: *Judäa unter den römischen Landpflegern – Krieg gegen die Römer –*

Belagerung und Zerstörung Jerusalems – Geschichte der Juden ausserhalb Palästina, von Alexander d. Gr. an, bis nach der Zerst. Jerusalems. Berlin.

(1857–9) *Geschichte des Judenthums und seiner Sekten.* 3 vols. Leipzig.

Kahle, P. E. (1959) *The Cairo Geniza.* 2nd edn. Oxford.

Kahles, W. (1976) *Strabo and Homer: the Homeric Citations in the Geography of Strabo.* PhD dissertation. Loyola University.

Kahn, J.-G. (1965) 'Did Philo Know Hebrew? The Testimony of the "Etymologies",' *Tarbiz* 34: 337–45. [in Hebrew]

Kamesar, A. (1993) *Jerome, Greek Scholarship, and the Hebrew Bible: a Study of the Quaestiones Hebraicae in Genesim* (Oxford Classical Monographs). Oxford.

(1994) 'Philo, *Grammatike*, and the Narrative Aggada', in *Pursuing the Text: Studies in Honor of Ben Zion Wacholder on the Occasion of his Seventieth Birthday*, ed. J. C. Reeves and J. Kampen (Journal for the Study of the Old Testament, Supplement Series 184). Sheffield: 216–42.

(1995) 'Philo and the Literary Quality of the Bible: a Theoretical Aspect of the Problem', *Journal of Jewish Studies* 46: 55–68.

(1997) 'The Literary Genres of the Pentateuch as Seen from the Greek Perspective: the Testimony of Philo of Alexandria', *Studia Philonica Annual* 9: 143–89.

(2002) 'Writing Commentaries on the Works of Philo: Some Reflections', *Adamantius* 8: 127–35.

(2004) 'The *Logos Endiathetos* and the *Logos Prophorikos* in Allegorical Interpretation: Philo and the D-Scholia to the *Iliad*', *Greek, Roman, and Byzantine Studies* 44: 163–81.

(2009) 'Biblical Interpretation in Philo', in *The Cambridge Companion to Philo*, ed. A. Kamesar. Cambridge: 65–91.

Karamanolis, G. E. (2006) *Plato and Aristotle in Agreement? Platonists on Aristotle from Antiochus to Porphyry* (Oxford Philosophical Monographs). Oxford.

Kassel, R. (1966) *Aristotelis De arte poetica liber* (Scriptorum classicorum bibliotheca Oxoniensis). Oxford.

Kerkhecker, A. (1999) *Callimachus' Book of Iambi* (Oxford Classical Monographs). New York.

Klinghardt, M. (1996) *Gemeinschaftsmahl und Mahlgemeinschaft. Soziologie und Liturgie frühchristlicher Mahlfeiern* (Texte und Arbeiten zum neutestamentlichen Zeitalter 13). Tübingen.

König, J. (2008) 'Sympotic Dialogue in the First to Fifth Centuries CE', in *The End of Dialogue in Antiquity*, ed. S. Goldhill. Cambridge: 85–114.

Kouremenos, T., Parássoglou, G. M. and Tsantsanoglou, K. (2006) *The Derveni Papyrus* (Studi e testi per il Corpus dei papiri filosofici greci e latini 13). Florence.

Kreuzer, S. (2004) 'Entstehung und Publikation der Septuaginta im Horizont frühptolemäischer Bildungs- und Kulturpolitik', in *Im Brennpunkt: Die Septuaginta: Studien zur Entstehung und Bedeutung der griechischen Bibel*, vol. II, ed. S. Kreuzer and J. P. Lesch (Beiträge zur Wissenschaft vom Alten und Neuen Testament 9.1 (No. 161)). Stuttgart: 61–75.

Kugel, J. L. (1990) *In Potiphar's House: the Interpretive Life of Biblical Texts*. San Francisco.

Kyriakou, P. (2006) *A Commentary on Euripides' Iphigenia in Tauris* (Untersuchungen zur antiken Literatur und Geschichte 80). Berlin.

Lamberton, R. (2002) 'Homeric Allegory and Homeric Rhetoric in Ancient Pedagogy', in *Omero tremila anni dopo. Atti del congresso di Genova 6–8 luglio 2000*, ed. F. Montanari (Storia e Letteratura 210). Rome: 185–205.

Lanfranchi, P. (2006) *L'Exagoge d'Ezéchiel le Tragique: Introduction, texte, traduction et commentaire* (Studia in Veteris Testamenti Pseudepigrapha 21). Leiden.

Lehrs, K. (1882) *De Aristarchi studiis Homericis*. 3rd edn. Leipzig.

Leonhardt, J. (2001) *Jewish Worship in Philo von Alexandria* (Texts and Studies in Ancient Judaism 84). Tübingen.

Lerner, M. (1882) *Anlage und Quellen des Bereschit Rabba*. Berlin.

Levenson, J. D. (1993) *The Death and Resurrection of the Beloved Son: the Transformation of Child Sacrifice in Judaism and Christianity*. New Haven.

Lévy, C., ed. (1998) *Philon d'Alexandrie et le langage de la philosophie. Actes du colloque international organisé par le Centre d'études sur la philosophie hellénistique et romaine de l'Université de Paris XII–Val de Marne (Créteil, Fontenay, Paris, 26–28 octobre 1995)*, Turnhout.

(2009) 'Philo's Ethics', in *The Cambridge Companion to Philo*, ed. A. Kamesar. Cambridge: 146–71.

Liddell, H. G. and Scott, R. (1996) *A Greek–English Lexicon*. 9th edn. Oxford.

Lieberman, S. (1962) *Hellenism in Jewish Palestine: Studies in the Literary Transmission, Beliefs and Manners of Palestine in the I century B.C.E. – IV century C.E.* (Texts and Studies of the Jewish Theological Seminary of America 18). New York.

Liebes, Y. (2009) 'The Work of the Chariot and the Work of Creation as Mystical Teachings in Philo of Alexandria', in *Scriptural Exegesis: the Shapes of Culture and the Religious Imagination. Essays in Honour of Michael Fishbane*, ed. D. A. Green and L. S. Lieber. Oxford: 105–20.

Loewenstamm, S. E. (1972) *The Tradition of the Exodus in its Development*. Jerusalem. [in Hebrew]

Lona, H. E. (2005) *Die Wahre Lehre des Kelsos: Übersetzt und erklaärt* (Kommentar zu frühchristlichen Apologeten 1). Freiburg im Breisgau.

Long, A. A. (1992) 'Stoic Readings of Homer', in *Homer's Ancient Readers: the Hermeneutics of Greek Epic's Earliest Exegetes*, ed. R. Lamberton and J. J. Keaney (Magie Classical Publications). Princeton, NJ: 44–66.

Ludwich, A. (1884–1885) *Aristarchs Homerische Textkritik nach den Fragmenten des Didymos*. 2 vols. Leipzig.

Lührs, D. (1992) *Untersuchungen zu den Athetesen Aristarchs in der Ilias und zu ihrer Behandlung im Corpus der exegetischen Scholien* (Beiträge zur Altertumswissenschaft 11). Hildesheim.

Männlein-Robert, I. (2001) *Longin, Philologe und Philosoph. Eine Interpretation der erhatenen Zeugnisse* (Beiträge zur Altertumskunde 141). Munich.

(2002) '"Wissen um die göttlichen und die menschlichen Dinge." Eine Philoso-phiedefinition Platons und ihre Folgen', *Würzburger Jahrbücher für die Alter-tumswissenschaft* N.F. 26: 13–38.

Marcovich, M. (2001) *Origen. Contra Celsum libri VIII* (Supplements to Vigiliae Christianae 55). Leiden.

Marcus, R. (1953) *Philo. Supplement I & II*. 2 vols. (Loeb Classical Library). London.

Marrou, H. I. (1950) *Histoire de l'éducation dans l'antiquité*. 2nd edn. Paris.

Martens, J. W. (2003) *One God, One Law: Philo of Alexandria on the Mosaic and Greco-Roman Law* (Studies in Philo of Alexandria and Mediterranean Antiquity 2). Leiden.

Massebieau, L. (1888) *Le classement des œuvres de Philon*. Paris.

McNamee, K. (1981) 'Aristarchos and "Everyman's" Homer', *Greek, Roman, and Byzantine Studies* 22: 247–55.

Meecham, H. G. (1935) *The Letter of Aristeas: a Linguistic Study with Special Ref-erence to the Greek Bible* (Publications of the University of Manchester 241). Manchester.

Meinel, R. (1915) κατὰ τὸ σιωπώμενον. *Ein Grundsatz der Homererklärung*. Ansbach.

Meyer, M. A. (1991) 'The Emergence of Modern Jewish Historiography: Motives and Motifs', in *Essays in Jewish Historiography*, ed. A. Rapoport-Albert (South Florida Studies in the History of Judaism 15). Atlanta, Ga.: 160–75.

Milikowsky, C. (2005) 'Rabbinic Interpretation of the Bible in the Light of Ancient Hermeneutical Practice: the Question of the Literal Meaning', in *'The Words of a Wise Man's Mouth are Gracious' (Qoh 10,12): Festschrift for Günter Stem-berger on the Occasion of his 65th Birthday*, ed. M. Perani (Studia Judaica 32). Berlin: 7–28.

Montanari, F. (1993) 'L'erudizione, la filologia e la grammatica', in *Lo spazio letterario della Grecia antica*, vol. 1: *La produzione e la circolazione del testo*, ed. G. Cambiano, L. Canfora and D. Lanze. Rome: 235–81.

(1995) 'Termini e concetti della Poetica di Aristotele in uno scolio a Odissea IV 69', in *Studi di filologia omerica antica II*, ed. F. Montanari (Biblioteca di studi antichi 50). Pisa: 21–5.

(1998) 'Zenodotus, Aristarchos and the Exdosis of Homer', in *Editing Texts = Texte edieren*, ed. G. W. Most (Aporemata 2). Göttingen: 1–21.

Most, G. W. (1989) 'Cornutus and Stoic Allegoresis: a Preliminary Report', *Aufstieg und Niedergang der Römischen Welt* II.36.3: 2014–65.

(1990) 'Canon Fathers: Literacy, Mortality and Power', *Arion* 3.1.1: 35–60.

Murray, O. (2007) 'Philosophy and Monarchy in the Hellenistic World', in *Jewish Perspectives on Hellenistic Rulers*, ed. T. Rajak, S. Pearce, J. K. Aitken and J. Dines (Hellenistic Culture and Society 50). Berkeley, Calif.: 13–28.

Naeh, Sh. (1992) 'Did the *Tannaim* Interpret the Script of the Torah Differently from the Authorized Reading?', *Tarbiz* 61: 401–48. [in Hebrew]

Najman, H. (2002) *Seconding Sinai: the Development of Mosaic Discourse in Second Temple Judaism* (Supplements to the Journal for the Study of Judaism 77). Leiden.

Nauck, A. (1848) *Aristophanis Byzantii grammatici Alexandrini fragmenta.* Halle.

(1886) *Porphyrii philosophi Platonici opusula selecta* (Bibliotheca scriptorum Graecorum et Romanorum Teubneriana). Leipzig.

Neuschäfer, B. (1987) *Origenes als Philologe.* (Schweizerische Beiträge zur Altertumswissenschaft 18.1–2). 2 vols. Basel.

Newman, H. I. (2006) *Proximity to Power and Jewish Sectarian Groups of the Ancient Period: a Review of Lifestyle, Values, and Halakhah in the Pharisees, Sadducees, Essenes, and Qumran* (Brill Reference Library of Judaism 25). Leiden.

Nickau, K. (1977) *Untersuchungen zur textkritische methode des Zenodotos von Ephesos* (Untersuchungen zur antiken Literatur und Geschichte 16). Berlin.

Niehoff, M. R. (1992) *The Figure of Joseph in Post-Biblical Jewish Literature* (Arbeiten zur Geschichte des antiken Judentums und des Urchristentums 16). Leiden.

(1993) 'Associative Thinking in the Midrash Exemplified by the Rabbinic Interpretation of the Journey of Abraham and Sarah to Egypt', *Tarbiz* 62: 339–60. [in Hebrew]

(1998a) 'Philo's Views on Paganism', in *Tolerance and Intolerance in Early Judaism and Christianity*, ed. G. N. Stanton and G. G. Stroumsa. Cambridge: 138–51.

(1998b) 'Zunz's Concept of Haggadah as an Expression of Jewish Spirituality', *Leo Baeck Institute Year Book* 43: 3–24 (originally published in Hebrew in *Tarbiz* 65 (1995): 423–59).

(1999) 'Alexandrian Judaism in 19th Century Wissenschaft des Judentums: Between Christianity and Modernity', in *Jüdische Geschichte in hellenistisch-römischer Zeit. Wege der Forschung: vom alten zum neuen Schürer*, ed. A. Oppenheimer (Schriften des Historischen Kollegs, Kolloquien 44). Munich: 9–28.

(2001) *Philo on Jewish Identity and Culture* (Texts and Studies in Ancient Judaism 86). Tübingen.

(2006) 'Creatio ex Nihilo Theology in Genesis Rabbah in Light of Christian Exegesis', *Harvard Theological Review* 99: 37–64.

(2007) 'Did the *Timaeus* Create a Textual Community?', *Greek, Roman, and Byzantine Studies* 47: 161–91.

(2008) 'Questions and Answers in Philo and Genesis Rabbah', *Journal for the Study of Judaism* 39: 337–66.

(2010a) 'The Joseph Story in Philo's Writings: From Text to Character', *Beit Mikra* (special issue devoted to the figure of Joseph; ed. L. Mazor) 55: 107–22. [in Hebrew]

(2010b) 'Philo's Role as a Platonist in Alexandria', *Études platoniciennes* 7: 37–64.

(2010c) 'The Symposium of Philo's Therapeutae: Displaying Jewish Identity in an Increasingly Roman World', *Greek, Roman, and Byzantine Studies* 50: 95–117.

(in press, a) 'Hellenistic Judaism in the Israeli Academy', in *Zemanim*. [in Hebrew]

(in press, b) 'Homer in Philo's Writings', in *Festschrift for Yehuda Liebes*, ed. M. R. Niehoff, M. Meroz and J. Garb. Jerusalem. [in Hebrew]

(in press, c) *Philo – an Intellectual Biography*. Yale University Press.

(in press, d) 'Philo', in *The Homer Encyclopaedia*, ed. M. Finkelberg. Oxford.

(in press, e) 'Philons Beitrag zur Kanonisierung der griechischen Bibel', in *Kanon in Konstruktion und Dekonstruktion*, ed. E.-M. Becker and S. Scholz. Berlin and New York.

(in press, f) 'The Scholarship of Celsus' Jew', in *Homer and the Bible in the Eyes of Ancient Interpreters*, ed. M. R. Niehoff (Jerusalem Studies in Religion and Culture). Leiden.

Niese, B. (1877) 'Apollodors Commentar zum Schiffskatalog als Quelle Strabo's', *Rheinisches Museum für Philologie* 32: 267–307.

Nikiprowetzky, V. (1977) *Le commentaire de l'écriture chez Philon d'Alexandrie. Son caractère et sa portée, observations philologiques* (Arbeiten zur Literatur und Geschichte des hellenistischen Judentums 11). Leiden.

(1983) 'L'exégèse de Philon d'Alexandrie dans le De Gigantibus et le Quod Deus', in *Two Treatises of Philo of Alexandria: a Commentary on the De gigantibus and Quod Deus sit immutabilis*, ed. D. Winston and J. M. Dillon (Brown Judaic Studies 25). Chico, Calif.: 5–75.

Nitzan, B. (2009) 'The *Pesher* Scrolls from Qumran', in *The Qumran Scrolls: Introductions and Studies*, ed. M. Kister. 2 vols. Jerusalem: vol. 1, 225–60. [in Hebrew]

Novick, T. (2009) 'Perspective, Paideia, and Accomodation in Philo', *Studia Philonica Annual* 21: 49–62.

Nünlist, R. (2006) 'A Neglected Testimonium on the Homeric Book-Division', *Zeitschrift für Papyrologie und Epigraphik* 157: 47–9.

(2009a) *The Ancient Critic at Work: Terms and Concepts of Literary Criticism in Greek Scholia*. Cambridge.

(2009b) 'Palaiphatos', in *Brill's New Jacoby*, ed. I. Worthington. Leiden. (available online: http://www.brillonline.nl)

Orlinsky, H. M. (1975) 'The Septuagint as Holy Writ and the Philosophy of the Translators', *Hebrew Union College Annual* 46: 89–114.

Papadoyannakis, Y. (2006) 'Instruction by Question and Answer: the Case of Late Antique and Byzantine Erotapokriseis', in *Greek Literature in Late Antiquity: Dynamism, Didacticism, Classicism*, ed. S. F. Johnson. Aldershot: 91–105.

Pearce, S. J. K. (2007) *The Land of the Body: Studies in Philo's Representation of Egypt* (Wissenschaftliche Untersuchungen zum Neuen Testament 208). Tübingen.

Pearson, L. (1983) *The Lost Histories of Alexander the Great* (American Philological Association: Monograph Series 20). Chico, Calif.

Pelletier, A. (1962) *Lettre d'Aristée à Philocrate* (Sources chrétiennes 89). Paris.

Pépin, J. (1958) *Mythe et allégorie. Les origines grecques et les contestations judéo-chrétiennes* (Philosophie de l'esprit). Aubier.

(1967) 'Remarques sur la théorie de l'exégèse allégorique chez Philon', in *Actes du Colloque international sur Philon d'Alexandrie (Lyon, 11–15 septembre 1966)*. Paris: 131–68.

(1987) *La tradition de allégorie de Philon d'Alexandrie à Dante*. Paris.

Perrot, C. (1984) 'La lecture de la Bible dans le Diaspora hellénistique', in *Études sur le judaïsme hellénistique. Congrès de Strasbourg, 1983*, ed. R. Kuntzmann and J. Schlosser (Lectio Divina 119). Paris: 109–32.

Perry, B. E. (1962) 'Demetrius of Phalerum and the Aesopic Fables', *Transactions of the American Philological Association* 93: 287–346.

Petit, F. (1978) *Philon d'Alexandrie. Quaestiones in Genesim et in Exodum: fragmenta Graeca* (Les œuvres de Philon d'Alexandrie 33). Paris.

Pfeiffer, R. (1949–53) *Callimachus*. 2 vols. Oxford.

(1968) *History of Classical Scholarship*, vol. 1: *From the Beginnings to the End of the Hellenistic Age*. Oxford.

Podlecki, A. J. (1969) 'The Peripatetics as Literary Critics', *Phoenix* 23: 114–37.

Pöhlmann, E. (1994) *Einführung in die Überlieferungsgeschichte und in die Textkritik der antiken Literatur*, vol. 1: *Altertum*. Darmstadt.

Pontani, F. (2005a). *Eraclito. Questioni omeriche sulle allegorie di Omero in merito agli dèi*. Pisa.

(2005b) *Sguardi su Ulisse. La tradizione esegetica greca all'Odissea* (Sussidi eruditi 63). Roma.

(2007) *Scholia Graeca in Odysseam*, vol. 1: *Scholia ad libros a–b*. Rome.

Porter, J. I. (1992) 'Hermeneutic Lines and Circles: Aristarchos and Crates on the Exegesis of Homer', in *Homer's Ancient Readers: the Hermeneutics of Greek Epic's Earliest Exegetes*, ed. R. Lamberton and J. J. Keaney (Magie Classical Publications). Princeton, NJ: 67–85.

Rajak, T. (2005) 'An Invitation from Ptolemy: Aristeas, Alciphron and Collective Memory', in *For Uriel: Studies in the History of Israel in Antiquity Presented to Professor Uriel Rappaport*, ed. M. Mor, J. Pastor, I. Ronen and Y. Ashkenazi. Jerusalem: 145*–165*.

(2009) *Translation and Survival: the Greek Bible of the Ancient Jewish Diaspora*. Oxford.

Richardson, N. J. (1980) 'Literary Criticism in the Exegetical Scholia to the *Iliad*: a Sketch', *Classical Quarterly* 30: 265–87.

(1992) 'Aristotle's Reading of Homer and its Background', in *Homer's Ancient Readers: the Hermeneutics of Greek Epic's Earliest Exegetes*, ed. R. Lamberton and J. J. Keaney (Magie Classical Publications). Princeton, NJ: 30–40.

(1994) 'Aristotle and Hellenistic Scholarship', in *La philologie grecque à l'époque hellénistique et romaine*, ed. F. Montanari (Entretiens sur l'antiquité classique 40). Vandoeuvres: 7–28.

Ritter, B. (1879) *Philo und die Halacha. Eine vergleichende Studie unter steter Berücksichtigung des Josephus*. Leipzig.

Roemer, A. (1911–12) 'Aristarchea', in *Homerische Probleme*, ed. E. Belzner and A. Roemer. 2 vols. Leipzig: vol. 1, 119–24.

Rokeah, D. (1991) *Judaism and Christianity in Pagan Polemics: Celsus. The True Doctrine; Porphyry. Against the Christians; Julian. Against the Galilaeans* (Kuntresim: Texts and Studies 72–3). Jerusalem. [in Hebrew]

Rose, V. (1886) *Aristotelis qui ferebantur librorum fragmenta*. Leipzig.

Rösel, M. (1994) *Übersetzung als Vollendung der Auslegung. Studien zur Genesis-Septuaginta* (Beihefte zur Zeitschrift für die alttestamentliche Wissenschaft 223). Berlin.

  (2008) 'Schreiber, Übersetzer, Theologen. Die Septuaginta als Dokument der Schrift-, Lese- und Übersetzerkulturen des Judentums', in *Die Septuaginta – Texte, Kontexte, Lebenswelten. Internationale Fachtagung veranstaltet von Septuaginta Deutsch (LXX.D), Wuppertal 20.–23. Juli 2006*, ed. M. Karrer and W. Kraus (Wissenschaftliche Untersuchungen zum Neuen Testament 219). Tübingen: 92–101.

Rosenbaum, H.-U. (1972) 'Zur Datierung von Celsus' ἀληθής λόγος', *Vigiliae Christianae* 26: 102–11.

Royse, J. R. (1976–7) 'The Original Structure of Philo's *Quaestiones*', *Studia Philonica* 4: 41–78.

  (2009) 'The Works of Philo', in *The Cambridge Companion to Philo*, ed. A. Kamesar. Cambridge: 32–64.

Runia, D. T. (1981) 'Philo's *De aeternitate mundi*: the Problem of its Interpretation', *Vigiliae Christianae* 35: 105–51.

  (1984) 'The Structure of Philo's Allegorical Treatises: a Review of Two Recent Studies and Some Additional Comments', *Vigiliae Christianae* 38: 209–56.

  (1986) *Philo of Alexandria and the Timaeus of Plato* (Philosophia Antiqua 44). Leiden.

  (1991) 'Secondary Texts in Philo's *Quaestiones*', in *Both Literal and Allegorical: Studies in Philo of Alexandria's Questions and Answers on Genesis and Exodus*, ed. D. M. Hay (Brown Judaic Studies 232). Atlanta, Ga.: 47–70.

  (1993a) *Philo in Early Christian Literature: a Survey* (Compendia Rerum Iudaicarum ad Novum Testamentum III.3). Assen.

  (1993b) 'Was Philo a Middle Platonist? A Difficult Question Revisited', *Studia Philonica Annual* 5: 124–33.

  (2001) *On the Creation of the Cosmos according to Moses: Introduction, Translation and Commentary* (Philo of Alexandria Commentary Series I). Leiden.

  (2008) 'The Place of *De Abrahamo* in Philo's Oeuvre', *Studia Philonica Annual* 20: 133–50.

Russell, D. A. (2003) 'The Rhetoric of the Homeric Problems', in *Metaphor, Allegory, and the Classical Tradition: Ancient Thought and Modern Revisions*, ed. G. R. Boys-Stones. Oxford: 217–34.

Russell, D. A. and Konstan, D. (2005) *Heraclitus. Homeric Problems* (SBL Writings from the Greco-Roman World 14). Atlanta, Ga.

Sandmel, S. (1956) *Philo's Place in Judaism: a Study of Conceptions of Abraham in Jewish Literature*. Cincinnati.

Sandnes, K. O. (2009) *The Challenge of Homer: School, Pagan Poets and Early Christianity* (Library of New Testament Studies 400). London.

Schäfer, P. (1997) *Judeophobia: Attitudes toward the Jews in the Ancient World.* Cambridge.

Schäublin, C. (1977) 'Homerum ex Homero', *Museum Helveticum* 34: 221–227.

Schenkeveld, D. M. (1970) 'Aristarchus and Ὅμηρος φιλότεχνος', *Mnemosyne* 23: 162–78.

  (1976) 'Strabo on Homer', *Mnemosyne* 29: 52–64.

  (1992) 'Prose Usages of AKOYEIN "To Read"', *Classical Quarterly* 42: 129–41.

  (1994) 'Scholarship and Grammar', in *La philologie grecque à l'époque hellénistique et romaine*, ed. F. Montanari (Entretiens sur l'antiquité classique 40). Vandoeuvres: 263–306.

Schenkeveld, D. M. and Barnes, J. (1999) 'Language', in *The Cambridge History of Hellenistic Philosophy*, ed. K. Algra, J. Barnes, J. Mansfeld and M. Schofield. Cambridge: 177–225.

Schimanowski, G. (2003) 'Der *Aristeasbrief* zwischen Abgrenzung und Selbstdarstellung', in *Persuasion and Dissuasion in Early Christianity, Ancient Judaism, and Hellenism*, ed. P. W. van der Horst, M. J. J. Menken and J. F. M. Smit (Contributions to Biblical Exegesis and Theology 33). Leuven: 45–64.

  (2007) 'Die jüdische Integration in die Oberschicht Alexandriens und die angebliche Apostasie des Tiberius Julius Alexander', in *Jewish Identity in the Greco-Roman World*, ed. J. Frey, D. R. Schwartz and S. Gripentrog (Ancient Judaism and Early Christianity 71). Leiden: 111–36.

Schironi, F. (2005) 'Plato at Alexandria: Aristophanes, Aristarchus and the "Philological Tradition" of a Philosopher', *Classical Quarterly* 55: 423–34.

  (2009) 'Theory into Practice: Aristotelian Principles in Aristarchean Philology', *Classical Philology* 104: 279–316.

Schmidt, M. (1976) *Die Erklärungen zum Weltbild Homers und zur Kultur der Heroenzeit in den bT-Scholien zur Ilias* (Zetemata 62). Munich.

  (1997) 'Variae Lectiones oder Parallelstellen: was notierten Zenodotus und Aristarch zu Homer?', *Zeitschrift für Papyrologie und Epigraphik* 115: 1–12.

  (2002) 'The Homer of the Scholia: what Is Explained to the Reader?', in *Omero tremila anni dopo. Atti del congresso di Genova 6–8 luglio 2000 (Storia e Letteratura 210)*, ed. F. Montanari. Rome: 159–83.

Schofield, M. (2003) 'Stoic Ethics', in *The Cambridge Companion to the Stoics*, ed. B. Inwood. Cambridge: 233–56.

Schorsch, I. (1977) 'From Wolfenbüttel to Wissenschaft: the Divergent Paths of Isaak Markus Jost and Leopold Zunz', *Leo Baeck Institute Year Book* 22: 109–28.

Schrader, H., ed. (1880) *Porphyrii Quaestionum homericarum ad Iliadem pertinentium reliquias.* Leipzig.

Schremer, A. (2010) *Brothers Estranged: Heresy, Christianity, and Jewish Identity in Late Antiquity.* Oxford.

Sedley, D. (2003) 'The School, from Zeno to Arius Didymus', in *The Cambridge Companion to the Stoics*, ed. B. Inwood. Cambridge: 7–32.

Severyns, A. (1928) *Le cycle épique dans l'école d'Aristarque* (Bibliothèque de la faculté de philosophie et lettres de l'Université de Liége 40). Liège.

Shroyer, M. J. (1936) 'Alexandrian Jewish Literalists', *Journal of Biblical Literature* 55: 261–84.

Siegert, F. (1996) 'Early Jewish Interpretation in a Hellenistic Style', in *Hebrew Bible / Old Testament: the History of its Interpretation*, vol. 1: *From the Beginnings to the Middle Ages (Until 1300). Part 1: Antiquity*, ed. M. Sæbø. Göttingen: 130–98.

(2004) 'Die Inspiration der Heiligen Schriften. Ein philonisches Votum zu 2 Tim. 3,16', in *Philo und das Neue Testament: Wechselseitige Wahrnehmungen 1. Internationales Symposium zum Corpus Judaeo-Hellenisticum Novi Testamenti (Eisenach/Jena, Mai 2003)*, ed. R. Deines and K.-W. Niebuhr (Wissenschaftliche Untersuchungen zum Neuen Testament 172). Tübingen: 205–22.

Siegfried, C. (1875) *Philo von Alexandria als Ausleger des Alten Testaments*. Jena.

Siker, J. S. (1991) *Disinheriting the Jews: Abraham in Early Christian Controversy*. Louisville, Ky.

Simon, A. (1973) 'Notes on the Story of the Binding of Isaac', *Biblical Thought* 1: 163–70. [in Hebrew]

Skinner, J. (1910) *A Critical and Exegetical Commentary on Genesis* (International Critical Commentary on the Holy Scriptures of the Old and New Testaments 1). Edinburgh.

Slater, W. J. (1982) 'Aristophanes of Byzantium and Problem-Solving in the Museum', *Classical Quarterly* 32: 336–49.

Snyder, H. G. (2000) *Teachers and Texts in the Ancient World: Philosophers, Jews, and Christians* (Religion in the First Christian Centuries). London.

Sodano, A. R. (1965) 'Gli omerici nell'esegesi di Porfirio. La methodologia fiologica-esthetica di Aristotele', *Atti Accademia Pontaniana* 15: 205–39.

Stein, E. (1935) *Alttestamentliche Bibelkritik in der späthellenistischen Literatur*. Lwow.

(1939) *Philo of Alexandria: the Writer and his Books, his Philosophy*. Warsaw. [in Hebrew]

Steinmetz, P. (1986) 'Allegorische Deutung und Allegorische Dichtung in der alten Stoa', *Rheinisches Museum für Philologie* 129: 18–30.

Sterling, G. E. (1991) 'Philo's *Quaestiones*: Prolegomena or Afterthought?', in *Both Literal and Allegorical: Studies in Philo of Alexandria's Questions and Answers on Genesis and Exodus*, ed. G. E. Sterling (Brown Judaic Studies 232). Atlanta, Ga.: 99–123.

(1999) '"The School of Sacred Laws": the Social Setting of Philo's Treatises', *Vigiliae Christianae* 53: 148–64.

(2004) 'The Place of Philo of Alexandria in the Study of Christian Origins', in *Philo und das Neue Testament: Wechselseitige Wahrnehmungen 1. Internationales Symposium zum Corpus Judaeo-Hellenisticum Novi Testamenti (Eisenach/Jena, Mai 2003)*, ed. R. Deines and K.-W. Niebuhr (Wissenschaftliche Untersuchungen zum Neuen Testament 172). Tübingen: 21–52.

(2008) 'Philo's *De Abrahamo*: Introduction', *Studia Philonica Annual* 20: 129–31.

Stern, J. (1996) *Palaephatus. On Unbelievable Tales.* Wauconda, Ill.

Stern, M. (1974–84) *Greek and Latin Authors on Jews and Judaism.* (Publications of the Israel Academy of Sciences and Humanities, Section of Humanities). 3 vols. Jerusalem.

Stoneman, R. (1997) *Alexander the Great* (Lancaster Pamphlets). London.

Struck, P. T. (2004) *Birth of the Symbol: Ancient Readers at the Limits of their Texts.* Princeton, NJ.

Susemihl, F. (1891–2) *Geschichte der griechischen Litteratur in der Alexandrinerzeit.* 2 vols. Leipzig.

Taran, L. (1981) *Speusippus of Athens: a Critical Study with a Collection of the Related Texts and Commentary* (Philosophia antiqua 39). Leiden.

Taylor, A. E. (1937 [1928]) *A Commentary on Plato's Timaeus.* Oxford.

Taylor, J. E. (2003) *Jewish Women Philosophers of First-Century Alexandria: Philo's 'Therapeutae' Reconsidered.* Oxford.

Taylor, Th. (1991) *Porphyry. On the Cave of the Nymphs.* Grand Rapids, Mich.

Tcherikover, V. A. (1958) 'The Ideology of the Letter of Aristeas', *Harvard Theological Review* 51: 59–85.

Terian, A. (1980) 'Syntactical Peculiarities in the Translations of the Hellenizing School', in *First International Conference on Armenian Linguistics: Proceedings. The University of Pennsylvania, Philadelphia, 11–14 July 1979*, ed. J. A. C. Greppin (Anatolian and Caucasian Studies). Delman, NY: 197–206.

(1981) *Philonis Alexandri de Animalibus: the Armenian Text with an Introduction, Translation and Commentary* (Studies in Hellenistic Judaism 1). Chico, Calif.

(1982) 'The Hellenizing School: Its Time, Place, and Scope of Activities Reconsidered', in *East of Byzantium: Syria and Armenia in the Formative Period. Dumbarton Oaks Symposium, 1980*, ed. N. G. Garsoïan, T. F. Mathews and R. W. Thomson. Washington, DC: 175–86.

(1988) *Philon d'Alexandrie. Alexander, vel De ratione quam habere etiam bruta animalia (De animalibus) e versione Armeniaca* (Les œuvres de Philon d'Alexandrie 36). Paris.

(1991) 'The Priority of the *Quaestiones* among Philo's Exegetical Commentaries', in *Both Literal and Allegorical: Studies in Philo of Alexandria's Questions and Answers on Genesis and Exodus*, ed. D. M. Hay (Brown Judaic Studies 232). Atlanta, Ga.: 29–46.

(1997) 'Back to Creation: the Beginning of Philo's Third Grand Commentary', *Studia Philonica Annual* 9: 19–36.

Thackeray, H. S. J. (1903) 'Translation of the Letter of Aristeas', *Jewish Quarterly Review* 15: 337–91.

Theodor, J. and Albeck, Ch. (1965) *Midrash Bereschit Rabba: Critical Edition with Notes and Commentary*, Jerusalem. [in Hebrew]

Tobin, T. H. (1983) *The Creation of Man: Philo and the History of Interpretation* (Catholic Biblical Quarterly, Monograph Series 14). Washington, DC.

Tramontano, R. (1931) *La lettera di Aristea a Filocrate: introduzione, testo, versione e commento.* Napoli.

Van den Hoek, A. (1997) 'The "Catechetical" School of Early Christian Alexandria and its Philonic Heritage', *Harvard Theological Review* 90: 59–87.

Van der Horst, P. W. (2003) *Philo's Flaccus: the First Pogrom* (Philo of Alexandria Commentary Series 2). Leiden.

Van der Kooij, A. (2008) 'The Promulgation of the Pentateuch in Greek according to the *Letter of Aristeas*', in *Scripture in Transition: Essays on Septuagint, Hebrew Bible, and Dead Sea Scrolls in Honour of Raija Sollamo*, ed. A. Voitila and J. Jokiranta (Supplements to the Journal for the Study of Judaism 126). Leiden: 179–91.

Van der Valk, M. (1963–4) *Researches on the Text and Scholia of the Iliad*. 2 vols. Leiden.

Vaux, R. de (1964) *Studies in Old Testament Sacrifice*. Cardiff.

Vermes, G. and Millar, F. (1973–87) *The History of the Jewish People in the Age of Jesus Christ (175 B.C.–A.D. 135): a New English Version of E. Schürer*. 4 vols. Edinburgh.

Villani, A. (2008) 'Origenes als Schriftsteller. Ein Beitrag zu seiner Verwendung von Prosopopoie, mit einigen Beobachtungen über die prosopologische Exegese', *Adamantius* 14: 130–50.

Vlastos, G. (1965) 'Creation in the *Timaeus*: Is It a Fiction?', in *Studies in Plato's Methaphysics*, ed. R. E. Allen. London: 401–19.

Wacholder, B. Z. (1968) 'Biblical Chronology in the Hellenistic World Chronicles', *Harvard Theological Review* 61: 451–81.

(1974) *Eupolemus: a Study of Judaeo-Greek Literature* (Monographs of the Hebrew Union College 3). Cincinnati.

Walter, N. (1964) *Die Thoraausleger Aristobulos. Untersuchungen zu seinem Fragmenten und zu Pseudoepigraphischen resten der judisch-hellenistischen Literatur* (Texte und Untersuchungen zur Geschichte der altchristlichen Literatur 86). Berlin.

Wan, S.-K. (1993) 'Philo's *Quaestiones et Solutiones in Genesim*: a Synoptic Approach', in *Society of Biblical Literature 1993 Seminar Papers*, ed. E. H. Lovering (SBL Seminar Papers 32). Atlanta, Ga.: 22–53.

Wasserstein, A. and Wasserstein, D. J. (2006) *The Legend of the Septuagint: From Classical Antiquity to Today*. Cambridge.

Watson, F. (2007) *Paul, Judaism, and the Gentiles: Beyond the New Perspective*. 2nd revised edn. Grand Rapids, Mich.

Weber, R. (1888) 'De Dioscuridis περὶ τῶν παρ᾽ Ὁμήρῳ νόμων libello', *Leipziger Studien zur classischen Philologie* 11: 87–196.

Weiler, G. (2007) 'Human Sacrifice in Greek Culture', in *Human Sacrifice in Jewish and Christian Tradition*, ed. K. Finsterbusch, A. Lange and K. F. D. Römheld (Studies in the History of Religions 112). Leiden: 35–64.

Weinstock, S. (1927) 'Die platonische Homerkritik und ihre Nachwirkung', *Philologus* 82: 121–53.

Wendland, P. (1896) 'Die Therapeuten und die philonische Schrift vom beschaulichen Leben', *Jahrbücher für classische Philologie, Supplementband* 22: 693–772.

West, M. L. (1997) *The East Face of Helicon: West Asiatic Elements in Greek Poetry and Myth*. Oxford.

(1998) 'The Textual Criticism and Editing of Homer', in *Editing Texts = Texte edieren*, ed. G. W. Most (Aporemata 2). Göttingen: 94–110.

(2001) *Studies in the Text and Transmission of the Iliad*. München.

West, S. (1967) *The Ptolemaic Papyri of Homer* (Wissenschaftliche Abhandlungen der Arbeitsgemeinschaft für Forschung des Landes Nordrhein-Westfalen, Sonderreihe: Papyrologica Coloniensia 3). Cologne.

Wevers, J. W. (1990) *Notes on the Greek Text of Exodus* (SBL Septuagint and Cognate Studies 30). Atlanta, Ga.

(1993) *Notes on the Greek Text of Genesis* (SBL Septuagint and Cognate Studies 35). Atlanta, Ga.

White, M. J. (2003) 'Stoic Natural Philosophy (Physics and Cosmology)', in *The Cambridge Companion to the Stoics*, ed. B. Inwood. Cambridge: 124–52.

Wilcken, U. (1923) 'Alexander der Grosse und die indischen Gymnosophisten', *Sitzungsberichte der Preussischen Akademie der Wissenschaften, Philosophisch-Historische Klasse*: 150–83.

Wilken, R. L. (1984) *The Christians as the Romans Saw Them*. New Haven.

Wolfson, H. A. (1947) *Philo: Foundations of Religious Philosophy in Judaism, Christianity, and Islam*. 2 vols. Cambridge, Mass.

Wright, B. G. (2006) 'Translation as Scripture: the Septuagint in Aristeas and Philo', in *Septuagint Research: Issues and Challenges in the Study of the Greek Jewish Scriptures*, ed. W. Kraus and R. G. Wooden (SBL Septuagint and Cognate Studies 53). Atlanta, Ga.: 47–61.

(2008) 'Transcribing, Translating, and Interpreting in the *Letter of Aristeas*: On the Nature of the Septuagint', in *Scripture in Transition: Essays on Septuagint, Hebrew Bible, and Dead Sea Scrolls in Honour of Raija Sollamo*, ed. A. Voitila and J. Jokiranta (Supplements to the Journal for the Study of Judaism 126). Leiden: 147–61.

Wyrick, J. (2004) *The Ascension of Authorship: Attribution and Canon Formation in Jewish, Hellenistic, and Christian Traditions* (Harvard Studies in Comparative Literature 49). Cambridge, Mass.

Yarbro Collins, A. (1983–5) 'Aristobulus', in *The Old Testament Pseudepigrapha*, ed. J. H. Charlesworth. 2 vols. New York: vol. II, 831–42.

Zuntz, G. (1959) 'Aristeas Studies II: Aristeas on the Translation of the Torah', *Journal of Semitic Studies* 4: 109–26.

Index of Greek terms

ἀδύνατος, 48, 49, 50
ἀκριβής, 35
ἁμαρτία, 115
ἀντιβολή, 21
ἀντιπίπτω, 54
ἀνωφελῶς, 172
ἀπίθανος, 49
ἀπρεπές, 128
ἁρμόττον, 43
ἀστερίσκος, 26
ἀφαίρεσις, 26, 28, 33, 113

γελοῖος, 49, 125
γραμματικός, 60

δηλόω, 63
διὰ τί, 42, 46, 47, 52, 149,
    161
διὰ τοῦτο, 52
διαβολή, 126, 127
διασκευή, 22, 23, 24, 113
διασώζω, 127
διερμηνεύω, 32
διόρθωσις, 21, 30
δύναμις, 62

ἐκπληκτικός, 65
ἐνέργεια, 62
ἐπιζητέω, 39
εὐπρεπές, 128
εὐτέλη, 128

ζητήματα, 180

θαυμάσιον, 64, 65

ἴσως, 69

κατὰ τὸ σιωπώμενον, 45, 57
κοινότερον, 69

λέξις, 69, 70
λύσις ἐκ τῆς λέξεως, 50

μάχομαι, 119
μεταγράφω, 32
μεταφέρω, 26, 28, 69
μυθῶδες, 68, 85, 88

νεώτεροι, 85

περιαιρέω, 33, 112
περισσός, 30, 138
πλάσματα, 86
προστίθημι, 26

σημαίνω, 33, 66, 69
σημεῖον, 33, 112, 113
συμφωνέω, 21, 53, 54
συντηρέω, 63

τί ἐστιν, 161

ὑπομνήμα, 11, 136

φυσικῶς, 68, 73
φύσις, 96

Index of sources

Index of modern authors

Amir, Yehoshua, 9, 133

Bauer, Walter, 155
Baumgarten, Albert, 30
Bickerman, Elias, 30
Birnbaum, Ellen, 7
Bousset, Wilhelm, 5
Brisson, Luc, 143

Cohn, Leopold, 7, 8, 158, 169

Dickey, Eleanor, 21
Dillon, John, 6

Fraser, Peter, 19, 58
Freudenthal, Jacob, 38, 54
Früchtel, Leopold, 89

Geiger, Abraham, 111
Goulet, Richard, 5
Gudemann, Alfred, 38

Hay, David, 5, 6, 77
Honigman, Sylvie, 19

Jacoby, Felix, 55
Jost, Isaac Marcus, 1

Kahle, Paul E., 33, 34
Kamesar, Adam, 9, 133

Lehrs, Karl, 12
Levenson, Jon, 99

Männlein-Robert, Irmgard, 173
Massebieau, Louis, 7, 169

Montanari, Franco, 11
Most, Glenn, 2

Nünlist, René, 85

Orlinsky, Harry, 22

Papadoyannakis, Yannis, 160
Pfeiffer, Rudolf, 44
Pontani, Filippo, 145

Richardson, N. J., 11
Rösel, Martin, 25, 83
Royse, James, 7
Runia, David, 158, 169
Russell, Donald, 145

Sandmel, Samuel, 100
Schironi, Francesca, 11, 44, 49
Shroyer, M. J., 6
Sterling, Gregory, 7, 163

Tcherikover, Victor, 22
Terian, Abraham, 169
Tobin, Thomas, 5

Walter, Nicolaus, 58
Wan, Sze-kar, 153
Wasserstein, Abraham, 37, 171
Wasserstein, David, 37, 171
Wendland, Paul, 7
West, Martin, 21

Zuntz, Günther, 19, 33
Zunz, Leopold, 111

General index

Aaron, 40, 127

Abraham, 53, 54, 56, 95, 96, 97, 98, 99, 101, 102, 108, 109, 110, 111, 119, 120, 121, 122, 124, 125, 128, 142, 154, 155, 172, 173

accent marks, 10

Achilles, 45, 48, 103, 104, 106, 109, 125

Adam, 110, 141, 148, 158, 163, 183

  daughters of, 148

additions, *see* interpolation

Adriatic coast, 105

Aeneas, 27

Aeschylus, 93, 102

Agamemnon, 43, 84, 128

agriculture, 147

Aias, 51

Alexander legends, 4

Alexander Polyhistor, 55

Alexander the Great, 55, 91, 108, 148

Alexander, Julius T., 164, 165, 167

Alexandria, 2, 3, 4, 5, 6, 9, 15, 30, 31, 34, 38, 39, 42, 44, 48, 51, 54, 55, 56, 58, 59, 60, 65, 73, 79, 89, 91, 92, 93, 102, 103, 111, 117, 118, 140, 144, 146, 148, 171, 174, 175, 176, 177, 180

  Ptolemaic, 4

Alexandrian scholarship, *see* scholarship

Allegorical Commentary, 7, 8, 96, 97, 126, 127, 133, 134, 135, 136, 137, 139, 145, 150, 151, 152, 153, 154, 155, 156, 157, 158, 159, 160, 161, 162, 163, 164, 168, 169, 170, 171, 172, 173, 174, 175, 177, 178, 179, 183, 185

allegory, 1, 3, 7, 14, 15, 44, 58, 59, 64, 68, 93, 94, 116, 118, 120, 127, 128, 133, 134, 135, 136, 137, 139, 141, 142, 143, 144, 146, 147, 148, 149, 150, 151, 152, 153, 156, 158, 159, 160, 162, 163, 167, 173, 177, 178, 179, 183

  Stoic, 13, 59, 151

Aloeidae, 81, 82

Amalek, 40, 41

analogy, 70, 72

Andreas, 32, 59

anthropomorphism, 62, 66, 68, 71, 155, 161, 181

Antiochus, 15

Antoninus Pius, 176

Aphrodite, 24, 50

Apion, 8, 14, 127, 176, 177, 185

Apollo, 49

Apollodorus, 60, 62, 71, 144, 149

apologetic, 107, 158, 160, 170, 182

Aporemata Homerica, 9, 41, 42, 43, 84, 103, 143, 153

aporetic inquiry, *see* question and answer

Aratus, 21, 62, 63, 112

Aristarchus, 4, 9, 10, 11, 12, 14, 19, 21, 23, 24, 25, 26, 27, 28, 29, 33, 34, 35, 38, 43, 44, 45, 46, 49, 50, 51, 54, 55, 56, 60, 61, 62, 63, 65, 71, 74, 79, 81, 82, 85, 89, 95, 106, 107, 112, 113, 115, 116, 119, 120, 121, 122, 124, 125, 128, 133, 137, 138, 139, 140, 144, 149, 180

  edition of Homeric text, 11

Aristeas, 4, 19, 20, 21, 24, 25, 26, 27, 28, 29, 30, 31, 32, 33, 34, 35, 36, 37, 39, 41, 60, 66, 71, 74, 79, 113, 124, 134, 182

  curse, 25, 27, 28, 29, 30, 37

Aristeas' colleagues, 27, 30, 34

Aristo, 15

Aristobulus, 4, 5, 8, 14, 30, 33, 58, 59, 60, 61, 62, 63, 64, 65, 66, 67, 68, 69, 70, 71, 72, 73, 74, 80, 112, 113, 140, 143, 144, 145, 147

  as a Stoic allegorist, 58

Aristobulus' colleagues, 74

Aristodemus, 149

Aristonicus, 11, 12, 14, 23, 24, 45, 50, 149

Aristophanes of Byzantium, 10

Aristotelian approach, *see* Aristotelian tradition

Aristotelian methods, 14, 49, 110

Aristotelian notion, *see* Aristotelian tradition

Aristotelian tradition, 2, 5, 14, 41, 44, 48, 50, 51, 58, 63, 65, 66, 71, 72, 73, 74, 83, 86, 92, 95, 103, 107, 108, 129, 139, 140, 141, 145, 147, 151, 160, 163, 168, 181